BOTH LITERAL AND ALLEGORICAL

Number 232

BOTH LITERAL AND ALLEGORICAL

edited by
David M. Hay

BOTH LITERAL AND ALLEGORICAL
Studies in Philo of Alexandria's *Questions and Answers on Genesis and Exodus*

edited by

David M. Hay

Scholars Press
Atlanta, Georgia

BOTH LITERAL AND ALLEGORICAL

Library of Congress Cataloging-in-Publication Data

Both literal and allegorical : studies in Philo of Alexandria's Questions and answers of Genesis and Exodus / edited by David M. Hay.
p. cm — (Brown Judaic Studies ; no. 232)
Papers presented at a meeting of the Society of Biblical Literature's Philo Consultation, Anaheim, Calif., Nov. 24, 1985.
Includes bibliographical references and indexes.
ISBN 1-55540-632-7
1. Philo, of Alexandria. Quaestiones et solutiones in Genesim et Exodum—Congresses. 3. Bible. O.T. Exodus—Criticism, interpretation, etc.—Congresses. I. Hay, David M., 1935- . II. Series.
BS1235.B668 1991 91–30913
222'.1106—dc20 CIP

Paperback edition published 2009 by Brown Judaic Studies.
ISBN 978- 1-930675-64-3 (alk. paper : paperback)

Printed in the United States of America
on acid-free paper

TABLE OF CONTENTS

INTRODUCTION

DAVID M. HAY

Philo of Alexandria's *Questions and Answers on Genesis and Exodus (Quaestiones et Solutiones in Genesim et Exodum* — hereafter abbreviated "*Quaestiones*") is the largest of his extant writings. It comments on passages in the two scriptural books in verse-by-verse sequence, often beginning with a query like "What is the meaning of the words. . . ?" Then one or more interpretations at the literal or allegorical level are presented; often a literal interpretation is succeeded by an allegorical one of the same text. It is especially characteristic of *Quaestiones* that Philo implies the acceptability of literal interpretations, even though non-literal ones receive much space and apparently more approval (as they usually do in Philo's other biblical commentaries[1]).

This collection of studies on the *Quaestiones* has grown out of a meeting of the Society of Biblical Literature's Philo Consultation in Anaheim, California on 24 November 1985. The papers presented there by Earle Hilgert, Abraham Terian, and myself have been revised and appear in print here for the first time. Publication plans were made at that meeting, but we also decided to expand the volume by inviting some other Philonists to prepare articles dealing with the *Quaestiones*. Invitations were issued and accepted, and the final essays were submitted in the spring of 1989. A number of scholars in recent years have emphasized the value of focussing on the shape and contents of individual Philonic works. So far as we know, however, ours is the first anthology of articles devoted to the *Quaestiones*. The quite numerous tables contained in the various essays in this volume suggest that the writers felt the contents of the *Quaestiones* require more analytical "mapping" than they have hitherto received.

Because of a history of neglect, one contributor to this volume (David Runia) has dubbed the *Quaestiones* Philo's "Cinderella."

---

[1]It is customary to distinguish three groups of exegetical writings within the Philonic corpus: the Allegorical Commentary (composed of the writings from *Legum Allegoriae* to *De Somniis*, which deal with various texts in Genesis), the Exposition of the Law (beginning with *De Abrahamo* and extending through *De Praemiis et Poenis*), and the *Quaestiones*. The *De Opficio Mundi* has features of style and content that mark it out from the other works; see esp. Nikiprowetzky 1977, 197-200.

Relatively few articles and no monographs have dealt with it, and no concordances to Philo cover it. In great measure the neglect is explained by the "pumpkin" vehicle in which most of the *Quaestiones* comes to us: an ancient Armenian translation remarkable for its stiffness and indications that the translator or translators were often baffled by the original Greek. Unfortunately most modern Philonists do not read Armenian. Apart from this linguistic problem, many readers have found the *Quaestiones* unattractive or simplistic by comparison with Philo's other writings. Again, just as Cinderella lost a glass slipper, some portions (perhaps very large portions) of the *Quaestiones* have been lost, although fragments continue to be discovered periodically. We need not press the metaphor so far as to imply that the neglect has been malicious or that Philo's other writings are inferior to the *Quaestiones*. But we hope that the present volume will encourage students of hellenistic Judaism to give this very extensive commentary more attention.

The convoluted history of manuscripts, translations, and published editions is traced in Earle Hilgert's essay. He surveys the evidence and scholarship dealing with the Greek and Latin fragments as well as the incomplete but fundamental Armenian version. He points out that, while we now have excellent translations of the Armenian into English (Ralph Marcus) and French (Charles Mercier and Abraham Terian), there is still no critical edition of the Armenian text itself.

For several years James Royse has been preparing a critical edition of all the Greek fragments of Philo. One expression of his efforts is presented in his study of *QE* 1.6,[2] a fragment discovered by Ludwig Früchtel. After comparing the Greek and Armenian evidence for the original form of this paragraph, he discusses its meaning in relation to Philo's frequent assumption that the finest wisdom of the Greeks was borrowed from the writings of Moses.

The remaining essays approach the contents of the *Quaestiones* from different angles, but each of them raises questions about this work's relationship to the Allegorical Commentary. Abraham Terian reviews the data and arguments of Ralph Marcus in favor of the view that the *Quaestiones* was written after the Allegorical Commentary and contains explicit references to that series of treatises. Terian shows that there is no solid basis for Marcus's position. He himself thinks that Philo wrote

---

[2]Throughout this anthology the *Quaestiones et Solutiones in Genesin* will be abbreviated as *QG* and the *Quaestiones et Solutiones in Exodum* as *QE*. Abbreviations of other works, including the remainder of the Philonic corpus, will be found in the Table of Abbreviations.

the *Quaestiones* before both the Allegorical Commentary and the Exposition of the Laws.

The *Quaestiones* is organized as a sequential commentary on passages in Genesis and Exodus but, as David Runia emphasizes, other scriptural texts are brought into Philo's discussion. Dr. Runia contends that interpretation of such "secondary texts" plays a smaller role in this work than in Philo's other commentaries. He also identifies 35 such texts for which there are no parallels in the Allegorical Commentary and argues that this favors the supposition that the *Quaestiones* is essentially an independent composition rather than merely a preliminary collection of materials intended for use in other treatises.

Scholars have often observed that Philo's exegetical writings explicitly mention other exegetes, both literalists and allegorists. My essay compares the references to other exegetes in the *Quaestiones* with those in Philo's other writings. The evidence in general supports the conclusion that the *Quaestiones* was written before the Allegorical Commentary. The number of references to such interpreters is proportionately greater in the *Quaestiones* than in the Allegorical Commentary, but even so these explicit references probably give only a partial indication of Philo's dependence on earlier and contemporary fellow exegetes.

Gregory Sterling urges that the *Quaestiones* be thought of as "prolegomena" to the Allegorical Commentary. He analyses *QG* 1 and then compares its contents with the portions of the Allegorical Commentary dealing with the same passages. For the most part the two series of commentaries offer interpretations in the same sequence. When both series comment on the same biblical text, Sterling thinks the Allegorical Commentary regularly offers interpretations of superior sophistication and coherence. In the *Quaestiones* Philo chose to present all exegetical options, in the Allegorical Commentary he concentrated on setting forth his own allegorical opinions.

The anthology is brought to a close with a detailed structural exploration of *QG* jointly written by two of the leading French Philonists of our time, Anita Méasson and Jacques Cazeaux. Their primary concern is to clarify the nature of the work by emphasizing its differences from Philo's other exegetical writings. Concentrating on *QG* 1 and 4, they point out some intricate patterns of repetition and correspondence. They also underline the great distance in genre between these "books" and treatises of the Allegorical Commentary. Only in the latter do they discern dynamic movement and the full range of Philo's profundity and literary skill.

The various essays included in this volume are far from uniform in methodology or conclusions. Yet they cumulatively constitute a strong case for regarding the *Quaestiones* as a distinctive work whose study is essential for a rounded appreciation of Philo's exegetical enterprise.

In closing I wish to express special thanks to Jeannine Hammond, Associate Professor of French at Coe College, for translating the article by Professors Méasson and Cazeaux. Earle Hilgert organized the original 1985 Philo Consultation and has given invaluable counsel and encouragement at various stages of this project, as has David Runia. The librarians of Coe College and the University of Iowa provided expert help in locating hard-to-find materials and information. Finally, I am grateful to Carole Butz of Coe's Development Office for helping to prepare the final copy for publication, in the process displaying great patience with corrections.

Cedar Rapids
22 July 1991

Abbreviations

The general guidelines pubished in *The Studia Philonica Annual* 1 (1989) are followed in this volume. The abbreviations of biblical books and other ancient Jewish and Christian literature as well as journals, monograph series, source collections, and standard reference works are taken from of the "Instructions to Contributors" in the *Journal of Biblical Literature* 107 (1988) 579-596. Classical and Patristic authors are cited according to the recommendations of H. G. Liddell, R. Scott, H. S. Jones (edd.), *A Greek-English Lexicon* (Oxford 1940) and G. W. H. Lampe (ed.), *A Patristic Greek Lexicon* (Oxford 1961). The following abbreviations are used for Philo's works:

Abr.=De Abrahamo
Aet.= De Aeternitate Mundi
Agr. = De Agricultura
Anim.=De Animalibus
Cher. = De Cherubim
Conf. = De Confusione Linguarum
Congr. = De Congressu Eruditionis Gratia
Contempl. = De Vita Contemplativa
Decal. = De Decalogo
Deo = De Deo
Det. = Quod Deterius Potiori Insidiari Soleat
Deus = Quod Deus Sit Immutabilis
Ebr. = De Ebrietate
Flacc. = In Flaccum
Fug. = De Fuga et Inventione
Gig. = De Gigantibus
Her. = Quis Rerum Divinarum Heres Sit
Hypoth. = Hypothetica
Ios. = De Iosepho
Leg. 1-3 = Legum Allegoriae I, II, III
Legat. = Legatio ad Gaium
Migr. = De Migratione Abrahami
Mos. 1-2 = De Vita Mosis I, II
Mut. = De Mutatione Nominum
Opif. = De Opificio Mundi
Plant. = De Plantatione

Post. = *De Posteritate Caini*
Praem. = *De Praemiis et Poenis, De Exsecrationibus*
Prob. = *Quod Omnis Probus Liber Sit*
Prov. 1-2 = *De Providentia I, II*
QE 1-2 = *Quaestiones et Solutiones in Exodum I, II*
QG 1-4 = *Quaestiones et Solutiones in Genesim I-IV*
Sacr. = *De Sacrificiis Abelis et Caini*
Sobr. = *De Sobrietate*
Somn. 1-2 = *De Somniis I, II*
Spec. 1-4 = *De Specialibus Legibus I, II, III, IV*
Virt. = *De Virtutibus*

Some standard works of Philonic scholarship are abbreviated as follows:

G-G — H. L. Goodhart and E. R. Goodenough, "A General Bibliography of Philo Judaeus," in E. R. Goodenough, *The Politics of Philo Judaeus: Practice and Theory* (New Haven: Yale, 1938), 125-321

PAL — Arnaldez, Roger, Jean Pouilloux and Claude Mondésert (eds.), *Philon d'Alexandrie Lyon 11-15 Septembre 1966.* Paris: Editions du Centre National de la Recherche Scientifique, 1967

PAPM — *Les œuvres de Philon d'Alexandrie*, French translation under the general editorship of R. Arnaldez, J. Pouilloux , and C. Mondésert. (Paris: Editions du Cerf, 1961-)

PCH — *Die Werke Philos von Alexandria in deutscher Übersetzung*, ed. L. Cohn and I. Heinemann. 7 vols. (Breslau and Berlin, 1909-64)

PCW — *Philonis Alexandrini opera quae supersunt*, ediderunt L. Cohn, P. Wendland, S. Reiter, 7 vols. (Berlin: De Gruyter, 1962)

PLCL *Philo*, with an English Translation, ed. F. H. Colson, G. H. Whitaker and R. Marcus. (Loeb Classical Library), 12 vols. Cambridge: Harvard, 1929-62.

SPh *Studia Philonica*

CHAPTER ONE

THE *QUAESTIONES*: TEXTS AND TRANSLATIONS

EARLE HILGERT

The Greek text of the *Quaestiones* is extant only in some two hundred fragments preserved in the works of other writers. Fortunately, however, four books of *QG* and two of *QE* exist in an ancient Armenian translation. These constitute our basic text. In addition to these sources there remains also a Latin translation containing approximately one-half of *QG* 4. Even so, it is clear that substantial portions of the original *Quaestiones* are lacking: the extant text of *QG* begins only at Gen 2:4 and ends abruptly at 28:9, while *QE* covers only from Ex 12:2 to 28:4; furthermore, Eusebius (*Hist Eccl* 2.18.5) speaks of five books of *QE* , while we have only two.

I. The Greek Fragments

The first scholar to publish fragments of Philo preserved as quotations in the works of other ancient writers was Thomas Mangey in 1742,[1] who in his edition of the Philonic corpus included fragments excerpted from a manuscript of John of Damascus' *Sacra Parallela*.[2] He was followed by the Armenian Mechitarist monk, Johannes Baptista Aucher(ean), who in his 1826 edition of the Armenian text[3] noted Greek fragments from thirty locations in the *Quaestiones*.[4] Shortly afterward Angelo Mai published a short section of *QE* (2.62-68), preserved in only one manuscript (Vat gr 379, 14th c.). In subsequent years Mai put forth three further collections containing fragments of Philo.[5]

[1]Mangey 1742. Cited from G-G, no. 404.

[2]Discussed in Harris 1886, xix.

[3]Aucher 1826 (G-G , no. 441).

[4]This fact has been generally ignored in subsequent scholarship and has only recently been pointed out by Royse 1984, 143, n.2, who lists the citations in question.

[5]Strictly speaking, the passage *QE* 2.62-68 published in Mai 1831 is not a "fragment" in the sense of a passage of Philo quoted by another writer, but a text of Philo in its own

Fragments of the *Quaestiones* were also included in J. B. Pitra's *Analecta Sacra* , vols 2 and 3.

The first collection of all thus far identified fragments of the *Quaestiones* was issued in 1886 by James Rendel Harris,[6] with extensive references to manuscript sources and previous editions. Harris was able to identify the location of many fragments published by Mangey but left unlocated by him. In 1890 Paul Wendland, in the course of collating manuscripts in Italy in preparation for his and L. Cohn's edition of Philo, discovered extensive fragments of the *Quaestiones* in the *Epitome* of Procopius of Gaza (6th c.). These, together with a few fragments of the *Quaestiones* found in Theodoret and Origen, he published the following year,[7] thus extending appreciably the collection of Harris. In their critical edition of the Greek text of Philo, Cohn and Wendland[8] discussed the manuscript sources of the fragments as they were known at the turn of the century, but did not include the actual texts. Harris's work was further extended by Émile Bréhier in 1908, who located three passages left unidentified by Harris.[9] Later Hans Lewy was able to add a dozen further fragments from John of Damascus and the *Catenae* .[10]

During the 1930's Ludwig Früchtel undertook a critical edition of the fragments of Philo. In 1937 he published several fragments of the *Quaestiones*:[11] eleven of these had already been included in Harris's collection as unlocated; Früchtel was able to locate these on the basis of a careful comparison with Aucher's Latin version.[12] He also added two additional fragments not in Harris's collection. Thereafter Früchtel continued to collect materials and succeeded in locating eleven more fragments,[13] but his project remained incomplete at the time of his death in 1963. His extensive files have been lodged with the Institutum Judaicum Delitzschianum at Münster i. W. While these files represent an

---

right, as Petit 1978, 13, points out. Accordingly in PAPM it is not included with the fragments (vol. 33) but is to be included in the forthcoming volume containing *QE*. The later publications were Mai 1834 and Mai 1837.

[6]Harris 1886, 12-75.

[7]Wendland 1891, 29-114.

[8]*PCW* 1.lvi-lx; lxii-lxx.

[9]Bréhier 1950, VII, n. 2.

[10]Lewy 1932 (G-G no. 438).

[11]Früchtel 1937.

[12]In this article Früchtel also included nine fragments from Clement of Alexandria, which, as Royse 1984, 146, has noted, "are not genuine fragments of the *Quaestiones* at all."

[13]Royse 1984, 148, and below, p. 23.

immense amount of labor, they were unfortunately based only on previously printed texts, and for the Armenian, on Aucher's Latin version, without recourse either to the manuscripts themselves or to the Armenian text as such. Früchtel's materials are therefore unpublishable as critical texts.

An attempt at a complete collection of all thus far identified fragments of the *Quaestiones* was brought together by Ralph Marcus in an appendix to his edition of the *Quaestiones* in 1953.[14] Marcus added no new material and worked only from printed editions[15] without attempting any more critical texts on the basis of the manuscripts than these editions had already achieved; neither did he make a clear distinction between genuine quotations and paraphrases,[16] nor was his collection actually complete to date, as he failed to include two fragments published previously by Früchtel.[17]

There thus remained a need for an edition of the Greek fragments which would be as complete as possible and also provide a genuinely critical text. This has now been provided by Françoise Petit in the Lyon edition of Philo.[18] Petit develops her text from manuscripts of three principal works: the exegetical *catenae* ("chains" of citations gathered from commentators on Scripture from the first six centuries and included in manuscripts of the Bible), the *Epitome* of Procopius of Gaza (d. ca. 538), who compiled a large collection of exegetical excerpts on the Heptateuch, and the various *florilegia* deriving from the parent work of John of Damascus (d. before 754), the *Sacra Parallela* or citations of patristic (as well as Philo's and Josephus's) comments arranged topically. In addition she presents a few fragments drawn from other patristic sources. In all she has used twenty-four manuscripts and thus is able to provide a critical apparatus for her text, fragment by fragment. She makes a clear distinction between actual quotations and paraphrases or "echoes" of Philo which occur across a wide body of patristic literature,

[14]Marcus 1953, 2.179-263.

[15]Chiefly those of Harris, Wendland and Früchtel (see above nn. 2,7,11).

[16]In addition to the editions cited above (n. 15), Marcus also included fragments published in Praechter 1896 and Staehle 1931 which, as Petit remarks, "livrent plutôt des échos philoniens que de véritables citations" (Petit 1978, 14).

[17]Früchtel 1937, 112, 113 n.1; cf Royse 1984, 146-47.

[18]Petit 1978. See also Petit 1979 and the fifteen fragments of *QG* contained in Petit 1977.

which she has not attempted to include.[19] Neither has she published the extensive borrowings from Philo by Ambrose, which are of course in Latin.[20] She has, however, noted these in those cases where they are from the *Quaestiones*. She also has located several previously unlocated fragments.

Since Petit's edition, further identifications of fragments have been made by James R. Royse, who for a number of years has been engaged in preparing a critical edition of all the Greek fragments of Philo. In the *Quaestiones* Royse has made important additions to the work of Petit: on the basis of Früchtel's studies, including his unpublished files, to which Royse has had access at Münster, and of his own investigation of manuscripts, he has been able to publish the locations of nine additional fragments not included by either Marcus or Petit;[21] three of these are his own discoveries.

The most recent critical project on the fragments of the *Quaestiones* is that of J. Paramelle,[22] who, in association with Enzo Lucchesi and Jacques Sesiano, has produced an elaborate edition of the fragments of *QG* 2.1-7 (on the construction of Noah's ark), as they are found in Codex Vatopedinus 659. This edition provides a critical text of the Armenian and Greek texts with apparatus, Latin and French translations, and extensive notes.

There remain a number of fragments published by Harris and Marcus which in the *florilegia* are attributed specifically to the *Quaestiones*, but which have not been found in our extant texts. It has been thought that these may be remains of those lost portions of the *Quaestiones* which appear in neither the Armenian nor the Latin versions, but Petit rejects this proposal as "guère probable"[23] on the ground that the text of the *Quaestiones* available to the compilers of the commentaries already had suffered losses analogous to those in the Armenian text.[24] Royse, however, has kept this possibility open.[25] Taking as his point of departure a suggestion of Marcus[26] that the

[19]Petit 1978,30: "On comprendra que nous ayons renoncé à nous engager dans un champ de recherche aussi vaste."
[20]See the detailed study of these in Lucchesi 1977.
[21]Royse 1984, 149-52.
[22]Paramelle 1984.
[23]Petit 1978, 28.
[24]*Ibid.,* 29-30.
[25]Royse 1984, 145.
[26]Marcus 1953 1.xii-xv.

original content and divisions of the *Quaestiones* followed the Pentateuchal lectionary readings of the Alexandrian synagogue (in analogy with those of the one-year cycle followed in Babylonia), he has demonstrated in great detail that these weekly sections or *parashiyyot* fit the apparent structure of the *Quaestiones* with striking precision.[27] The resultant picture of the original scope of the *Quaestiones* reveals numerous lacunae in the extant text and strengthens the possibility that some, if not all, thus far unlocated fragments may be from these missing materials.

The foregoing discussion demonstrates how complex is the problem of the Greek fragments of those treatises of Philo for which we have only Armenian or Latin versions. If the history of this research teaches us anything, it is that one can never claim to have located all existing fragments; but that the vast bulk of them are now in hand seems equally certain. With the increasing number of patristic texts, as well as that of Philo, now becoming available in machine readable form, and the existence of a computerized concordance to Philo[28] (unfortunately not yet generally available), it can be hoped that further fragments may yet be identified.

II. The Latin Version[29]

Our earliest modern scholarship on any part of the *Quaestiones* was devoted to the editing and publishing of the old Latin version, which contains *QG* 4.154-245, as well as material between §§195 and 196 not found in the Armenian text. Manuscripts of this version first attracted the attention of scholars during the Renaissance. The text was published initially at Paris in 1520 by Agostino Giustiniani, Bishop of Nebbio and professor at the Sorbonne, under the title, *Philonis Judaei quaestiones centrum et duae, et totidem responsiones morales super Genesin, latine.*[30] Subsequently an improved edition based on better manuscripts was issued by J. Sichard (Basel: Adam Petri, 1527) and reprinted by Heinrich Petri

[27]Royse 1976-77.

[28]Developed by Peder Borgen with assistance from the Norwegian Scientific Research Council. See Borgen and Roald Skarsten 1971, 37-39, 50.

[29]The following discussion is based in large part on Petit 1973; see also *PCW* 1.l-lii; 6.xii-xvi.

[30]G-G no. 444.

(Basel) in 1538 and again in 1550.[31] There was also an edition in 1599.[32] Sichard's 1538 edition was reprinted by Aucher beneath his Armenian text of 1826. Aucher was thus the first in recent times to bring the existence of the Latin version to the attention of scholars, after a hiatus of more than two hundred years. Critical study of the text began with Johannes Baptista Pitra, librarian of the Vatican, who in an essay, "De vetere Philonis interprete Latino,"[33] noted peculiarities in vocabulary and assigned the translation to "African Latin" of the time of Tertullian. Paul Wendland, in discussing fragments of Philo, noted that the unique material in the Latin *QG* shows evidence of being authentically from Philo.[34] Frederick C. Conybeare, in his edition of *De Vita Contemplativa*,[35] continued the discussion of the date and provenance of the Latin version (which also contains *De Vita Contemplativa*, both it and *QG* being quite clearly the work of the same translator). Conybeare concluded for the latter part of the fourth century and pointed to evidence for Italian provenance rather than African.[36] Cohn, writing concurrently, accepted his conclusions.[37] Since their time, there has been unanimity among scholars that the old Latin translation is a fourth century version.

The definitive edition of the Latin version was published by Françoise Petit in 1973.[38] Following Conybeare, Petit concludes that it was produced in Italy during the last quarter of the fourth century.[39] In support of this she adduces the following evidence: the peculiarities of the vocabulary and syntax are typical of the fourth century; the biblical text shows no evidence of the Vulgate, but accords with many readings of the Old Latin; none of the glosses in the text appears to be later than the translation, but they do reflect the Apollinarian controversy of the latter third of the fourth century; finally, Ambrose probably and Augustine certainly were familiar with this version.[40]

---

[31]Sichard 1527 (G-G no. 445). The 1538 and 1550 editions are numbers 446 and 448 respectively in G-G.
[32]Not listed by G-G, but referred to by Marcus 1953, 2.267.
[33]Pitra 1884, cited by Marcus 1953, 2.267; not listed in G-G .
[34]Wendland 1891, 85, n.2.
[35]Conybeare 1895.
[36]Conybeare 1895, 144-45.
[37]*PCW* 1.li.
[38]Petit 1973. See n. 29 above.
[39]Petit 1973, 1.13.
[40]Petit 1973, 1.8-13.

With Petit's work we now have a fully critical edition of the Latin text. After analyzing the fifteen known manuscripts,[41] ranging in date from the eleventh to the fifteenth centuries, she concludes that only the following are of value for establishing the text:[42]

- L X-XI c Originally at the Monastery of Lorsch; now lost. Used by Sichard in his edition of 1527, and now available only through his notations. Petit cites as *Sich.*
- F XI c Originally at Fulda; now at Cassel (Theol 4°, no 3.) This, with additions from L where F is lacking, was the basis of Sichard's text.
- A XI c Originally at the Abbey of Admont (Styria). Now in the Goodhart Collection at Yale (Petit gives New York, as formerly).
- B XII c Of unknown provenance, now at Budapest (Lat m ae 23).
- G Late XV c Formerly at Coblenz, now in Berlin (Görries 132).

These six manuscripts, along with the extant Greek fragments and the Armenian version, constitute the basis of Petit's text and apparatus. They, with the remaining extant manuscripts, all derive from a single exemplar which must have contained *QG, De Vita Contemplativa,* and the pseudo-Philonic *Liber antiquitatum*, and which probably was brought to Germany from Italy during the Carolingian renaissance as one of two hundred volumes with which Angilbert enriched the library of his abbey of St. Riquier. This accords with the fact that all of the oldest manuscripts were preserved in Benedictine monasteries in Germany and Austria, while no manuscripts of the Latin text are to be found in France, and only late ones, dependent on those in Germany, appear in Italian libraries.[43]

The Latin version is characterized by Petit as "très mauvaise." She goes on to say: "Lorsque le traducteur se croit, à tort ou à raison, en possession du sens, il modifie à son gré la syntaxe de l'original et se permit de grandes libertés. Dans les passages plus obscurs, il tombe dans

---

[41]Cohn has listed eleven mss. (*PCW* 6.xv-xvi); G-G mistakenly list two mss. twice (306/321; 318/323) plus a third which is not Latin but Greek (their no. 324). I am indebted to Abraham Terian for this information.

[42]Petit 1973, 1.30-43; the *editio princeps* of Giustiniani (1520) was based on an inferior ms. of the 14th c., Urbino lat. 73, which Petit (pp. 40-41) judges "parfaitement inutile à l'établissement du texte, de même que l'édition princeps."

[43]Petit 1973, 1.14-15.

le charabia."[44] In preparing her edition, Petit has attempted to choose not simply the best reading found in the extant manuscripts, but in as far as possible to go behind them to the probable reconstruction of the text produced by the fourth-century translator — a leap backward of at least six hundred years for which there is no manuscript evidence. Since it is clear that all extant manuscripts derive from a single (9th c.?) archetype, the restoration of its text can be achieved with a fair degree of certainty. Behind this point, however, she is forced to rely on conjecture, governed by the necessity of distinguishing between anomalies that arose in the process of transmitting the Latin text, and those that are due to the translator. In the latter case, discernable errors in translation (as distinguished from scribal errors) are retained if they can be explained on the basis of the Greek fragments or the Armenian.[45] Accordingly, in addition to a critical apparatus, Petit has provided a 192-page linguistic commentary in which with much erudition she explains the basis for her readings, and also cites numerous parallels elsewhere in Philo.

III. The Armenian Version

The Armenian version, which is our sole source for much of the *Quaestiones*, in the early nineteenth century was adjudged by its first editor, the Mechitarist Johannes Baptista Aucher, to have been made at the beginning of the fifth century by a disciple of Mesrop, the inventor of the Armenian alphabet and translator of the Bible, and thus to have been a part of what is known as "the Golden Age" of Armenian translation of Greek texts. This opinion was endorsed by Conybeare[46] and incorporated into the Prolegomena of Cohn and Wendland's critical edition of the Greek text.[47] It was also followed by Marcus as late as 1953, who cites Aucher as his authority.[48] Already, however, in 1936, Hans Lewy, working on the basis of modern critical scholarship on the history of early Armenian literature, had demonstrated that the translation of Philo belongs not to the "golden Age" of the fifth century, but to that of the subsequent "Hellenizing School" of the late sixth century, located in Constantinople. Lewy's conclusions rest in the main on two observations: that our earliest external evidence of the Armenian

[44]Petit 1973, 1.13.
[45]Petit 1973, 1.29.
[46]Conybeare 1895, 155.
[47]*PCW* 1.liv, n. 1.
[48]Marcus 1953 1.vii.

version is in the work of the Armenian historian Eliseus, who was active in Constantinople shortly after 570; and that the extremely Hellenistic syntax of the version fits this later period, whereas the translations produced in the previous century exhibit a pure Armenian style. Lewy's conclusions have been accepted by subsequent scholars.[49]

Aucher provided both an Armenian text and a Latin translation. The *Quaestiones* as a whole thus entered the world of Philonic scholarship almost three centuries after the Greek corpus had become available through the *editio princeps* of Adrien Turnèbe in 1552. Aucher based his edition on five manuscripts, available to him in the library of San Lazaro in Venice. These were the following:[50]

A No. 1040 1296 C.E.
B A copy of Istanbul (Galata) 69 1791 C.E.[51]
C No 1334 XIII c.+ (*QG* 1-4)
D No 1376 (?) XVIII (?) (*QG* 4 only)
E Apparently a lexicon

Of these Aucher took A as his base, and depended largely on it and B and C.[52] Since Aucher's time, some sixty other manuscripts have been located containing all or portions of the extant Armenian version. These range in date from the twelfth to the nineteenth centuries, and while more than half of them are preserved in the Matenadaran Library of the Academy of Sciences of the Armenian Soviet Socialist Republic in Erevan, others are to be found at Jerusalem (St. James' Monastery), Galata (Istanbul), Paris (Bibliothèque Nationale), Bzommar (Lebanon), New Djulfa (near Isfahan), Tabriz and Ankara, as well as Venice. The bulk of the manuscripts have, however, exercised relatively little influence on scholarship. Aucher's edition remains our working text of the Armenian version, and stands at the base of our modern language translations.

There has been a certain amount of confusion in the identification and listing of the Armenian manuscripts. In 1936 Hans Lewy listed

49Petit 1973, 1.15-16; Terian 1981, 6-9.

50Of these, G-G list only Venice 1040 (G-G no. 350) and 1334 (G-G no. 352).

51There has been some confusion as to the identity of Aucher's Ms. B: Mercier 1979, 17, identifies it as Venice 253, while Terian 1985-86, 187-189, correcting his statement in Terian 1981, 17-18, points out that "Aucher's B . . . was copied from Galata MS 69, which in turn was copied from Jerusalem MS 333," while Venice 253 "contains none of the works of Philo."

52Mercier 1979, 17; Marcus 1953, 1.v.

twenty-two manuscripts, all that were known at the time.[53] Goodhart and Goodenough in their *Bibliography* published a list (prepared by Robert P. Casey) of twenty-seven manuscripts, plus thirteen more that they identified as containing scholia on Philo.[54] As with their listing of Latin manuscripts, there are also several errors in their list of Armenian texts, arising from mistaken comparisons of entries in various catalogues. Terian notes that in two instances they list manuscripts that cannot otherwise be identified (G-G nos. 343, 361), and in three instances they mistakenly give the same manuscript twice (355/356; 357/359; 365/373).[55] Marcus, in his translation of the *Quaestiones* , undertook no discussion of the manuscripts and based his work on Aucher's edition.

Mercier[56] lists twenty-four manuscripts as containing all or portions of the extant text of *QG*, thirty-one others which are entitled "Collections" (*Recueils*), and twelve further that appear to have some relationship to *QG* . His list, however, contains a number of errors, as pointed out by Terian.[57] His system of sigla ignores the fact that most of the latest manuscripts are copies of earlier, extant texts (Erevan 2056 of Erevan 1500; Jerusalem 157 of Erevan 2595, Galata 69 of Jerusalem 333; Paris 159 of Venice 1040). Galata 69 should be dated 1791 rather than 1298 (the colophon of its exemplar, Jerusalem 333, was copied into it). Venice 253 in Mercier's list contains only a short scholion on *De Providentia* , but no works of Philo. Similarly Erevan 59 and Venice 1376 contain only scholia. Conversely, Erevan 2595, which he includes in his list of manuscripts containing scholia and catenae, is a genuine text copied from Jerusalem 333. Several other manuscripts containing scholia not in his list have been identified by Terian.

Most recently our fullest description and most accurate list of Armenian manuscripts of Philo has been given by Terian,[58] who identifies twenty-seven manuscripts and notes that in addition there are about fifty more containing scholia and catenae of Philonic quotations (he lists thirty-eight of these that are at the Matenadaran).[59]

[53]Lewy 1936, 4-6.
[54]G-G pp. 182-85.
[55]Terian 1981, 14, n. 33.
[56]Mercier 1979, 17-22.
[57]Terian 1985-86.
[58]Terian 1981, 14-25, supplemented and corrected in Terian 1985-86.
[59]Terian 1981, 13, n. 28.

Of the twenty-seven manuscripts identified by Terian, he indicates twenty-one as containing material from the *Quaestiones*. These are:[60]

	Date	*QG*	*QE*
Erevan 5239	1274	4.35-	1-2
Erevan 3932	1275	1-3	1-2
Erevan 1500	1282	1-4	1-2
Venice 1040	1296	1.49-4.75	1.10-21; 2.44-
Jerusalem 333	1298	1-4	1-2
Erevan 3935	13 c.	1-3	1-2
Bzommar 121	13-14 c	1-3	1-2
Erevan 2104	1318	2.61-63	1-2
Erevan 2100	1325	4.1-	
Erevan 2057	1328		1-2
Erevan 2102	1342	1.3-3	1-2
Erevan 2058	14 c.	4	
Erevan 4275	14 c.	1-3.55	
Venice 1334	14 c.	1-4	1-2
Jerusalem 1331	14 c.	1-4.156	
Erevan 2056	1646	(copy of Erevan 1500)	
Istanbul 114	18 c.	Contains the Philonic corpus	
Jerusalem 157	1758	(copy of Jerusalem 333)	
Erevan 2595	1786/87	(copy of Jerusalem 333)	
Istanbul (Galata) 69	1791	(copy of Jerusalem 333)	
Paris(B.N.) 159	1816	(copy of Venice 1040)	

Terian also lists the catalogues of the following libraries containing Armenian manuscripts of Philo:[61]

60Of the manuscripts listed here, the following are available in microfilm in the collection of the Philo Institute at McCormick Theological Seminary in Chicago: Erevan 3932, 3935, 2104, 2100, 2057, 2102, 4275, 2056 and 2595. These were graciously made available by the Matenadaran Library in Erevan.

61Terian 1981, 15 and n. 35.

Matenadaran, Erevan, ASSR: O. Eganyan et al., *Cowc'ak jeṙagrac' Maštoc'i anvan matenadarani*, I-II Erevan, 1965, 1970.

St.James's Monastery, Jerusalem: N. Bogharian, *Grand Catalogue of St . James Manuscripts*, I-VII Jerusalem, 1966-74.

Monastery at Bzommar, Lebanon: M. Keschischian, *Katalog der armenischen Handschriften in der Bibliothek des Klosters Bzommar* Vienna, 1946.

Bibliothèque Nationale, Paris: F. Macler, *Catalogue des manuscrits arméniens et géorgiens de la Bibliothèque Nationale* Paris, 1908.

Monastery at New Djulfa: S. Tēr-Awetisian, *Katalog der armenischen Handschriften in der Bibliothek des Klosters in Neu-Djoulfa,* I-II Vienna, 1970-72.

As for the relative value of the Armenian manuscripts, Terian endorses Lewy's conclusion that those best suited for establishing a critical text are six, all dating from before the middle of the fourteenth century and all containing the entire Armenian corpus; these six derive from a single archetype, and may be subdivided into two recensions, α and β, of which the latter is generally superior. These six manuscripts are: Erevan 1500 (α), Erevan 2057 (α), Erevan 2104 (α), Venice 1040 (β), Jerusalem 333 (β), and Erevan 2100 and 2102 (originally one manuscript, α/β mixed). These all contain the *Quaestiones*. While Lewy's judgment of their preeminence was based primarily on his study of the text of one treatise, *De Jona* , Terian has amplified his verdict to include the whole corpus: "Lewy's pronouncements . . . seem to apply to the entire text of the Armenian Philo, of which the corpus and textual tradition [of] the *De Jona* is an integral part."[62]

Aucher's Latin translation remained, until recent years, the only access to the *Quaestiones* available to scholars unacquainted with the Armenian. Initially printed by the Mechitarist fathers of Venice, it was soon republished (without the Armenian text) in Leipzig as part of C. E. Richter's edition of Philo,[63] and thus became more widely available in a handy form. This edition was reprinted twice.[64] Portions of *QE* were

[62]*Ibid.*, 22.

[63]Richter 1828-30. *QG* 1-2 are in vol. 6.250-371; *QG* 3-4 and *QE* in 7.3-350.

[64]Leipzig: Tauchnitz, 1851-53; Leipzig: Otto Holtze, 1880-93 (G-G no. 420).

also published by Angelo Mai and Constantin von Tischendorf.[65] Aucher's translation of *QG* 1-2 is also included with Mercier's French translation in the Lyon edition of Philo.[66]

Aucher's translation, while displaying great erudition in the realm of classical Armenian, is seen today by scholars expert in both Armenian and Hellenistic Greek to suffer at many points from the frailties of the ancient Armenian translator, who often was incapable of understanding the Greek text and who, in striking contrast to the more liberated Latin translator, solved his problem simply by rendering the Greek word for word into Armenian on the basis of lexical lists available to him. At numerous points he thus produced a translation that was virtually unintelligible in Armenian,[67] but which, thanks to its very woodenness, for a modern scholar who knows Philo's Greek vocabulary and style, is essential for reconstructing the Greek *Vorlage*.[68]

In spite of the fact that the whole of the extant *Quaestiones* has thus been available to scholars since the first half of the nineteenth century, it has exercised relatively little influence on Philo scholarship. It was not included in the major critical edition of Philo produced by Cohn and Wendland, nor in the German translation edited by Cohn and I. Heinemann (PCH). The first publication of the *Quaestiones* in a modern language did not appear until 1953, with Marcus' English translation in two supplemental volumes to the Loeb Classics edition of Philo. Marcus had been engaged for more than a quarter of a century in the preparation of this translation. As early as 1930 he had discussed the nature of the Armenian version.[69] In his translation, Marcus followed Aucher's Armenian text, but went beyond him in making extensive use of the greater number of Greek fragments now available and particularly in identifying the Greek terms represented by the Armenian translator's

[65]"Ex opere in Exodum selectae quaestiones" in Mai 1831 (see n.5 above); Tischendorf 1868, 144-55.

[66]Mercier 1979.

[67]Terian 1981, 13-14, states: "As for the medieval and later scribes, they must have copied the seemingly obscure works of Philo with little or no understanding."

[68]For a detailed discussion of the Armenian translator's technique, see Terian 1981, 9-14; cf. Marcus 1930, 61-64; Lewy 1936, 16-24; Petit 1973, 1.16-17; and Mercier 1979, 26-38.

[69]It should also be noted that, concurrently with the work of Marcus, Hans Lewy had projected a critical edition of the Armenian corpus of Philo, which was to be sponsored by the Preussische Akademie der Wissenschaften. Political developments in Germany after 1933, together with Lewy's untimely death in Israel, precluded his publishing the text of more than one treatise, that of *De Jona* (see n. 53 above).

vocabulary. Marcus' method is reflected in his publication in 1933 of "An Armenian-Greek Index to Philo's *Quaestiones* and *De Vita Contemplativa*."[70] On the basis of the Greek fragments of the *Quaestiones* published by Harris and those of *De Vita Contemplativa* edited by Conybeare, he was able to establish a list of Armenian terms with their Greek equivalents in Philo's vocabulary. Through his conversance with Hellenistic Greek Marcus was successful repeatedly in recognizing equivalences in the Armenian translator's Hellenizing style that had escaped Aucher. In his second volume Marcus also included the Greek fragments of the *Quaestiones* and of those portions of *QG* extant in the old Latin version.

French translations of *QG* 1-2 and *QG* 3-6 were made by Charles Mercier (d. 1978) for the Lyon edition and published in separate volumes.[71] The former was prepared for the press after his death by J. P. Mahé, Jacques Cazeaux and Enzo Lucchesi; the latter by Madeleine Petit with the aid of J. P. Mahé. This second volume also contains the old Latin version of *QG* 6 edited by Françoise Petit (substantially as published previously in Petit 1973) together with a French translation and notes by her. Mercier went beyond Marcus in expanding his manuscript base and also drew on the Greek fragments and the old Latin version. As he was a philologist and not a Philonist, it is understandable that his notes are almost entirely linguistic. Terian judges Mercier's work to be "a very readable translation of a most problematic text," which he attributes to his "mastery of the Armenian translators' method, especially his recognition of the underlying Greek syntax and the redundant use of synonyms which often represent a single word in the original Greek."[72]

The volume in the Lyon edition containing *QE* is now in press, translated by Terian, who has based his version on a full comparison of the vocabularies of all treatises of Philo extant in both Greek and Armenian. His is the first translation of the *Quaestiones* to be so grounded. As with the other volumes in this series that have been translated from Armenian, that text is, by an infelicitous decision of the editors, not included. For this we are still dependent on Aucher's publication of 1826.[73]

---

[70]Marcus 1933.

[71]Mercier 1979; Mercier and Petit 1984.

[72]Terian 1985-86, 187, 189.

[73]*The National Union Catalogue, Pre-1956 Imprints*, ALA-Bemrose Microfiche no. 6314, p. 317, lists only eight libraries in the U.S. in which it is available: University of

Substantial work remains to be done on the Armenian *Quaestiones*. There is no critical text. Our basis for study thus remains in a primitive condition as compared with the exemplary editions we possess of the fragments in Greek and of the old Latin translation, both prepared by Petit, or indeed of the Greek Philonic corpus as a whole.

California, Berkeley; University of Chicago; Harvard University; Library of Congress; Hebrew Union College, Cincinnati; New York Public Library; Union Theological Seminary, New York; and Dumbarton Oaks, Washington, D. C. Fortunately, however, a reprint edition was issued at Hildesheim, 1988.

CHAPTER TWO

PHILO'S *QUAESTIONES IN EXODUM* 1.6

JAMES R. ROYSE

The search for Greek fragments of Philo's *Quaestiones* has occupied many scholars over the years, and has resulted in a gradual accumulation of a large collection of texts, ranging from a few words to the extensive extract of *QE* 2.62-68. One of those whose work is closely linked with this search is Ludwig Früchtel, and in an earlier article I reported on some of his contributions to this search which have been in part overlooked.[1] However, I there failed to note a further fragment which Früchtel had identified for the first time. This text comes from *QE* 1.6 and permits, with some emendation, the establishment of virtually the entire Greek text of this section.

The primary witnesses to the Greek are two manuscripts of the *Sacra parallela*.[2] It happens that the section itself, as found in the Armenian version,[3] divides into two parts, the first introduced by "in the first place," and the second by "but in the second place." These introductory phrases have not been preserved in the Greek extracts, and of course make little sense unless read in the context of the entire section.[4] But, apart from these phrases and the question that begins the section, the first fragment contains precisely the first half of the section, and the second fragment begins precisely where the first leaves off and

[1]Royse 1984.

[2]The standard survey of the florilegia is found in Richard 1964; see cols. 476-86 on the *Sacra parallela*.

[3]The Armenian with a Latin translation was published by Aucher 1826, 451. The section is translated into English in Marcus 1953, 2.13-14.

[4]Such phrases are in fact retained within the Greek fragments of the *Quaestiones* only in rather few places: *QG* 2.11 and 13 (as found in the chains), 2.2 and 7 (as found in Vatopedinus 659), and *QE* 2.66 and 68 (as found in Vaticanus 379).

then continues to the end. This division of fragments is paralleled in a few other cases.[5]

The first fragment (ὑπερβολὴ ... ἄγαν) is found in Vaticanus 1553 (K), with the lemma assigning it to the first book of *QE*, and was first published by Mai in 1833 without being located.[6] Harris identified the text in 1886,[7] and it was further printed by Marcus[8] and Petit.[9] The second fragment (ἡ αὐτάρκεια ... καθαιρεῖν) is found in Berolinensis 46, the famous codex Rupefucaldinus (R), and was printed by Harris as one of his unidentified fragments,[10] noting that the first portion of it (through βίον) is also found in the florilegium of Pseudo-Antonius.[11] Since this second fragment is not explicitly attributed to the *Quaestiones* in the manuscripts, but merely to Philo, it was not included among the unidentified fragments of the *Quaestiones* edited by Marcus and Petit. But in his collection of fragments Früchtel did correctly locate the text, and even provided some useful emendations of the Greek, relying in part on the (Latin version of the) Armenian.

First, let us look at the Greek text, as I believe it may be reconstructed for the entire section after the opening question.

> <Πρῶτον μὲν> ὑπερβολὴ καὶ ἔλλειψις ἀνισότητα ἐγέννησαν· ἀνισότης δέ, ἵνα αὐτὸς μυθικώτερον χρήσωμαι τοῖς ὀνόμασιν, μήτηρ ἀδικίας ἐστὶν ὡς ἔμπαλιν ἰσότης δικαιοσύνης· ὑπερβολῆς δὲ καὶ ἐλλείψεως μέσον τὸ αὔταρκες, ἐν ᾧ τὸ ἱερὸν γράμμα περιέχεται τὸ "μηδὲν ἄγαν." <δεύτερον δὲ> ἡ αὐτάρκεια πηγὴν ἔχουσα σωφροσύνης μέτρον ἐστὶ τῶν ἀναγκαίων καὶ χρησίμων εἰς τὸν βίον - ταύτης ἀδελφὰς <εἶναι> συμβέβηκεν ὀλιγοδείαν, εὐκολίαν,

---

[5]See, for instance, *QE* 2.9, as cited by Petit 1978, 244-45. There the second citation from the *Sacra parallela* (surviving in R alone) begins precisely where the first citation (found in S, H, A, and at another place in R) ends.

[6]Mai 1833, 106a; reprinted in *PG* 86^2, col. 2092A (6) 7-12.

[7]Harris 1886, 47.

[8]Marcus 1953, 2.238.

[9]Petit 1978, 234-35.

[10]Harris 1886, 101.

[11]This florilegium was originally published by Conrad Gessner (or Gesner) 1546, 1-162; reprinted in *PG* 136, cols. 765-1244. On this florilegium, see Richard 1964, cols. 492-94.

ἀπερίττους ἀρετάς ⌝, πάντα ὅσα τῦφος
διαίρει πρὸς ὕψος ἐπιχειροῦσα καθαιρεῖν.

1-7 (ὑπερβολή – ἄγαν):
K, f. 245ʳ (2) 3-8: (scil. f. 244ᵛ 13: Φίλωνος)
ἐκ τοῦ α τῶν ἐν ’Εξόδῳ ζητημάτων
8-13 (ἡ – καθαιρεῖν)
R, f. 220ʳ (31) 31-34: τοῦ αὐτοῦ (scil. f. 220ʳ 14: Φίλωνος)
8-10 (ἡ – βίον):
Antonius, Gessner, p. 38 = *PG* 136, 881A8-9
(Φίλωνος [Philonis] on previous text, p. 38 [= 881A4])

---

1 Πρῶτον μὲν add. Früchtel ex Arm ὑπερβολή coni. Petit (in app.) ex Arm: ὑπερβολαί K ἔλλειψις coni. Petit (in app.) ex Arm (ad litteram ἔκλειψις cum verbis additis): ἐλλείψεις K 7 δεύτερον δὲ add. Früchtel ex Arm 10 εἶναι add. Früchtel post συμβέβηκεν 12 ἀπερίττους ἀρετάς scr. Früchtel ex Arm (inexcessiva virtus = ἀπέριττον ἀρετήν): ἀπερίττους ἄρτους R 13 πρὸς R: εἰς Harris per errorem 13 διαίρει et καθαιρεῖν scr. Harris Früchtel: διαιρεῖ et καθαίρειν R

We turn first to a consideration of the text. The Armenian[12] for the most part clearly supports the above Greek text, and the reader is referred to Marcus's Armenian-Greek index[13] for confirmation of many

---

[12] For the sake of reference here is the Armenian of the entire section following the question (Aucher 1826, 451): naxaṙǰin gerazanc‘ut‘iwn ew pakasut‘iwn zugut‘ean ew hasarakut‘ean (hawasarut‘ean) cnaw anzugut‘iwn ew anhawasarut‘iwn. zi ew es aṙaspelagoyn inč‘ var arkic‘ zanuanc‘d, mayr dora anirawut‘iwn ē, orpēs darjcal isk andstin, zugut‘iwn ew hawasarut‘iwn ardarut‘iwn ē. isk gerazanc‘ut‘ean ew pakasut‘ean miǰak ē bawakann. yorum astuacayin girn zays ed, zi mi ic‘ē yoyž. erkrord isk iwr ašxatut‘iwnn zerkir varelov, parkeštut‘ean č‘ap‘ ē harkaworac‘n ew pitaworac‘n aṙ ənd marmnoyn keans. ew sora k‘ors dēp ełew linel sakawapitut‘iwn, diwrut‘iwn, ew anaṙawel aṙak‘inut‘iwn. ew amenayn or inč‘ miangam hpartut‘iwn bažanē aṙnu jeṙnarkeal tapalel. Aucher's translation reads: Primum quidem excessus defectusque aequitatis sive paritatis generavit inaequitatem ac imparitatem. Ut autem et ego fabulosum quidquam usurpabo de his nominibus, mater istius iniquitas est, sicut itidem paritas sive aequalitas justitia est. Inter autem excessum, et defectum medium tenet sufficiens; in quo divinus liber hoc constituit, ut Nihil erit nimis. Secundo, proprius labor suus in agro colendo mensura est moderata necessariorum utiliumque ad corporalem vitam. Sorores autem isti contigere frugalitas, facilitas, et inexcessiva virtus, et omne quidquam, quod superbiam sibi sumit evertendam.

[13] Marcus 1933, 251-82. Armenian-Greek correspondences are also noted in Awetik‘ean 1836-37.

of the equivalences. However, a few points are worth further discussion, and are here treated in order.

The addition of Πρῶτον is certain, and although μέν is never, it seems, expressed in the Armenian, the context here appears to require it, since δεύτερον δέ is later supported by the Armenian.

The readings ὑπερβολή and ἔλλειψις, suggested by Petit in her apparatus, may be considered quite certain. The readings of K differ only by two extremely common itacisms. The Armenian supports the singular, as does the context, and the singular forms occur in the Greek in the next sentence.[14] Actually, for the second word the Armenian more literally corresponds, as Petit notes, to ἔκλειψις,[15] and also adds a phrase, rendered by Aucher as "aequitatis sive paritatis,"[16] which is literally "of equality" (as Marcus translates), since ἰσότης is rendered by this doublet. Petit suggests that these terms are added "pour préciser qu'il s'agit de morale et non d'astronomie."

We now come to a problem in the Armenian, even though the Greek seems quite clear. Petit comments:[17]

> Le membre ἀνισότης δέ – δικαιοσύνης, parfaitement cohérent dans la citation grecque, semble altéré dans l'arménien. L'origine de la faute paraît être l'omission accidentalle de ἀνισότης δέ, réinséré par la suite en mauvaise place.

There are, in fact, several problems here. The object of the first clause, ἀνισότητα, comes before the verb in the Greek, but in the Armenian, which usually respects the Greek word order, the verb *cnaw* immediately follows the clarifying genitives already cited, as Aucher's literal translation shows. I believe that there are at least three possible textual sequences here.

1. It may well be that the punctuation, as printed by Aucher at any rate, is incorrect. Note that *ew anhawasarut'iwn* might correspond perfectly with ἀνισότης δέ, since *ew* is often used for δέ, but is not postpositive. We could then take *anzugut'iwn* as corresponding to ἀνισότητα, with the slight problem that it comes after the verb in the

---

[14] Petit (1978, 235, n. a) points out that the Armenian verb is also in the singular; perhaps the comments on agreement made by Jensen (Jensen 1959, 141 §374) provide some clarification.

[15] The Armenian *pakasut'iwn* renders ἔκλειψις twice at *Prov.* 2.100, although both occurrences have an added *lusoy* ("of the light") to clarify that astronomical phenomena are being discussed.

[16] This translation assumes Aucher's correction of ***hasarakut'ean*** (literally κοινωνίας) into ***hawasarut'ean*** (literally ἰσότητος).

[17] Petit 1978, 235, n. b.

Armenian rather than before. (In Armenian the nominative and accusative of these two words are the same.) It is true that it is puzzling that there is this shift in rendering of ἀνισότης, but there are some parallels to such inconsistent translation.[18] This is the explanation adopted by Marcus.[19]

2. Another explanation is that ἀνισότης was originally rendered here both times by the same doublet, that what we have after *cnaw* is in fact the translation of ἀνισότης δέ, and that the translation of ἀνισότητα has fallen out of the Armenian because of its similarity to the clarifying genitives. Indeed, we may postulate that what originally stood in the Armenian text was:

> pakasut'iwn zugut'ean ew hawasarut'ean anzugut'iwn ew anhawasarut'iwn cnaw anzugut'iwn ew anhawasarut'iwn zi . . .

The occurrence of at least similar doublets three times in such a short space would naturally invite confusion.

3. It is also possible that ἀνισότητα was originally rendered in its correct place, and that the clarifying genitives after the word for ἔλλειψις are a corruption of this original text.

When we turn to the second part of the section, it seems that both the Greek and the Armenian have been corrupted. Indeed, the first four words in the Greek fragment are completely transformed in the Armenian. I believe that the most natural explanation is that the Greek here is correct, and that the Greek manuscript lying before the Armenian translator was only partially readable. The Greek words ἡ αὐτάρκεια πηγὴν ἔχουσα are rendered as: *iwr ašxatut'iwnn zerkir varelov*. These words correspond (it seems) literally to: αὐτοῦ κόπος γῆν χρωμένῳ.[20] We can thus see that about half of the original letters (αυτ- -κ- -π- -γην- -χ-) were utilized, although the sense is entirely altered, leading to Marcus's translation: "one's own labor in tilling the soil. . . ." The Greek that we have clearly goes better with the thought of this section, and with σωφροσύνης the Greek and Armenian begin anew their close correspondence.

Note, though, that the Armenian seems to understand the phrase here as "measure of moderation," while in the Greek σωφροσύνης

---

[18] See Terian 1980, 197-207 (esp. 201-204).

[19] He comments (Marcus 1953, 2.13, n. *g*) on ***anhawasarut'iwn*** : "Aucher mistakenly takes this noun as the second object of 'produce' in the preceding sentence."

[20] The Armenian *varelov* is the instrumental case of the participle of the verb which is equivalent to χρῶμαι.

seems to depend on πηγήν, giving a somewhat awkward reading. The phrase πηγὴν ἔχουσα σωφροσύνης is most closely paralleled in Philo at *Op*. 21 and *Dec*. 122, although neither provides an example with a genitive dependent on πηγή. But the Armenian does have its rendering of σωφροσύνης in the genitive, and I suppose that the meaning must be that self-sufficiency has its source from temperance.

A little further on, for the Greek βίον, which is usually rendered by *keans* alone, we find *marmnoyn keans*. The term *marmnoyn* literally is σώματος, and I have found no example of its addition, although here it may serve to clarify that the necessities are for the "bodily life," a thought perhaps suggested by the earlier (incorrect) reference to "the earth."

Früchtel added εἶναι after συμβέβηκεν, and it certainly seems as though such an addition is necessary for the sense. However, I propose to add it before in order to avoid the subsequent hiatus. Philo's own placement varies, but there is at least some justification for the proposed arrangement.[21]

R's reading ἄρτους was judged by Früchtel to be corrupt, and so he wrote ἀπερίττους ἀρετάς, using Aucher's rendering "inexcessiva virtus" but keeping R's plural. Now, in fact the Armenian *ar̄ak'inut'iwn* corresponds to the singular ἀρετήν,[22] since in the *Quaestiones*, at least, the Armenian number is always the same as the Greek: at *QG* 1.51, 100; 3.8; and *QE* 1.7, both are singular, while at *QG* 4.204 both are plural. Adopting, then, Früchtel's reading, we must suppose that the Armenian originally translated it as *anar̄awel ar̄ak'inut'iwns*, differing only by the final letter (since the adjective could be the same with singular or plural). At some point this final *s* was omitted. With this change the position of the phrase, originally standing in apposition to the names of the two virtues, is even less clear, and consequently *ew* (= καί) was inserted before the phrase, thus giving Aucher's "et inexcessiva virtus." The corruption in the Greek can be readily explained as a kind of harmonization: after writing the ending -τους once, a scribe imposed that ending on the following word.[23]

21 See, e.g., *Sacr*. 2; *Det*. 82; *Dec*. 19 and 29 for some possible positions.

22 Marcus (1933, 252) cites this as almost a perfect one-to-one correspondence of Armenian and Greek.

23 While I believe that Früchtel's conjecture must be correct, it is remarkable that Philo on occasion finds extensive lessons in ἄρτος. Note that at *Spec*. 1.173 the twelve ἄρτοι are even related by him to εὐκολία and ὀλιγοδεία, while at *QG* 4.205 the

Note, by the way, that these two virtues, ὀλιγοδεία and εὐκολία, are often used by Philo together: *Sacr.* 27; *Spec.* 1.173; 4.101; *Virt.* 8; *Prob.* 77, 84. And they also appear to occur at *QE* 2.12, which is extant only in the Armenian, where we find the same two words as at *QE* 1.6.[24]

Given the above text, the section may be translated as follows:[25]

> First, excess and deficiency generate inequality, and inequality, if I may use rather mythological words, is the mother of injustice as again equality is of justice. But sufficiency is the mean of excess and deficiency, in which Holy Scripture includes "Nothing too much." Secondly, sufficiency, having its source from moderation, is the measure of things necessary and useful for life — its sisters happen to be frugality and contentment, inexcessive virtues —, undertaking to bring down all those things which delusion raises on high.

The overall theme of Philo's comments here is determined by the notion of "sufficiency," as called to his mind by the biblical text. Indeed, at the other two places where he comments on Exod 12:4, *Leg.* 3.165-66 and *Her.* 192-93, Philo makes similar points, and takes the occasion to discourse on the nature of equality.[26] However, this is the only occurrence of αὐτάρκεια in Philo's extant Greek, and is, of course, suggested by τὸ ἀρκοῦν in the biblical lemma; elsewhere the term Philo uses is τὸ αὔταρκες, as earlier in this section.

The points made, in the first part especially, would seem to be primarily Aristotelian, although the leading idea is nicely found in the following fragment of Democritus: καλὸν ἐν παντὶ τὸ ἴσον· ὑπερβολὴ δὲ καὶ ἔλλειψις οὔ μοι δοκέει.[27] And of course the

---

Armenian corresponds (Marcus 1953, 1.205, n. *i*) to the statement that bread (ἄρτος) is σύμβολον τῆς ὀλιγοδείας.

[24] Marcus (1953, 2.47) translates the relevant phrase as "the related virtues of frugality and contentedness," and adds in his note *h:* "ταῖς ἀναγκαίαις ἀρεταῖς, ὀλιγοδείᾳ καὶ εὐκολίᾳ." It is thus curious that, when dealing with *QE* 1.6, where he translates "frugality and contentment," he adds on the second noun in his note *n* : "Prob. εὐφροσύνη: Aucher 'facilitas.'"

[25] Besides the translation of Marcus, one may compare the following Latin translation in *PG* of the line preserved in Antonius: Frugalitas, ex temperantia ceu fonte scaturiens, rerum ad vitam necessariarum et utilium mensura est.

[26] Goodenough (1932, 118-19) discusses the notion of equality in *Heres* and says that *Her.* 156 "recalls Aristotelian moral terminology" (119, n. 5). In fact, *QE* 1.6 is much closer to the terminology he cites.

[27] Diels-Kranz, B102.

thought here is a major theme of Aristotle's theory of values. See, for example, the following passage from the *Nicomachean Ethics*:[28]

> τὸ δ' ἴσον μέσον τι ὑπερβολῆς καὶ ἐλλείψεως. . . . μεσότης δὲ δύο κακιῶν, τῆς μὲν καθ' ὑπερβολὴν τῆς δὲ κατ' ἔλλειψιν· καὶ ἔτι τῷ τὰς μὲν ἐλλείπειν τὰς δ' ὑπερβάλλειν τοῦ δέοντος ἔν τε τοῖς πάθεσι καὶ ἐν ταῖς πράξεσι, τὴν δ' ἀρετὴν τὸ μέσον καὶ εὑρίσκειν καὶ αἱρεῖσθαι.

When we turn to the second part of the section, we find similar ideas. Self-sufficiency comes from moderation, which has as its sister virtues[29] frugality and contentment. These latter two are then called "inexcessive virtues," presumably because their essence consists in avoiding any kind of excess. Such a claim fits in with the notion of virtue as a mean, of course, although I have not found any other explicit reference to "inexcessive virtue" in Philo or elsewhere.[30]

Returning now to the end of the first part of the section, we find an interesting issue raised by Petit concerning the proper interpretation of: τὸ ἱερὸν γράμμα περιέχεται τὸ "μηδὲν ἄγαν." The Armenian *astuacayin girn* here might literally be rendered as "divine writing,"[31] and Aucher, not knowing the Greek, translated the Armenian: "in quo divinus liber hoc constituit, ut Nihil erit nimis." Marcus, with the Greek before him, translated "In this passage Holy Scripture lays down (the rule), 'Nothing too much.'" Petit, however, disputes the line taken by Aucher and Marcus:[32]

> Il est impossible de comprendre ici τὸ ἱερὸν γράμμα comme désignant le texte biblique (contre Aucher et Marcus). Il faut interpréter: «l'inscription sacrée», en se rappelant que les murs du pronaos du temple d'Apollon à Delphes portaient des devises attribuées aux Sept sages, parmi lesquelles Μηδὲν ἄγαν.

Now, it is clear that Philo calls this writing "holy." The problem is whether it appears on the temple at Delphi or in the Bible. However, while it might be possible for Philo to refer to a pagan temple as

[28] *Eth. Nic.* 2.6 (1106a 28-29, 1107a 2-6). For another parallel in Philo see *Spec.* 4.168: ὁδὸν τὴν μέσην, ὑπερβολῆς καὶ ἐλλείψεως οὖσαν μεθόριον.

[29] Philo uses ἀδελφὰς ἀρετάς also at *Leg.* 3.242.

[30] But cf. Clement of Alexandria, *Paedagogus* 3.55 (p. 287 Potter): εὐκολία δέ ἐστιν ἕξις ἀπέριττος . . . . This text is cited by von Arnim 1903, 3.68.

[31] According to Marcus 1933, *astuacayin* corresponds most often to θεῖος, but also to ἱερός, and *gir* corresponds to γράμμα (and once to γραφή).

[32] Petit 1978, 235, n. d.

containing "holy" writing, it would at least be unexpected.[33] In fact, his usage for such phrases is as follows. The phrase ἱερὸν γράμμα occurs elsewhere in Philo's Greek only at *QE* 2.19, where it is used of the Bible. The similar phrase ἱερώτατον γράμμα occurs twice, *Deus* 6 and *Migr.* 139, both times of the Bible. And the plural, ἱερὰ γράμματα, occurs twelve times, eleven of which refer to the Bible: *Mos.* 2.290, 292; *Spec.* 2.159, 238; *Praem.* 79; *Contempl.* 28, 75, 78; *Legat.* 195; *QE* 2.62; and one unidentified fragment.[34] The sole exception is *Mos.* 1.23 where, writing of the sacred books of the Egyptians, Philo says: ἐν τοῖς λεγομένοις ἱεροῖς γράμμασιν. Here, of course, the additional adjective makes all the difference.

Moreover, note that Philo says that the holy writing περιέχεται the famous maxim. Aucher's and Marcus's translations, although literally correct for the Armenian *ed* (which is the aorist of the verb corresponding to τίθημι[35]), suggest too strongly that the rule is actually to be found in the holy writing,[36] which of course would not be true if it were the Bible. Rather, we must remember that Philo in fact held that *all* of the best of Greek wisdom is to be found in the Bible, that is, in the Old Testament. Now, of course, Philo does not suppose that the words μηδὲν ἄγαν are literally to be found in (the Greek rendering of) some verse of the Bible. But he can still think that the Bible includes or contains[37] this teaching of "Nothing too much."[38] In fact, such a belief is at the heart of his allegorical method. And elsewhere Philo makes this clear for a number of sayings which are not literally present.

---

[33] Philo refers to the most famous of the Delphic writings, "Know thyself," as τὸ Δελφικὸν γράμμα (*Legat.* 69), but not as "holy."

[34] Printed by Marcus 1953, 2.259 (no. 5); Petit 1978, 288 (*QE* no. 8).

[35] See Marcus 1933, 261 (*dnem*).

[36] It is true, of course, that a common meaning of περιέχω is to refer to specific passages; see 1 Peter 2:6.

[37] Philo uses περιέχω at *Congr.* 120 in a way that is perhaps parallel to *QE* 1.6 ; there he refers (as Colson translates) to the "ordinances containing commandments positive and prohibitive." Philo's method of interpretation would seem to require that "containing" (περιεχόντων) go beyond the literal words.

[38] Aucher (1826, 451, n. 1) expresses the same point in a note on his translation of this sentence: Sensus auctoris simpliciter id asserere videtur, quod illud axioma majorum, *nihil* vel *nequid nimis*, facile continetur etiam in mandatis Scripturae sacrae.

For example, consider his treatment in *QG* 4.8 of the "three measures" of Gen 18:6.[39] Philo finds support for the notion that "all things are measured by three" in Homer (*Il.* 15.189) and in the Pythagorean doctrines. And he goes on to say: "So that truly and properly, God alone is the measure of all things, both intelligible and sense-perceptible. . . ." Now this true and proper meaning of what is expressed in Gen 18:6 is nothing but a quotation from Plato, *Laws* 4.716C 4-5: ὁ δὴ θεὸς ἡμῖν πάντων χρημάτων μέτρον ἂν εἴη μάλιστα.

And a similar observation may be made concerning Philo's treatment of the saying, "Know thyself" (γνῶθι σεαυτόν), also inscribed on the temple at Delphi. Philo often cites or alludes to this maxim,[40] and at *Migr.* 8 finds its substance in the biblical admonition "Give heed to thyself" (πρόσεχε σεαυτῷ), as found at Exod 34:12 and elsewhere:[41]

> πάντα τὸν αἰῶνα γίνωσκε σεαυτόν, ὡς καὶ Μωυσῆς πολλαχοῦ διδάσκει λέγων "πρόσεχε σεαυτῷ". . . .

Philo is thus telling us that the Delphic maxim, "Know thyself," is often taught by Moses, although in different words.[42]

Of course, Philo actually believes that the movement occurred in the reverse order. That is, it is not the case that Moses is here paraphrasing the Delphic maxim, or that Moses is presenting in a corrupted or obscure form what is presented purely and clearly at Delphi. To see this, consider what Philo says in *QG* 4.152, where he is discussing Gen 25:8: "failing, Abraham died in a good old age, old and full of days." There he compares this line to the saying of Heraclitus, "We live their death, and we die their life" (ζῶμεν τὸν ἐκείνων θάνατον, τεθνήκαμεν δὲ

---

[39] The section is translated in Marcus 1953, 1.278-83 and in Mercier and Petit 1984, 165-71. The Greek fragments of this section, which partially cover the material discussed here, may be found in Marcus 1953, 2.214 and in Petit 1978, 147-48.

[40] See Courcelle 1971, 245-50.

[41] Courcelle (245) cites the biblical verse as occurring at Exod 34:12; Deut 4:9, 6:12, 8:11. It also occurs in the LXX at Gen 24:6; Exod 10:28, 23:21; Deut 11:16; 12:13,19,30; 15:9; 24:8; Tob 4:12,14; Sir 29:20. Incidentally, the phrase at Deut 15:9 is the basis of a homily by Basil ("Homilia in illud, 'Attende tibi ipsi'" [*PG* 31, cols. 197-218]), in which he also finds the substance of the maxim "Know thyself," as noted briefly by Karsten 1838, 78. However, Basil does not explicitly cite the Delphic maxim here, although one manuscript does make the explicit connection at the end (see *PG* 31, col. 217, n. 60).

[42] In fact, at *Deo* 2 (Aucher 1826, 614), where the Greek possibly had ἱερὸν γράμμα, we find yet another reference to "Know thyself."

τὸν ἐκείνων βίον).[43] And the similarity, which to us may seem remote and forced, is sufficient for Philo to say that Heraclitus is "like a thief taking law and opinions from Moses." Thus for Philo the "Heraclitean" saying is actually a biblical saying, which Heraclitus has simply stolen.

Of course, the same is true of "Know thyself," although Philo does not make a point of insisting upon its being stolen. And, we can conclude, "Nothing too much" is in the same state. It actually is, for Philo, a point made by Moses, although not using those words, and naturally the Greeks stole it from him. And thus Philo can reasonably say that it is contained in Scripture.

Finally, we may note some parallels to Philo's claim here which may be found in comments on a line from Homer, *Il.* 10.249:

> Τοδεΐδη, μήτ' ἄρ με μάλ' αἴνεε μήτε τι νείκει.

Now, this line may seem to us to be straightforward, but to some of those who found their ancient wisdom in the Homeric poems it suggested the maxim μηδὲν ἄγαν. And beyond noting a mere parallelism of thought, some went on to claim that the traditional maxim was in fact derived from this Homeric line.[44] Thus we find as a scholium on the line: ἐντεῦθεν Χίλων τὸ "μηδὲν ἄγαν" φησίν. Or, again: ἐντεῦθεν τὸ "μηδὲν ἄγαν" δηλοῦται.[45] The ἐντεῦθεν makes it clear that derivation, and not simply parallelism, is understood.[46]

In summary, then, it is likely that Philo did mean that Scripture contained the Greek maxim μηδὲν ἄγαν and felt free to use it to explain the meaning of a biblical verse, just as he felt free to incorporate terminology from Aristotle's ethical theory.

---

43 Cited from *Leg.* 1.108 (see Marcus 1953, 1.434, n. *l*); the wording in Diels-Kranz, fragment B62, is slightly different.

44 See Wilkins (1926, 141-42), who cites the verse from Homer and some of these comments on it. Wilkins also cites the discussion of the verse in Plutarch, *Septem sapientium convivium* 21 (164C), where Aesop says that Chersias finds both "Know thyself" and "Nothing too much" in Homeric lines, citing for the latter *Il.* 10.249. Wilkins comments (142): "This last passage in the *Banquet of the Seven Wise Men* , half-playful though it is, affords a conspicuous instance of the tendency of late Greek writers to refer the Delphic maxims back to Homer, even as men of a later day came to look for some statement of every truth in the Hebrew Bible."

45 These scholia may be found in Erbse 1974, 3.48.

46 Similarly, in his commentary on the *Iliad*, Eustathius finds the maxim anticipated by Homer, without (it seems) claiming an actual derivation: see Eustathius, p. 801, 44-47, found in van der Valk, 3.57.

CHAPTER THREE

THE PRIORITY OF THE *QUAESTIONES* AMONG PHILO'S EXEGETICAL COMMENTARIES

ABRAHAM TERIAN

Ralph Marcus in his brief introduction to Philo's *Quaestiones et Solutiones in Genesim et in Exodum* invites attention to the problem of their place within the Philonic corpus. Thinking that the *Allegoriae*, the long allegorical commentary on Genesis which constitutes the bulk of Philo's works, was written first, Marcus notes:

> That the *Quaestiones* is later than the *Allegoriae* is indicated by the fact that in the former Philo occasionally refers to the larger commentary, *e.g.* in *QG* ii. 4, *QE* ii. 34, 113. Schürer (*GJV* iii, 3rd ed. 501) believes that the *Quaestiones* is partly earlier, partly later than the *Allegoriae*. That is possible.[1]

More recently, V. Nikiprowetzky[2] and S. Sandmel[3] have expressed some doubt about the validity of one or another of the passages cited by Marcus while apparently agreeing somewhat with Schürer, who in his later editions seems to rely on the questionable views of L. Massebieau and E. Bréhier.[4] Various other arguments whereby the *Quaestiones* are assigned to a primary, secondary or some ambivalent place among

[1]Marcus 1953, 1.x, n. *a*. Ch.Mercier refrains from commenting on its place in the Philonic corpus; nor does he annotate the crucial line in *QG* 2.4 (PAPM 34A, 191).

[2]Nikiprowetzky 1977, 231-232n. 216 (cf. 199, 222 n. 190); see also Nikiprowetzky 1983*a*, 67-69.

[3]Sandmel 1979, 181.

[4]Massebieau and Bréhier 1906. In this methodologically very questionable study, arranging the works of Philo in accordance with the political turns of the time, the *Quaestiones in Exodum* and the first two books of the *Quaestiones in Genesim* are placed with the *Expositiones* at the beginning of the corpus, and the remaining two (or four) books with the *Allegoriae* at the end (pp. 279-284). In an earlier study Massebieau treats the *Quaestiones* first, without attempting to establish their chronological place in the corpus: Massebieau 1889, 7-10. See Schürer 1909, 3.648 n. 43 and 687 n. 154; cf. the new English edition: Schürer 1987, 3.2 826 n. 43 and 842 n. 116.

Philo's major commentaries on the Pentateuch have been raised by others in earlier decades.[5]

Establishing the proper place of this segment of Philo's commentaries alongside the *Allegoriae* and the *Expositiones*[6] is crucial for understanding his exegetical method and perhaps also for discerning other literary and apologetic tendencies in his works — if not a development in his thought. Thus, the specific passages cited by Marcus, and other passages as well, call for serious consideration. Notwithstanding the seemingly insoluble difficulties of determining the chronological sequence of Philo's major commentaries and his works in general, we shall methodically examine the internal evidence in the commentaries so as to ascertain whether the *Quaestiones* are the earliest of his exegetical undertakings. In the course of treating all passages ever brought to bear on this subject, we shall deal with hitherto unresolved textual complexities not only in the Armenian version but also in the Greek. The disentanglement of such complexities would be our primary task in this renewed inquiry into the matter.

A note on the tripartite division of Philo's major biblical commentaries is deemed necessary in view of Nikiprowetzky's following conclusion in his *magnum opus* on Philo:

> Nous pensons que Philon a écrit en réalité non pas trois commentaires de l'Ecriture, mais seulement deux. La série des *Quaestiones* forme l'un de ceux-ci avec son caractère et ses problèmes particuliers; l'ensemble du *Commentaire allégorique* et de l'*Exposition de la Loi* constitue le seconde.[7]

But much of the material Nikiprowetzky presents in the preceding pages and in their corresponding notes negates his hasty and sweeping conclusion.[8] Note particularly the very passages he employs to establish his view (*Mos.* 2.46-47 and *Praem.*1-2); these passages indicate the Scriptural divisions underlying the *Expositiones* as a separate

---

[5] Dähne 1833, 1037, places the *Quaestiones* at the end of the corpus; so also Grossmann 1841-1842, 2.14-17; Ewald, 1858, 6.270-271, argues that the *Quaestiones* are first because of their brevity and because they are presupposed in the later, amplified works; Cohn 1899, 391, relies on Eusebius (*HE* 2.18.1) in placing them after the *Allegoriae.*

[6] Whereas the designation *Exposition of the Law* is commonplace in Philo scholarship, we prefer the plural *Expositiones* to distinguish between the *Allegoriae* and the subsequent works beginning with *De Opificio* and ending with *De Praemiis.*

[7] Nikiprowetzky 1977, 202; cf. 241-242. Elsewhere he calls this second division "le *Commentaire allégorique* - l'*Exposition de la Loi,*" "le *Grand Commentaire* ," or, simply, "le *Commentaire,*" (232).

[8] *Ibid.* 192-202, 214-234.

commentary. Note also the arguments he brings to distance *De Opificio* from the *Allegoriae*. There is, to be sure, a structural continuity not only between the *Allegoriae* and the *Expositiones* but also between the *Quaestiones* and the *Allegoriae* — if not also between some of the rest of Philo's works and the exegetical commentaries as a whole.[9] Nevertheless, the tripartite division of these commentaries is justifiable on the basis of the passages mentioned and there is no good reason to depart from the traditionally accepted view. In the final analysis, neither view is pertinent to the immediate issue of determining the place of the *Quaestiones* chronologically within the Philonic corpus.

I. The Internal Evidence in the *Quaestiones*

A. *QG* 2.4 (on Gen 6:14)

> Accordingly this ark [i.e. of Noah] is overlaid with bitumen inside and out for the beforementioned reason. But that (other ark) in the temple, which is overlaid with gold, is a likeness of the intelligible world, as is shown in the treatise concerning this subject. (tr. Marcus)[10]

In recent years, a substantial Greek fragment containing most of *QG* 2.1-7 was located in Codex Vatopedinus 659 and published by J. Paramelle.[11] Although the fragment has omissions immediately before, in the middle and immediately after the lines quoted above, it preserves the crucial last line in its entirety: ὡς ἐν τοῖς περὶ αὐτῆς λόγοις δείκνυται. The line in question agrees with the Armenian word for word. Paramelle translates it as follows: "comme il est montré dans le textes qui en traitent," and hastens to observe very perceptively:

> Le présent δείκνυται est sans doute a interpréter comme un futur, l'auteur annonçant le sujet qu'il se prépare a développer plus loin, tandis qu'il emploi le même verbe à l'aoriste pour renvoyer à un ouvrage antérieur: *De specialibus legibus* II 224. . . :

[9]See esp. Borgen and Skarsten 1976-77, 1-13; also Terian 1984, 292-294.

[10]The Armenian of this passage shows no inherent difficulties and has been harmoniously translated since Aucher's edition of the text. "*Haec ergo arca bitumine linitur ob dictam causam intrinsecus et extrinsecus. Quae vero in Sanctis (sanctorum) auro linitur, intelligibilis mundi similitudo est, sicut in sermone de illa declaratur*" (tr. Aucher). "Cette arche-ci est donc enduite de goudron à l'intérieur et à l'extérieur pour la raison qui a été dite. Mais celle qui, dans le Temple, est enduite d'or, est l'image du monde intelligible, comme le montre le traité qui la concerne" (tr. Mercier).

[11]Paramelle 1985.

καθάπερ ἐν τοῖς ἰδίᾳ περὶ αὐτοῦ λόγοις ἔδειξα, allusion qui vise . . . *De decalogo* 106-120.[12]

The tense of the verb δείκνυται is clearly a present of anticipation — of what is immediate, likely, or certain.[13] Quite justifiably, the cognate verb ἐπιδείκνυμι in its present tense is at times rendered with a sense of the future in the German, English, and French translations of Philo.[14] One such instance, *Sobr.* 9 (where Philo contrasts Ishmael, the sophist, with Isaac, the sage), shows striking syntactical similarities when compared with the passage in question; it reads: ὡς . . . ἐν τοῖς ἰδίᾳ λόγοις ἐπιδείκνυμεν, translated as "wie wir in einer eigenen Abhandlung, wann wir beide charakterisieren werden, zeigen wollen" (tr. Adler); "as we propose to shew in the special treatise" (tr. Colson); and "comme nous le montrerons dans un traité spécial"(tr. Gorez).[15]

We may also observe that very rarely does Philo use λόγος or λόγοι in the sense of σύνταξις,[16] the usual word for treatise, which he employs repeatedly when referring to a work as a whole — often in conjunction with its title.[17] A more common meaning of λόγος or λόγοι in contexts such as the above is "subject," "discourse," "discussion," "an account," or "a passage," that is, as part of a treatise.[18] In the light of

[12]*Ibid.* 144-147 and n. 23

[13]See Smyth 1956, 421-422.

[14]*Det* . 41; *Sobr* 9; and *Spec.* 1.205.

[15]Alluding either to *Mut.* 201-263 or, less likely, to the lost *On Isaac.* Adler notes: "Eine solche Charakteristik Ismaels und Isaaks lesen wir bei Philo De mutat. nomin. §201-263. Wahrscheinlich verweist hier Philo aber auf das uns nicht erhaltene Leben Isaaks" (PCH 5.82 n. 2). On the questionable translation of λόγοι (better rendered as "Ausführungen," "discussion," and "commentaire" in *Spec.* 2.224, referring to *Dec.* 106-120), see below and n. 16.

[16]For example, in *Prob.* 1 λόγος alludes to the lost treatise *Every Bad Man is a Slave;* in *Opif.* 15 and 52 it alludes to the lost treatise Περὶ ἀριθμῶν; on the meaning of λόγοι in *Sobr.* 9, see the preceding note.

[17]*Plant.* 174, ref. to treatises collectively; *Her.* 1, ref. to a lost work on Gen 15:1; *Mut.* 53, ref. to the lost Περὶ Διαθηκῶν; *Abr.* 2 and 13, ref. to *De Opificio; Mos.* 2.1, ref. to *Mos.* 1; *Dec.* 1, ref. to the preceding treatises of the *Expositiones; Spec.* 1.1, ref. to *De Decalago*; *Spec.* 2.1, ref. to *Spec.* 1; *Spec.* 4 (title), ref. to the whole of the four books; *Virt.* 52, ref. to *Mos.* 1-2; *Virt.* 101, ref. to *De Specialibus Legibus* collectively; and *Praem.* 3, ref. to the preceding treatises of the *Expositiones.* Cf. Nikiprowetzky 1977, n. 179: "Surtout, dans l'usage de Philon, le terme de σύνταξις désigne invariablement *un traité et un seul.*"

[18]See, for example, *Leg.* 2.65; 3.54, 139; *Det.* 13; *Agr.* 107; *Plant.* 149, 177; *Conf.* 14; *Mut.* 53; *Opif.* 15, 52; *Abr.* 276; *Mos.* 2.105; *Spec.* 1.189; 2.223-224, 243; 4.130; *Prob.* 16. Another common usage of the term(s) is with reference to the Holy

these observations, a more accurate translation of the last line in the above quote (ὡς ἐν τοῖς περὶ αὐτῆς λόγοις δείκνυται) would be: "as is to be shown in the discussion regarding this subject."[19]

Marcus is equally misleading in his annotation, where he points to *Ebr.* 88-90 as the earlier treatment which is referred to here.[20] Instead, we are compelled to consider the passage in question as follows: having envisaged the scope of his immediate work, Philo is referring to the *Quaestiones in Exodum,* the only place where the subject of the ark of the tabernacle is fully discussed, especially in 2.53-68, and where no further reference is made either to a previous or to a forthcoming discussion of the subject.

B. *QE* 2.34 (on Exod 24:7)

> Concerning the divine covenant we have already spoken in detail, so that it is not proper to discuss the subject again at the present time. (tr. Marcus)[21]

Marcus notes: "Philo here apparently alludes to his (lost) work Περὶ Διαθηκῶν in two books, see *De Mut. Nom.* 53."[22] This lost work, an exposition of Gen 6:13-9:19, belongs to the *Allegoriae* and falls between *Quod Deus* and *De Agricultura.* The work is mentioned explicitly in *Mut.* 53, the latter book being an exposition of Gen 17:1-22.

More than suggesting a work by name or a whole treatise devoted to a specific subject, the allusion in *QE* 2.34 seems to point to an immediate discussion. The Armenian of the first line above reads: *yaghags astuatsayin ktakaranin chshgrteal ē yaṙajagoyn,* the Greek equivalent of which would be περὶ τῆς διαθήκης θεοῦ ἠκριβώσαμεν πρότερον,

---

Scriptures: the *scriptura sacra* in general, a *locus biblicus* in particular, or a named book in the Pentateuch.

[19]Cf. the translation of καθάπερ ἐν τοῖς ἰδίᾳ περὶ αὐτοῦ λόγοις ἔδειξα (*Spec.* 2.224, referring to *Dec.* 106-120) in PCH, PLCL, and PAPM, respectively: "wie ich in den ihm eigens gewidmeten Ausführungen gezeigt habe" (tr. Heinemann); "as I have shewn in the discussion devoted to this in particular" (tr. Colson); and "comme je l'ai montré dans un commentaire que je lui ai consacré spécialement" (tr. Daniel). On the questionable translation of λόγοι as "Abhandlung," "treatise," and "traité" in ὡς. . . ἐν τοῖς ἰδίᾳ λόγοις ἐπιδείκνυμεν (*Sobr.* 9, referring to *Mut* . 201-263), see above and n. 12.

[20]Marcus 1953, 1.72 n. *f.* See the criticism of this in Nikiprowetzky 1977, 231-232 n. 216; Nikiprowetzky 1973, 67.

[21]"*De Divino Testamento certius accuratiusque jam dictum fuit, ita ut vix oporteat nunc temporis replicare* " (tr. Aucher). No textual difficulties are discernible here.

[22]Marcus 1953, 2.76 n. *a.*

which Marcus translates correctly. Note the singular διαθήκης, "covenant." As for ἠκριβώσαμεν, "we have spoken in detail" or "we have investigated accurately," it is often used by Philo when referring to any previous discussion of some length.[23] There are a number of such references in the extant *QE*, several of which have the same phrase that we find in 2.34 — e.g., 1.12 (alluding to 1.10); 2.12 (alluding to 2.11), 23 (alluding to the preceding biblical verses), 37 (alluding to 2.29, 33 and 37 itself), 47 (alluding to 2.45), 49 (alluding to *QG* 1.25; 2.14; 4.154), 81 (alluding to 2.73-80), and 100 (alluding either to a lost part of *QE* or to the lost Περὶ ἀριθμῶν).[24]

It seems that in *QE* 2.34 (on Exod 24:7) Philo is alluding either (a) to some lost part of *QE* (possibly on Exod 6:4-5, the only other reference to divine covenant in those parts of Exodus covered by the original six books of *QE*),[25] or (b) to the covenant between God and Abraham as interpreted in considerable detail in *QG* 3.40-60, treating Gen 17:1-22 (as in *De Mutatione Nominum*). There is good reason to favor the second of these two possibilities since it is inconceivable that Philo would have devoted more detailed discussion by way of questions and answers to Exod 6:4-5 than to Gen 17:1-22 (it should be observed that Gen 17 contains as many references to the covenant as the entire book of Exodus). Moreover, equally important for the argument against Marcus is the fact that in *QG* 3.40-60 no allusion is made to any previous work on the covenant(s) — neither to the lost Περὶ Διαθηκῶν nor to *De Mutatione Nominum*. One would expect at least a passing allusion to either of these treatises (especially the latter, which treats the same scriptural passage) if the *Allegoriae* already existed when Philo was writing the *Quaestiones*.

---

[23]See the various uses of the verb in *Migr*. 176; *Her*. 125, 215; *Fug*. 87; *Mut* . 69; *Somn*. 1.4, 133, 172, 197; 2.8, 155, 206; *Mos*. 2.46, 115; *Dec* . 18, 82; *Spec*. 1.269; 2.200. At times ἠκριβώσαμεν refers to a whole treatise; see, e.g., *Abr*. 2; *Dec*. 1; *Spec*. 1.1; 2.1.

[24]Cf. *QE* 1.1, 8, 18; 2.51, 77, 84, 92, 94, 97, 99, and 113.

[25]On the biblical passages covered and the original extent of *QE*, see Royse 1976-1977, 61.

C. *QE* 2.113 (on Exod 28:20)

As I have said, there is between them [i.e. the four rows which make up the annual seasons in the zodiac] an intervening space and interval of clear and pure ether. (tr. Marcus)[26]

The Armenian *orpēs asats'in* has as its Greek equivalent ὡς ἔλεγον, which may be taken either as first person singular or as third person plural. The Armenian translator wrongly opts for the third person plural, leaving the reader with the impression that here Philo is endorsing what others have said. Marcus, like Aucher, prefers the first person singular reading, erring, however, in thinking that here Philo is alluding to the *Allegoriae*.[27] Rightly understood, the reference is to what has just been said in the preceding lines of the same section. The form of the statement has a number of parallels in the same Book. For example, in *QE* 2.37, "the divine essence, of which I have spoken earlier," refers to section 33; in 2.77, "as has been said," refers to section 76; in 2.81, "as I said a little while ago," refers to sections 73-80. Sandmel rightly remarks on the passage in question: "I do not see the aptness of the citation of *QE* II,113."[28]

We may conclude that the three passages cited by Marcus are not convincing; the references they contain seem to point to the *Quaestiones* themselves.

There still remains another passage in the *Quaestiones* which, together with *Spec.* 1.269 (treated below, Part III), has given rise to some misunderstanding about the extent of the commentary. We ought to consider this passage as the last bit of internal evidence from the *Quaestiones* with some implications for our subject.

D. *QG* 4.123 (on Gen 24:36)

What is here said as a blessing of Reuben stands first, and (then) that of Judah. But it is for him alone, while the other is as a part, for he is placed above with the sole

[26]The first "and" is supplied by Marcus and should therefore be parenthesized. The text, however, does not require a conjunction at this juncture where a comma and an indefinite article would make better sense. "*Ut dixi, est inter illas intervallum spatiumque purissimi ac nitidissimi aetheris* " (tr. Aucher).
[27]Marcus, as in the "Introduction" (Marcus 1953, 1.x, n. *a*), gives no specific reference in the translation notes.

> and elder. But what the principle of these things is will be explained when we inquire into the blessings. (tr. Marcus)[29]

Partly because of the inherent difficulties of the passage, these last lines of the section were misunderstood by Marcus, as his ambiguous translation and puzzling notes at this juncture indicate. Following the second period he observes: "This obscure statement may refer to Judah's being associated with Reuben, or to Judah's entering into his people (Deut. xxxiii. 7) or to Simeon's being included with Levi (Deut. xxxiii. 8)." At the end of the section he notes: "These Pentateuchal passages, Gen. ch. xlix and Deut. ch. xxxiii, are not discussed in the extant text of the *Quaestiones*."[30] It is obvious that Marcus in his perception of this passage is dependent on Aucher, whose equally ambiguous translation is followed with the note: "*Sed desideratur locus promissus.*"[31] Following the reference to Deut 33:6 and 7, and perhaps also the accompanying note by Aucher, Massebieau[32] and Cohn[33] were quick to conclude that Philo intended to have his *Quaestiones* cover the whole Pentateuch. We shall say more about the original extent of this commentary in our discussion of *Spec.* 1.269 below; but first, we shall provide a revised translation of the passage under consideration with a comment.

> What is said (as) a blessing for Reuben [Deut 33:6] stands first, then that (said) for Judah [vs. 7]. But his [i.e. Judah's] is a whole (blessing), whereas the other's [i.e. Reuben's] is as a part. Thus he [i.e. Judah] is placed above the other [i.e. Reuben], even the elder. And what the principle of these things is will be explained when we inquire into the blessings.

While commenting on Gen 24:36b in the first part of this section, Philo presents Abraham as giving a blessing to Isaac; that is, nature granting a ready gift to the self-taught, contrasted with "whatever over a long period of time teaching enables one to acquire" by way of hearing.

---

[28]Sandmel 1979, 181 n. 82.

[29]"*Haec autem prolata Rubeni, benedictio, imprimus est de Judae: verum illi, ut soli; huic autem, ut pars; super enim ponitur cum altera majori. Quae vero ratio sit istorum, dicetur, quum benedictiones examinemus* " (tr. Aucher). "La bénédiction qui a été dite pour Ruben est première, puis (celle) de Juda, mais pour celui-là elle est pour lui seul, et pour celui-ci, (elle est) comme une partie, car il est placé au-dessus avec un autre plus grand. Et comment ces (choses) sont conformes à la raison, ce sera dit lorsque nous examinerons les bénédictions" (tr. Mercier).

[30]Marcus 1953, 1.408, n. *b*.

[31]Aucher 2.341 n. 3.

[32]Massebieau 1889, 7 n. 5.

[33]Cohn 1899, 403.

There seems to be a contrast here between Isaac, the self-taught,[34] and the unnamed Ishmael, who in Philo's allegory stands for "hearing" and "one taught" by others.[35] Now it is possible to trace Philo's thought in what follows, for we find him contrasting the greater blessing the younger brother receives with the lesser blessing the elder brother receives.[36] Accordingly, he refers to the brevity of the blessing given by Moses to the tribe of Reuben and compares it with the lengthier, more complete blessing given to the tribe of Judah (Deut 33:6,7). Then, by placing the younger brother above the elder, he seems to be drawing an analogy between Judah and Reuben on the one hand and the unnamed Jacob and Esau on the other (Gen 27:27-29, 39-40). Moreover, since the section is primarily on Isaac, the self-taught or the one taught by God, who is contrasted with Ishmael, the one taught by hearing others, Philo would be thinking of the complementary symbolism represented by Jacob, the one taught by training or practice,[37] and Esau, who exemplifies folly or ignorance.[38] Thus, the promised treatment of the subject of blessings appears to be that of Gen 27, and not of Gen 49 and/or Deut 33. In *QG* 4.196-242 Philo apparently fulfills the commitment he makes in section 123.

Thus far we may conclude that there is neither reference nor allusion in the *Quaestiones*, as we have them, to either the *Allegoriae* or any of Philo's other extant works.

II. The Internal Evidence in the *Allegoriae*

A. *Leg.* 3.139

Some possible evidence for the priority of the *Quaestiones* may be seen in *Leg.* 3.139, in the reference to a previous discussion having to do with the four passions. The line in question has been mistranslated:

---

[34]*QG* 3.59, 88; 4.91, 122, 127, 129, 144; *Congr.* 36; *Abr.* 52; etc.

[35]*QG* 3.32, 59; 4.147, 245; *Fug.* 208; *Mut.* 201. Elsewhere Ishmael represents the sophist: *QG* 3.33; *Cher.* 8; *Sobr*. 9.

[36]A similar pattern of thought is discernible in the earlier books, in the treatment of Abel and Cain (*QG* 1.59, 61) and the sons of Noah: Shem, Ham, and Japheth (*QG* 2.79).

[37]*QG* 4.162-244 *passim;* often in contrast with Esau (see note below).

[38]*QG* 4.161-238 *passim; Leg.* 3.2, 88; *Sacr*. 17, 120, 135; *Det.* 45; *Ebr.* 9; *Sobr*. 26; *Migr.* 153; *Her.* 252; *Congr.* 61, 175; *Fug.* 39.

as has been mentioned in a treatise specially devoted to that subject (ὥς τις κατ' ἐξαίρετον λόγος μέμνηται). (tr. Whitaker)

In spite of the compounded error in the accompanying note, "This treatise was never written or is lost,"[39] a likely allusion to the *Quaestiones* is discernible here.

The problem is similar to that noted above, in our observations on *QG* 2.4 and the use of λόγος or λόγοι with reference to writings.[40] Here again, the word "treatise" in the above periphrastic translation is both unnecessary and misleading, giving rise to unwarranted speculation. A more literal translation with less grounds for conjecture would be "as has been mentioned regarding this subject in particular" — or, as I. Heinemann translates and notes, "wie die besondere Lehre von ihnen [i.e. die Lehre von den vier Affekten] ergibt."[41] While previously in *Leg.* 2.8, 102 and 3.113 Philo speaks of the four passions (and the allusion could be to these passages), in the *Quaestiones* he devotes more attention to the subject, speaking repeatedly of sensual pleasure, desire, grief, and fear — whether separately or in combination — e.g., *QG* 1.72, 76; 2.56-57; 3.9-10; 4.15-19, 51-53, 197-198, 230; *QE* 1.15, 22; 2.21-22 and 51.

B. *Sacr.* 51

The following is a more decisive passage:

With good reason then is Abel who refers all that is best to God called a shepherd, while Cain who refers them to himself and his own mind is called a tiller of the soil (γῆς ἐργάτης). But what is meant by a tiller of the soil (Gen. iv. 2) I have shown in earlier books (τί δέ ἐστι τὸ γῆν ἐργάζεσθαι, διὰ τῶν προτέρων βιβλίων ἐδηλώσαμεν). (tr. Colson)[42]

Colson goes on to note in the "Appendix to the Sacrifices of Abel and Cain" that "No such passage in the earlier books survives. But in *De*

[39]PLCL 1.394 n. d. After providing a similar translation, Cl. Mondésert dependently observes: "Traité dont on ne peut rien dire de plus: peut-être perdu, peut-être jamais écrit" (PAPM 2.250 n. 1).

[40]See above, n. 16.

[41]PCH 3.130 n. 1.

[42]"So wird Abel, der das Beste auf Gott bezieht, ein Hirte genannt, Kain aber, der es auf sich selbst und seinen eigenen Geist bezieht, ein Ackerbauer. Was es aber heißt, den Acker zu bebauen (1 Mos. 4,2), haben wir in den früheren Büchern erklärt" (tr. Leisegang). "Aussi est-ce à juste titre qu'Abel, celui qui rapporte à Dieu les choses les meilleures, est appelé 'pasteur' tandis que Caïn, qui les rapporte à lui-même et à son propre esprit, est appelé 'travailleur de la terre'. Or, qu'est-ce que travailler la terre? Nous l'avons montré dans des ouvrages antérieures (*Gen.* 4,2)" (tr. Méasson).

Agr. 21 ff. a 'tiller of the soil' is explained as one who lives to satisfy the wants of the body."[43] Obviously, Colson limits himself to the earlier books of the *Allegoriae*, and, at this point, seems to rely on H. Leisegang, who observes: "Die Stelle über den Ackerbau, den Kain treibt, ist uns in den vorausgehenden Büchern wahrscheinlich verloren gegangen. Im Buche De agricultura §§21-25 jedoch findet sich eine Erörterung über 1 Mos. 4,2, die die Lücke hier vollständig ausfüllt."[44] Likewise, in the French translation of *Sacr.* 51, A. Méasson follows Leisegang and Colson:"Il est bien difficile de savoir à quel ouvrage Philon fait allusion ici. On peut seulement citer *Agric.* 21 s., où il définit le travailleur de la terre par opposition au cultivateur."[45] Yet the above passage abounds with clues that lead to the *Quaestiones*. But reluctance to use Aucher's Latin translation has somehow caused Colson and the early German translators, on whose annotations he often relies in his explanatory notes, to ignore this third of the Philonic corpus. In fact, the *Quaestiones* are referred to but twice in the footnotes of the first ten Loeb Classical Library volumes[46] and rarely in the appendices.[47]

The passage poses no difficulties; on the contrary, it is very clear even in its allusion to the *Quaestiones*. The plural "books" seems to be a fitting designation for these writings[48] and suggests the possibility of having the meaning of "tiller of the soil" explained in more than one book. Moreover, the scriptural reference (Gen 4:2) and the names of Abel and Cain make the search in the *Quaestiones* very compelling.

---

[43]PLCL 2.490-491.

[44]PCH 3.235 n. 4.

[45]PAPM 4.117 n. 3.

[46]PLCL 3.470, n.*b;* 4.370 n. *a*; cf. 7.254-255 n. *c* — merely mentioned.

[47]PLCL 3.486, 511; 5.608; 6.605; 7.615; 8.450; and 9.512.

[48]Cf. *Virt.* 16-17, where Philo employs the same word (plural) in referring to earlier works where he had "dealt fully with each of the rules which promote simplicity (ἀτυφία)." These "scattered precepts which appear in different places," seem to be his directives against "vanity" (τῦφος). At best, they are to be found in the allegorical interpretation of circumcision in the *Quaestiones* (*QG* 3.46-52; *QE* 2.2; see also *QG* 2.24; 3.25, 30, 56; 4.15, 19, 28, 48, 100, 133, 142, 149, 156, 161, 224, 237; *QE* 1.6, 13, 15; 2.14, 25, 37, 54; quite often, the Armenian text allows the substitution of "vanity" for "arrogance" or "pride," and "simplicity" for "humility") and, to a lesser extent, in the *Allegoriae* (*Migr.* 92; *Somn.* 2.25; see also *Cher.* 42; *Ebr.* 124; *Fug.* 25, 35; *Somn.* 2.40, 47, 63-64, 95, 139-140) and the prior works in the *Expositiones* (*Spec.* 1.8-11; see also *Abr.* 104; *Mos.* 2.96; *Dec.* 4-6, 162;*Spec.* 1.309). Elsewhere, and with reference to his own writings, Philo employs the singular: βιβλίον in *Plant.* 1, referring to *De Agricultura;* and βίβλος in *Ebr.* 1, referring to *De Plantatione.* The designation is otherwise reserved for the Scriptures.

Surely, in *QG* 1.59 (on Gen 4:2) Philo compares the work of the shepherd, Abel, with that of the tiller of the soil, Cain:

> For one of them labors and takes care of living beings even though they are irrational, gladly undertaking the pastoral work which is preparatory to rulership and kingship. But the other occupies himself with earthly and inanimate things.[49]

Again, in *QG* 2.66 (on Gen 9:20), Philo compares the work of the planter, Noah, with that of the tiller of the soil, "the fratricide," of whom he says: "For symbolically the body is called 'earth' (since) by nature our (body) is earthy, and it works basely and badly like an unskilled hireling," and adds that "the worker-mind of the body, in accordance with its bodily (nature), pursues bodily pleasures."[50] A similar explanation of "what is meant by a tiller of the soil" is found in *QE* 1.6 (on Exod 12:4): "One's own labor in tilling the soil is a measure of moderation in the things necessary and useful for bodily life." (The word γῆ is variously rendered as "soil," "ground," or "earth," and this should help us to comprehend the derivation of the word "earthly" and the further derivation of "body" and "bodily" in these passages.)

It may be stated with fair certainty that "the earlier books" mentioned in *Sacr.* 51 are the *Quaestiones.*

C. *Sobr.* 52

Equally overwhelming evidence for the priority of the *Quaestiones* may be seen in this line:

> We have said before that Shem bears a name which means "good" (ἔφαμεν πάλαι, ὅτι Σὴμ ἐπώνυμός ἐστιν ἀγαθοῦ). (tr. Colson)[51]

Commenting on where Philo had said this before, Colson notes: "Probably, as Adler suggests, in the lost discourse on Noah's nakedness."[52] What leads to such a conclusion is discernible in Colson's

[49]The Greek fragment, cited in Marcus 1953, 2.184-185, shows a paraphrased conflation of this passage with *QG* 2.66; Fr. Petit omits it in PAPM 33.56.
[50]Cf. *Agr.* 5, 21-25.
[51]"Wir haben schon früher einmal gesagt, daß Sem vom Guten benannt ist" (tr. Adler). "Nous avons dit plus haut que Sem est le nom qui sert à désigner le bien" (tr. Gorez).
[52]PLCL 3.471 n. c; for more on this lost work, see *ibid.* 308-309; Adler 1929, 1-8, especially 3; cf. *idem,* PCH 5.93 n. 4: "Weder in der Schrift Ü. d. Nüchternheit findet sich vorher eine solche Erklärung des namens Sem, noch in einer anderen der uns erhaltenen Schriften. Es ist mir höchst wahrscheinlich, daß im 2. Buche Ü. d. Trunkenheist, in dem Abschnitte über die γυμνότης, der Bibelvers Gen. 9,23 behandelt

further remarks on this passage in the "Appendix to *De Sobrietate*": "The interpretation of 'Shem' as = 'name' and thence, as the best of names, 'the good,' does not appear elsewhere in what we have of Philo."[53]

Colson and others would have been correct had we been limited to the Greek corpus of Philo's works, for indeed in the two instances where the name Shem appears in treatises of the *Allegoriae* which precede *De Sobrietate* (*Leg.* 2.62 and *Post.* 173) it is without the given meaning. In the *Quaestiones,* however, the name Shem occurs twice with the meaning "good": in *QG* 1.88: "These names [i.e., of the three sons of Noah] are symbols of three things in nature — of the good, the bad, and the indifferent"; and in 2.79 (following several allusions to Shem and what his name represents in the immediately preceding sections, 65-78): "Shem, Ham, Japheth. . . these three, the good, the bad, and the indifferent."

The last two of these references from the *Allegoriae* add considerably to the little yet sufficient evidence for the priority of the *Quaestiones.*

III. The Internal Evidence in the *Expositiones*

The following two passages in the *Expositiones* have commanded much attention in previous studies dealing with the chronology, the classification, and the extent of Philo's exegetical commentaries. With the treatment of these two we complete our task of accounting for all the passages ever brought to bear on the subject.

A. *Opif.* 52

> There are several other powers of which 4 has the command, which we shall have to point out in fuller detail in the special treatise devoted to it (ἃς ἀκριβέστερον καὶ ἐν τῷ περὶ αὐτῆς ἰδίῳ λόγῳ προσυποδεικτέον). (tr. Whitaker)[54]

---

und bei dieser Gelegenheit die allegorische Deutung Sems gegeben war, auf die sich nun Philo hier bezieht." Colson is, in turn, followed by J. Gorez in PAPM 11-12.150-151 nn. 4-5: "Peut-être dans le passage perdu sur la nudité de Noé . . . Sem, dans ce seul passage de Philon [*Sobr*. 52], est l'équivalent de 'nom'."

[53]PLCL 3.512; so also J. Gorez in PAPM 11-12.150 n. 6: "Sem, dans ce seul passage de Philon, est l'équivalent de 'nom'."

[54]"Noch viele andere Beteutungen hat die Vierzahl, die genauer in einer besonderen Abhandlung erörtert werden sollen" (tr. Cohn; he notes: "Diese auch sonst von Philo

In all previous considerations of this passage, the promised discussion pertaining to the tetrad is taken as an allusion to the lost arithmological treatise Περὶ ἀριθμῶν, with the understanding that this work was not yet written at the time when Philo wrote his *De Opificio;* whereas in *QG* 4.110, 151, *QE* 2.87, and *Mos.* 2.115 he mentions the Περὶ ἀριθμῶν as a written work.[55] The inevitable conclusion, then, is that the *Quaestiones* and *De Vita Mosis* are posterior to *De Opificio,* and that the latter treatise is to be separated from the rest of the *Expositiones* (of which *De Vita Mosis* is a part).[56]

Before considering *Opif.* 52, however, it is imperative that we consider the completely overlooked and somewhat conflicting allusion to the lost Περὶ ἀριθμῶν in *Opif.* 15:

> We must recount as many as we can of the elements embraced in it [i.e., in the "one"]. To recount them all would be impossible. Its pre-eminent element is the intelligible world, as is shown in the treatise dealing with the "One" (ὡς ὁ περὶ αὐτῆς λόγος μηνύει). (tr. Whitaker)

Following Whitaker's reliable translation, we see an equally clear allusion to the same lost treatise and an apparent contradiction between *Opif.* 15 and 52. Moreover, the allusion made in *Opif.* 15 is in keeping with all the other allusions and direct references to the long-lost work as an existing document at the time when Philo was writing his respective works. Cohn was probably aware of the contradiction within *De Opificio* and apparently tried to resolve it by translating *Opif.* 15 as follows (*Opif.* 52 had already gained much attention in Philo scholarship because of its inflated chronological significance; therefore, it was easier — if not necessary — it seems, to twist the meaning of *Opif.* 15):

---

zitierte Abhandlung ist verloren gegangen" [PCH 1.44 n. 2]). "La tétrade jouit de beaucoup d'autres propriétés, dont il nous faudra faire l'exposé avec plus de précision dans le traité qui lui sera consacré" (tr. Arnaldez; he notes: "Traité perdu" [PAPM 1.174 n. 1]).

[55]The direct references to the Περὶ ἀριθμῶν in *QG* 4.151 and *QE* 2.87 were not noticed by Aucher, Marcus and Mercier in their respective translations. For more on this work, see Staehle 1931, 1-18.

[56]Nikiprowetzky 1977, 217 n. 154, 232; on the place of these works within the *Expositiones,* see p. 197.

> Von dem Inhalt (dieses Tages) müssen wir das anführen, was wir zu sagen imstande sind; denn alles sagen ist unmöglich. Er ist nämlich vor allen bevorzugt und umfasst die Schöpfung der gedachten Welt, wie der Bericht (der Bibel) über ihn besagt.[57]

The minor translational differences aside, Cohn's taking τὸν νοητὸν κόσμον ἐξαίρετον as the antecedent of αὐτῆς is not grammatically justifiable, whereas Whitaker's taking μίαν or τὴν μονάδος as the antecedent of the feminine pronoun is correct. Moreover, Whitaker's translation is consistent with the immediate context, which is about the first day of creation (τὴν πρώτην); not so with Cohn's translation. Consequently, Whitaker's translation of *Opif.* 15 must stand and *Opif.* 52 must be reconsidered in the light of the latter passage.

Except for the last word in ἅς ἀκριβέστερον καὶ ἐν τῷ περὶ αὐτῆς ἰδίῳ λόγῳ προσυποδεικτέον, the German, English, and French translations of *Opif.* 52 are basically correct. To amplify our point, however, some grammatical and lexical observations on the last four words of this crucial line are necessary. The antecedent of the pronoun αὐτῆς is τετράς, "the tetrad," or "the number four." The first of the next two words, ἰδίῳ λόγῳ, points to a locus in a "particular," "special" or "specific" work or treatise. In our above treatment of *QG* 2.4 and *Leg.* 3.139 we dealt with the recurring problem of rendering λόγος as "treatise" instead of "discussion," that is, part of a treatise (Philo had no special treatise devoted entirely to one number or another). But it seems proper to render λόγος as "treatise" in arithmological contexts such as the above since we are certain of such a work by Philo, to which, as noted above, he refers several times by its title.[58] The last Greek word, προσυποδεικτέον, is a compound, impersonal verb which occurs but once in the extant Philonic corpus: only here; and, curiously, Liddell and Scott give only one example of its use: our very passage, with "one must show besides" as its meaning.[59] As for its various parts, the usual meaning of the prepositional προσυπ- is "beyond," "besides," or "in addition"; that of δείκνυμι, as observed in several of the above passages, is "to show"; and the impersonal construction with -τέον is equivalent to

[57]Unfortunately, Arnaldez follows Cohn to some extent in translating this passage as follows: "Il faut noter la plus grande partie possible de ce que renferme ce jour, puisqu'il n'y a pas moyen de tout dire; il enferme, en effet, le monde intelligible séparé, comme le dit le passage qui en parle."

[58]If taken as "discussion," λόγος in *Opif.* 15 could refer to all that precedes on the number one, and in *Opif.* 52 to all that precedes on the number four (cf. our translation of the latter passage further below).

[59]q.v., LSJ, 1529; cf. the uses of προσυποδείκνυμι in the *Letter of Aristeas* 136 and 168 (cited, *ibid.*).

δεῖ, meaning "it is necessary," "it is possible," "one must," "one could," etc. We notice that the sense of "beyond," "besides," or "in addition" has been dropped from the various translations of προσυποδεικτέον in *Opif.* 52. The common error stems from an early misreading of this extremely rare word, the mistranslation of which has been perpetuated in the various translations of Philo. We prefer its fuller meaning given in Liddell and Scott and would therefore translate the lines in question as follows (retaining as much as possible of Whitaker's translation given above):

> There are several other powers of which four has the command, which could be pointed out besides those detailed in the special treatise devoted to it.

Our translation of *Opif.* 52 (a) resolves the seeming contradiction between it and *Opif.* 15, (b) renders both passages harmoniously with all other passages in which the Περὶ ἀριθμῶν is mentioned — whether directly or indirectly, and (c) does justice to the immediate context and to the rhetorical overtones of the passage — as Philo goes on to cite a few additional examples of the powers of four and to prolong his comments on "day four" (*Opif.* 52-61).

We maintain that the significance of *Opif.* 52 has been inflated and consider all chronological conjectures based on this passage alone (including the separation of *De Opificio* from the remainder of the *Expositiones*) rather unfounded.

B. *Spec.* 1.269

An equally problematic passage is *Spec.* 1.269, the misinterpretation of which has had a substantial effect on misunderstanding the *Quaestiones,* especially the extent of their coverage. We shall focus on the problem posed by the passage and shall then suggest a solution.

> What these things [i.e., pertaining to the offering of the heifer, Num 19:1-9] symbolically indicate has been described in full elsewhere where we have expounded the allegory (τίνα δε διὰ τούτων ὡς διὰ συμβόλων αἰνίττεται, δι' ἑτέρων ἠκριβώσαμεν ἀλληγοροῦντες). (tr. Colson)[60]

[60] "Was aber hierdurch symbolisch angedeutet wird, haben wir an andrer Stelle in allegorischer Erklärung ausgeführt" (tr. Heinemann). "Ce que ces choses-là représentent symboliquement, nous l'avons dit ailleures en détail, dans nos interprétations allégoriques" (tr. Daniel).

In view of the fact that the biblical passage commented on here does not occur elsewhere in Philo, and that any mention of it in the missing sections of *QG* and *QE* is unlikely, Cohn concluded that Philo is alluding to *Quaestiones* that extend beyond Exodus, namely, the supposed *Quaestiones et Solutiones in Numeros*.[61] Recently, however, J. Royse has convincingly reaffirmed the original extent of the *Quaestiones* through Genesis and Exodus and has clarified for the record the problem surrounding four *lemmata* introducing, in one of the manuscripts of the *Sacra Parallela* (Vaticanus gr. 1553), excerpts purportedly derived from *Quaestiones* extending beyond Exodus.[62] Royse's illuminating study helps us interpret the passage under consideration even though he remarks: "Philo could have brought in a discussion of Num 19:1-9 at various places in the missing sections of the allegorical exposition, since his ability to connect texts and topics of the most disparate sorts is well known."[63]

But the above quoted lines, especially the Greek, do not necessarily imply that Num 19:1-9 has been expounded elsewhere. The reference is to the symbolism rather than to the scriptural passage; that is, Philo is alluding to the symbolic significance of offering a heifer rather than to a previous discussion of Num 19:1-9. We shall therefore suggest that in *Spec.* 1.269 Philo is referring to *Her.* 100-236, where he allegorizes at length on Abraham's offering a heifer among other animals (Gen 15:9-11). A shorter discussion of the same scriptural passage is found in *QG* 3.3-8. While it is tempting to think that the reference in *Spec.* 1.269 could be to the *Quaestiones*, the lengthier discussion in the *Allegoriae* is more in keeping with the inherent meaning of the text.

IV. Summary and Conclusion

Textual arguments that do not allow the *Quaestiones* to stand at the beginning of Philo's exegetical commentaries can no longer be maintained. The three passages cited by Marcus from the *Quaestiones* as referring to the *Allegoriae* are better understood as referring to the

---

[61]Cohn 1899, 403. Colson notes: "No such account survives. Heinemann suggests that it belongs to the *Quaestiones* of which we have nothing beyond Exodus" (PLCL 7.255 n. c, referring to PCH 2.86 n. 1: "Wahrscheinlich in der verlorenen Forsetzungen der Quaestiones et Solutiones"). S. Daniel adds: "Sans doute dans un traité qui ne nous a pas été conservé" (PAPM 24.171 n. 6).

[62]Royse 1976-77, esp. 42-43 (cf. Lucchesi 1976).

[63]*Ibid.*, 43.

Quaestiones themselves: *QG* 2.4, on the basis of the anticipatory present tense, refers to *QE* 2.53-68; *QE* 2.34 refers to *QG* 3.40-60; and the reference in *QE* 2.113 is to the preceding lines of the same section. Moreover, the closing lines of *QG* 4.123 allude to Gen 27 and not to Gen 49 or Deut 33; thus, they point to sections 196-242 of the same book and not to some missing or other contemplated *Quaestiones* on the rest of the Pentateuch. So also *Spec.* 1.269: after a discussion of Num 19:1-9, it seems to allude to a lengthy discussion of Gen 15:9-11, and thus points to *Her.* 100-236 rather than to some projected *Quaestiones* on Numbers. Furthermore, three puzzling passages in the *Allegoriae*, hitherto regarded as referring to lost works, are explained as referring to the *Quaestiones: Leg.* 3.139 seems to point to the more than twenty remarks on the four passions in the *Quaestiones* — if not to some such passages earlier in *Leg.* (2.8, 102 and 3.113); *Sacr.* 51 refers to the meaning of "tiller of the soil" given in *QG* 1.59, 2.66, and *QE* 1.6; while *Sobr.* 52 refers to the meaning of the name "Shem" given in *QG* 1.88 and 2.79.

Except for the references to the lost treatise Περὶ ἀριθμῶν in *QG* 4.110, 151, and *QE* 2.87 (see the discussion of *Opif.* 52, above), Philo is altogether silent in the *Quaestiones* about his other works. We would expect a passing reference to one or another of his numerous biblical treatises had either of the lengthier commentaries, the *Allegoriae* and the *Expositiones,* existed at the time when he was treating the same scriptural passages in the *Quaestiones.* Conversely, we find more than possible allusions to the *Quaestiones* in the *Allegoriae* (and to the *Allegoriae* in the *Expositiones* — as in *Spec.* 1.269). However few these references, the cumulative internal evidence seems sufficient for us to conclude against Marcus and others that the *Quaestiones* are the earliest of Philo's exegetical commentaries. We find no evidence to the contrary.

CHAPTER FOUR

SECONDARY TEXTS IN PHILO'S *QUAESTIONES*

DAVID T. RUNIA

I. The Problem[1]

The *Quaestiones in Genesim et Exodum* may justifiably be regarded as the Cinderellas of Philonic studies. Clothed in the unfamiliar garb of a literal (and frequently inscrutable) Armenian translation, they cannot match the attractions of their more glamorous sister writings, and so in practice have been relegated to the kitchen of the collective scholarly enterprise. One need cast only a swift glance at the editions, translations and studies of Philo's writings to realize how inadequately the material of the *Quaestiones* has been integrated into Philonic scholarship as a whole. This is a great pity. Certainly, even in the extremely unlikely event that the fairy godmother should wave her wand and produce a complete Greek text,[2] the repetitive form and procedure of the *Quaestiones* would remain a drawback. But not only do these texts have an intrinsic interest of their own. It is gradually emerging that they can provide us with important information on other problematic aspects of Philonic research as well.

In recent years there has been a growth of interest in the more formal aspects of Philo's writings. Most of this interest has focussed on the treatises of the Allegorical Commentary. Instead of merely complaining about Philo's repetitions and seemingly aimless ramblings, scholars have now decided to try to understand what may have induced

---

[1]This paper was prepared with the financial support of the Netherlands Organization for the Advancement of Pure Research (Z.W.O.). It was written while the author was in residence at The Institute for Advanced Study in Princeton, N.J. during the year 1986-87. The author wishes to express his thanks to the Director for the opportunity to use its wonderful facilities during a most memorable year.

[2] But let us thankful for small mercies, e.g., for the Greek text of (most of) *QG* 2.1-7, published by Paramelle 1984.

him to embark on them in the way he did. Independently of each other V. Nikiprowetzky and the Norwegian scholars P. Borgen and R. Skarsten suggested that the germ of Philo's method in the Allegorical Commentary should be sought in the question and answer method such as may have been practised in the Alexandrian Synagogue.[3] In the *Quaestiones*, they argue, Philo retains this method fairly much unchanged. In two articles on the structure of Philo's allegorical treatises I examined this theory and was able, in broad terms, to confirm it.[4] In addition I made three observations. Firstly I drew attention to the way Philo habitually invokes other biblical texts in order to give depth to his explanation of the main biblical text on which the treatise concentrates. This led me to make the following distinction:[5]

> One can thus speak of *primary exegesis*, which concentrates on direct exegesis of the *main biblical lemma*, and of *secondary exegesis*, which gives exegesis of *subordinate biblical lemmata* to the extent the exegete deems fit for the full understanding of the main biblical text (to which, sooner or later, he always returns).

The term 'secondary texts' in the title of the present article is based on this this distinction (it will emerge in the course of it that the term 'secondary exegesis' is not suitable). Secondly it became apparent in the course of my analyses that when Philo moves from primary to secondary exegesis the 'mode of transition' from the one text to the other is surprisingly often of a *verbal* rather than of a merely *thematic* nature, i.e., the texts are associated primarily on account of their *wording*.[6] Thirdly I argued that in writing an allegorical treatise Philo achieves a loose kind of unity rather than a tight-knit structural coherence, and that this unity can be described in terms of a main directive idea.[7]

---

[3]Nikiprowetzky 1977 (but this work was already completed in 1970), 170-80; the theory was further examined in Nikiprowetzky 1983*a*, 5-58 (esp. 5-9, 53-4); Borgen and Skarsten 1976-7. Note that the evidence for Alexandrian synagogal practice is wholly drawn from Philo (and esp. *Contempl.* 75-8), and is not independently confirmed by other Judaeo-Hellenistic writings. If the Pseudo-Philonic *De Jona* is a Jewish homily from Alexandria, which is by no means certain, it makes no use of the *quaestio* procedure whatsoever.

[4] Runia 1984 and Runia 1987.

[5] Runia 1984, 238.

[6] Cf. *ibid.* 239-40, 245.

[7] Cf. Runia 1987, 23ff., arguing against Cazeaux 1983. The term 'main directive idea' taken over from Radice 1984.

In the second of the two articles it was noted in passing that the *Quaestiones* differ from the treatises of the Allegorical Commentary in that they contain very little secondary exegesis, i.e. the individual *quaestio* concentrates almost exclusively on the main biblical lemma which furnishes its exegetical problem, and seldom refers to other biblical texts.[8] This observation was at the time based on an impression, and its validity was not adequately put to the test. In the present article I shall present a comprehensive examination of the use that Philo makes of secondary biblical references in the books of the *Quaestiones* still extant. As a result we will be able to conclude whether the above-mentioned observation was correct or not. In addition it is to be hoped that this limited piece of research will give some more general new insights into Philo's aims and methods in an undeservedly neglected series of writings.

II. Method

Since there are no previous studies to guide us, a method will have to be devised to deal with our subject. But this can be done quite straightforwardly. I shall commence by presenting the *evidence,* i.e, a complete list of the occasions on which Philo refers to secondary biblical lemmata.[9] For each case the following information will be supplied:

(i) The number of the text and its location (page & line) in Marcus.[10]

(ii) The main biblical lemma (MBL) under discussion.

(iii) The secondary biblical lemma (SBL) adduced.

(iv) The form of reference (FR) to the secondary biblical text, whether allusion, paraphrase or quotation.

---

[8] Runia 1987, 29: 'The most distinctive feature of Philo's allegorical treatises from the literary point of view is his desire to connect together his exegetical explanations [i.e., of primary and secondary texts] into a continuous chain. This distinguished these works from the *Quaestiones*. . . .' Cf. Runia 1986a, 381: 'Adhering strictly to the biblical lemma which supplies the problem, it functions as an independent exegetical unit and is almost never complemented with references to other texts (rare exceptions at *QG* 2.59, 4.87).'

[9] In compiling this list I have made extensive use of the invaluable supplement to the *Biblia Patristica* prepared by the Centre d'Analyse et de Documentation Patristiques at Strasbourg (= Allenbach 1982), which in turn is indebted to identifications made by Aucher, Marcus, Petit and other scholars.

[10] I use the two volumes of Marcus 1953 because it is the only complete translation of the *Quaestiones* in a modern language. The translation of Mercier 1979-84 (which also contains the text of Aucher's Latin translation) is superior in some aspects, but it as yet does not include the *Quaestiones in Exodum.*

(v) The type of exegesis (TE) involved, whether literal or figurative or arithmological.[11] If the type of exegesis is explicitly introduced, as often occurs in the *Quaestiones* , it will be indicated by lit. or fig.; if it is implicit, the same abbreviations will be bracketed. Arithmological examples will be indicated by fig./-arithm.

(vi) The context and subject matter (CSM) of the passage.

(vii) The type of usage (TU) involved in the selection and application of the secondary biblical text.

(viii) The mode of transition (MOT) involved in moving from the primary to the secondary biblical text (if relevant — none is given for arithmological examples). Note that a verbal MOT usually includes a thematic MOT as well, but the reverse does not apply.

(ix). Parallels (P) for the exegesis in other Philonic writings. Parallel passages are introduced by cf., contrasting passages by cp. Parallels in which both the main and the secondary text in the *Quaestio* occur are marked by an asterisk. Parallels referring to usage of the main text elsewhere have MBL added in brackets; otherwise it may be assumed that the parallel refers to usage of the secondary text. Priority will be given to parallels located in the Allegorical Commentary, because of the importance of the question of the relation between the *Quaestiones* and the Allegorical Commentary (see below §4g).

(x) Additional comments (if required).

It will be understood that, though it would be highly desirable to make a detailed analysis of each passage containing a secondary text,[12] this will not be possible within the limited scope of our study.

In the fourth section of the study the *results* accruing from the analysis of the evidence will be presented under various headings. The results thus gained will allow us to draw some more general conclusions that will shed light on the vexed questions of Philo's purpose in writing the *Quaestiones* and the relation they have to the Allegorical Commentary (which not seldom discusses the very same biblical texts). These *conclusions* will be summarized in the final section.

There remains one question that needs to be resolved before we can begin. What are the criteria by which we judge a biblical lemma to be

---

[11] Though strictly speaking arithmological exegesis is a sub-set of figurative or typological exegesis.

[12] The detailed interpretation of the contents of the *Quaestiones* remains almost wholly virgin territory.

secondary rather than primary? Strictly speaking any biblical text referred to in a *quaestio* which differs from the main biblical text upon which the *quaestio* is based is a secondary text. So when in *QG* 2.31 Philo compares the diminution of the flood (as the ark comes to rest in Gen 8.4) at the autumnal equinox with its commencement at the vernal equinox (cf. Gen 7.11), in the light of the above-mentioned criterion the second text should be regarded as secondary. But this approach is too mechanical and presents us with quite a few texts which are not secondary in the sense that I intend. I have thus included in my list only those texts which fall outside the immediate biblical context of the main biblical text (note that this rule is not always easy to apply; no. 26 below is clearly a borderline case).[13]

III. The Evidence

1. *QG* 1.32 19.25 Marcus. MBL Gen 3:1. SBL Gen 6:4. FR allusion. TE (lit.). CSM excellent senses and giant magnitude of the first men. TU background. MOT thematic. P cf. *QG* 1.92, cp. *Gig*. 58.

2. *QG* 1.55 32.27 Marcus. MBL Gen 3:22. SBL Lev 23:9. FR quotation. CSM discussion of scriptural use of anthropomorphisms concerning God. TU standard text. P two texts Lev 23:9 and Deut 8:5 cited together at frag. p.8 Harris*, *Deus* 53-4, 68, *Somn*. 1.237, *QG* 2.54 (Lev 23:9 also at *Sacr*. 94, *Migr*. 113).

3. *QG* 1.55 33.1 Marcus. MBL Gen 3:22. SBL Deut 8:5. FR quotation. CSM see above. TU standard text. P see above.

4. *QG* 1.55 33.19 Marcus. MBL Gen 3:22. SBL Gen 1. FR allusion. TE (fig.). CSM God's lack of envy shown in creation. TU example. MOT thematic. P cf. *Opif*. 21, *Deus* 108 etc.

5. *QG* 1.55 33.23 Marcus. MBL Gen 3:22. SBL Gen 2:9. FR allusion. TE (fig.). CSM God's lack of envy shown in planting the tree of life. TU example. MOT thematic. P none specific, cf. *Leg*. 3.52, *Plant*. 44.

6. *QG* 1.64 39.7 Marcus. MBL Gen 4:7. SBL Gen 1. FR allusion. TE (fig.). CSM importance of correct division shown in creation of cosmos. TU example. MOT thematic. P cf. *Her*. 133, *Spec*. 2.151.

7. *QG* 1.64 39.27 Marcus. MBL Gen 4:7. SBL Deut 26:1-11. FR allusion. TE (fig.). CSM thanksgiving (through division) as required response to creation. TU proof. MOT thematic. P cf. *Spec*. 1.208-10, but theme not in *Sacr*. (cf. 72ff.).

8. *QG* 1.86 54.14 Marcus. MBL Gen 5:24. SBL Deut 34:5-6. FR allusion. TE (lit.). CSM Moses like Enoch receives the gift of 'translation'. TU comparison. MOT

[13] Secondary text located in fragments of the *Quaestiones* (e.g., Deut 32:5 in *QG* fr. 13 Petit) have not been included because their original context is unclear.

thematic. P cf. *Sacr*. 8-10, *Mut*. 25-6, 34; but direct connection Enoch-Moses not found elsewhere.

9. *QG* 1.86 54.16 Marcus. MBL Gen 5:24. SBL 2 Kgs 2:11-12. FR allusion. TE (lit.). CSM Elijah like Enoch receives the gift of 'translation'. TU comparison. MOT thematic. P none (Elijah elsewhere only at *Deus* 136).

10. *QG* 1.89 56.6 Marcus. MBL Gen 6:1. SBL Gen 41. FR allusion. TE (lit.). CSM grace precedes judgment, as in the case of the seven years of plenty and the seven years of want in Egypt. TU example. MOT thematic. P none (cp. *Ios*. 110, 114).

11. *QG* 1.90 57.2 Marcus. MBL Gen 6:3. SBL Exod 31:3. FR quotation (incomplete). TE (fig.). CSM nature of divine spirit indicated by Bezalel's being equipped with σοφία and ἐπιστήμη. TU example. MOT verbal (πνεῦμα). P cf. *Gig*. 23*, *Leg*. 3.95 etc.

12. *QG* 1.91 58.22 Marcus. MBL Gen 6:3. SBL Num. 8:24. FR allusion. TE fig./arithm. CSM 25 sacred number since associated with the Levites. TU arithmology. P cf. *Det*. 64 and below no. 77.

13. *QG* 1.93 62.6 Marcus. MBL Gen 6:6. SBL Gen 2:7. FR allusion. TE (lit.). CSM man on the earth and made from the earth, hence his proneness to evil. TU example. MOT verbal (γῆ). P none specific; cf. *Leg*. 3.69, but not at *Deus* 33ff.

14. *QG* 1.100 67.22 Marcus. MBL Gen 6:13. SBL Num. 14:9. FR quotation. TE (fig.). CSM time deified by the wicked. TU comparison/proof. MOT verbal (καιρός). P cf. *Post*. 121-2, cp. *Mut*. 265.

15. *QG* 2.4 72.4 Marcus. MBL Gen 6:14. SBL Exod 25:11. FR allusion. TE (fig./-symb.). CSM comparison of the two arks, one coated with gold, the other with bitumen. TU comparison. MOT verbal (κιβωτός). P none (cp. *Plant*. 43, *Conf*. 105f.). On the cross-reference cf. Paramelle 1984 147 and Terian's essay in the present volume.

16. *QG* 2.5 76.15 Marcus. MBL Gen 6:15-16. SBL Lev 25:8-17. FR allusion. TE (fig./arithm.). CSM 50 as number of jubilee year and thus of freedom and release. TU arithmology. P cf. *Sacr*. 122, *Mut*. 228, *Spec*. 2.176ff. (and below nos. 39, 43, 54).

17. *QG* 2.12 86.19 Marcus. MBL Gen 7:2-3. SBL Lev 13:15. FR allusion. TE fig. CSM twin unclean animals represent the fool, who is like the unclean leper with his defiled thoughts. TU example. MOT verbal (μὴ καθαρῶν/ἀκάθαρτος). P cf. *Deus* 123-36, *Leg*. 1.49, *Sobr*. 49, *QG* 2.29 (favorite exegetical theme, but here no emphasis on the paradox, as below in no.21).

18. *QG* 2.12 87.16 Marcus. MBL Gen 7:2-3. SBL Gen 2:9. FR allusion. TE fig. CSM man's comprehension of and inclination to both good and evil indicated by tree of knowledge. TU background. MOT thematic. P cf. *QG* 1.11, but no proper parallels in Allegorical Commentary (cp. *Leg*. 1.61, 3.107).

19. *QG* 2.17 97.6 Marcus. MBL Gen 7:11. SBL Gen 1. FR quotation. TE (fig./arithm.). CSM Noah's 600 years related to 6 as the number of creation. TU arithmology/background. P on hexad and creation cf. *Opif.* 13 etc.

20. *QG* 2.26 104.17 Marcus. MBL Gen 8:1. SBL Isa 51:2. FR quotation. TE (lit.). CSM mention of Abraham and Sarah proves that mention of Noah includes his family. TU proof. MOT thematic. P none.

21. *QG* 2.29 108.7 Marcus. MBL Gen 8:2. SBL Lev 13:23. FR allusion. TE fig. CSM beginning of healing is constraint of sickness, as in the case of leprosy. TU proof. MOT thematic. P cf. above no.17.

22. *QG* 2.31 109.19 Marcus. MBL Gen 8:4. SBL Gen 1. FR allusion. TE lit. CSM flood's diminution begins at autumnal equinox, whereas creation took place on the vernal equinox. TU comparison. MOT thematic. P cf. *Spec.* 2.150-2, *QG* 2.17 and below nos. 25 & 85.

23. *QG* 2.38 116.5 Marcus. MBL Gen 8:8. SBL Lev 5:7. FR allusion. TE (lit.). CSM Noah despatches his dove because it is a clean animal. TU background. MOT thematic. P cf. *Her.* 127, *Mut.* 233, *QG* 3.3.

24. *QG* 2.43 122.6 Marcus. MBL Gen 8:11. SBL Isa 1:9. FR paraphrase (?). TE fig. CSM through God's goodness a residual seed remains, as also indicated by the prophet. TU proof. MOT verbal/thematic (via σπέρμα, which not in MBL, but taken from Gen 7:3, cf. *QG* 2.12, 66, *Mos.* 2.60). P the SBL nowhere else used; for the theme cf. *Praem.* 172 (seed), *Somn.* 2.191-2 (Sodom).

25. *QG* 2.45 123.13 Marcus. MBL Gen 8:12. SBL Exod 12:2. FR quotation. TE (lit.). CSM two equinoxes again. TU proof. MOT thematic. P see above no.22.

26. *QG* 2.45 125.5 Marcus. MBL Gen 8:12. SBL Gen 6:9. FR quotation. TE fig. CSM Noah associated with genesis and hexad, hence his righteousness qualified as 'in his generation'. TU proof. MOT thematic. P none, but cp. *Abr.* 27, *Deus* 117ff.

27. *QG* 2.47 128.5 Marcus. MBL Gen 8:14. SBL Gen 1:9-13. FR allusion. TE (lit.). CSM earth grows plants in one day, just as happened in creation. TU comparison/proof. MOT thematic. P cf. *Opif.* 40.

28. *QG* 2.54 135.7 Marcus. MBL Gen 8:21. SBL Lev 23:9. FR quotation. CSM God's repentance must be understood in light of scripture's use of anthropomorphisms. TU standard text. P see above no.2.

29. *QG* 2.54 135.8 Marcus. MBL Gen 8:21. SBL Deut 8:5. FR paraphrase. CSM see above. TU standard text. P see above no.2.

30. *QG* 2.56 140.14 Marcus. MBL Gen 9:1-2. SBL Gen 1:27-28. FR quotation (abbreviated). TE lit. CSM comparison of first man and Noah, both of whom are blessed. TU comparison. MOT verbal (two texts almost identical). P none (Adam and Noah differently correlated in *Abr.* 56).

31. *QG* 2.56 142.2 Marcus. MBL Gen 9:1-2. SBL Gen 2:5, 7. FR quotation. TE lit. CSM Noah compared with incorporeal, not moulded man. TU comparison. MOT thematic. P see above.

32. *QG* 2.59 145.8 Marcus. MBL Gen 9:4. SBL Gen 2:7. FR quotation. TE lit. CSM blood indicates not rational but sense-perceptive soul. TU background. MOT thematic. P two texts Gen 2:7 and Lev 17:11 also found together in *Det.* 80, *Her.* 55-6, *Spec.* 4.123, i.e., a standard exegetical theme.

33. *QG* 2.59 145.11 Marcus. MBL Gen 9:4. SBL Lev 17:11. FR quotation. TE lit. CSM see above. TU background. MOT verbal (αἷμα). P see above.

34. *QG* 2.65 156.6 Marcus. MBL Gen 9:18-19. SBL Deut 32:49. FR allusion. TE lit. CSM Canaan singled out, with an eye to the future. TU background (answering *quaestio*). P none.

35. *QG* 2.66 157.10 Marcus. MBL Gen 9:20. SBL Gen 3:23. FR allusion. TE lit. CSM scripture compares Noah to first moulded man, the one leaving paradise, the other leaving the ark, to become a farmer. TU comparison. MOT verbal/thematic (parallelism Gen 3:23 ἐξαπέστειλεν... ἐκ τοῦ παραδείσου, Gen 8:16 ἔξελθε ἐκ τοῦ κιβωτοῦ, and fact that both are tillers of the soil). P none (but cf. above no. 30-1). Note that Armenian is confused; Greek paraphrase at Petit 1978 120 helpful.

36. *QG* 2.66 157.13 Marcus. MBL Gen 9:20. SBL Gen 1:9. FR quotation. TE lit. CSM see above. TU proof (supporting above comparison). MOT thematic. P cf. *Opif.* 38 (flooding).

37. *QG* 2.66 158.5 Marcus. MBL Gen 9:20. SBL Gen 4:2. FR allusion. TE fig. CSM difference between Noah, who becomes farmer, and Cain, who works the earth. TU comparison. MOT verbal (*difference* in wording). P cf. *Agr.* 20-5*, but not exploited at *Sacr.* 51, *QG* 1.59 (on which see below §4g).

38. *QG* 2.67 159.11 Marcus. MBL Gen 9:20. SBL Gen 2:6. FR allusion. TE (lit.). CSM God produces necessities (water, wheat), man superfluities (wine). TU comparison (contrast). MOT thematic. P none (cp. *Opif.* 131, *QG* 1.3, *Post.* 127 etc.).

39. *QG* 2.78 170.3 Marcus. MBL Gen 9:28. SBL Lev 25:4ff. FR allusion. TE (fig./arithm.). CSM Noah's years after flood are 350, 350 = 7 x 50, 7 and 50 are special years, as set out in the book Leviticus. TU arithmology. P cf. *Spec.* 2.110 (and nos. 16, 43, 54).

40. *QG* 2.79 170.8 Marcus. MBL Gen 10;1. SBL Gen 5:32, 6:10. FR allusion. TE in *quaestio*. CSM why different name order of Noah's sons in different biblical passages? TU comparison/*quaestio*. P none.

41. *QG* 3.1 176.5 Marcus. MBL Gen 15:7. SBL Gen 12:1. FR allusion (subtle). TE fig. CSM Abraham removed from one land and given/shown another. TU parallel text (see below §4i). MOT verbal (γῆ). P cf. *Migr.* 36ff., *Det.* 159 etc.

42. *QG* 3.38 225.17 Marcus. MBL Gen 16:16. SBL Exod 7:7. FR allusion. TE (fig./arithm.). CSM Abraham 80 + 6 when Ishmael born, Moses 80 when began to give oracles. TU arithmology. P none (only discussion of number 80 in Philo).

43. *QG* 3.39 228.3 Marcus. MBL Gen 17:1. SBL Lev 25:4, 10. FR allusion. TE (fig./arithm.). CSM Abraham is 99, 90 = 50 + 49 (= 7 x 7), 7 and 50 are significant years. TU arithmology. P cf. above nos. 16 & 39.

44. *QG* 3.46 241.11 Marcus. MBL Gen 17:10-11. SBL Deut 10:16. FR quotation. TE fig. CSM double circumcision, of the flesh and the mind. TU proof. MOT verbal (περιτέμνω). P cf. *Spec.* 1.305 (but not at 1.1-11).

45. *QG* 3.52 252.14 Marcus. MBL Gen 17:14. SBL Num. 35:10ff. FR allusion. TE lit. CSM how can it be that the uncircumcised infant should be put to death when the law pardons even him who commits manslaughter? TU background (leading to a question). MOT thematic. P cf. *Fug.* 86ff., *Sacr.* 128 etc. (but MBL nowhere else commented on).

46. *QG* 3.56 258.27 Marcus. MBL Gen 17:17. SBL Num. 18:26ff. FR allusion. TE (fig./arithm.). CSM Sarah's 90 years significant, for 90 = 100 – 10 (i.e., minus decad = tenth), as in the offering of the first fruits. TU arithmology. P cf. *Mut.* 2, 190-1 (see further below 4g).

47. *QG* 3.56 259.12 Marcus. MBL Gen 17:17. SBL Gen 21:33. FR allusion. TE (fig./arithm.). CSM as above, but in praise of 100 as related to 90. TU arithmology. P as above (also cited at *Plant.* 73ff.).

48. *QG* 3.61 263.14 Marcus. MBL Gen 17:24-5. SBL Deut 16:16. FR allusion. TE (fig./arithm.). CSM Ishmael's 13 years recall the thrice-yearly festal offering. TU arithmology. P none specific; allegorical parallel at *Leg.* 3.11 shows that Marcus' reference can be made more precise.

49. *QG* 4.4 275.22 Marcus. MBL Gen 18:3. SBL Gen 4:13. FR quotation (?). TE (fig.). CSM Cain illustrates the limit of wickedness, that God should abandon the soul. TU example. MOT thematic. P cf. *Det.* 141-4, *Conf.* 165, *QG* 1.73.

50. *QG* 4.4 275.25 Marcus. MBL Gen 18:3. SBL Exod 19:22. FR quotation. TE (fig.). CSM another example of threat of abandonment by God. TU example. MOT thematic. P none.

51. *QG* 4.8 282.14 Marcus. MBL Gen 18:6-7. SBL Exod 33:13. FR quotation. TE (fig.). CSM quest for vision of the One exemplified by Moses. TU example. P cf. *Leg.* 3.101, *Post.* 13, *Mut.* 8, *Spec.* 1.41ff. (a favorite text).

52. *QG* 4.10 284.7 Marcus. MBL Gen 18:8. SBL Gen 14:14. FR allusion. TE (lit.). CSM Abraham attends on visitors, though he himself has a host of servants. TU background. MOT thematic. P cf. *Det.* 14 (n.b.), *Abr.* 232.

53. *QG* 4.16 290.8 Marcus. MBL Gen 18:12. SBL Exod 4:14. FR quotation. TE (fig.). CSM both Sarah and Aaron show true rejoicing (as freedom from passion).

TU comparison/proof. MOT verbal (ἐγέλασεν ἐν ἑαυτῇ, χαρήσεται ἐν ἑαυτῷ), as Philo himself emphasizes. P *Mut.* 166-8*, *Det.* 126.

54. *QG* 4.27 301.19 Marcus. MBL Gen 18:24-32. SBL Lev 25:10. FR allusion. TE (fig./arithm.). CSM 50 sacred number of release. TU arithmology. P cf. *Congr.* 109* and see further above nos. 16, 39, 43.

55. *QG* 4.29 304.14 Marcus. MBL Gen 18:33. SBL Gen 28:11ff. FR allusion. TE (fig.). CSM ascent and descent of soul illustrated by ladder of Jacob's dream. TU example. MOT verbal (τόπος). P cf. *Somn.* 1.70-1*, 133ff.

56. *QG* 4.29 304.16 Marcus. MBL Gen 18:33. SBL Exod 19:17-25? FR allusion. TE (fig.). CSM ascent and descent of soul illustrated by Moses on the mountain. TU example. MOT thematic. P *Post.* 136, *Somn.* 1.71 (see discussion below §4i); Moses as νοῦς *QE* 2.40ff.

57. *QG* 4.60 340.4 Marcus. MBL Gen 20:2. SBL Gen 12:13. FR allusion (subtle). TE (lit.). CSM why doublet (Abraham twice calls Sarah his sister)? TU comparison (raises *quaestio*). P none specific, but cf. *Abr.* 89ff., *Her.* 258.

58. *QG* 4.80 360.2 Marcus. MBL Gen 23:9. SBL Exod 26:33. FR allusion. TE fig. CSM double cave and double plan of tabernacle compared and allegorized. TU comparison/proof. MOT thematic. P for comparison none; on tabernacle cf. *Mut.* 43.

59. *QG* 4.87 366.13 Marcus. MBL Gen 24:3. SBL Exod 5:2. FR quotation. TE (fig.). CSM Pharaoh admits God as creator, but not as ruler, whereas Abraham recognizes both. TU comparison/proof (contrast). MOT verbal (κύριος). P cf. *Leg.* 3.12, 243, *Post.* 115, *Ebr.* 19, 77-9, *Somn.* 2.182, *Mos.* 1.88 (SBL common text, but note that avoided at *Mut.* 19!).

60. *QG* 4.88 367.1 Marcus. MBL Gen 24:3. SBL Gen 28:1. FR allusion. TE in *quaestio*. CSM comparison courtship procedure of Isaac and Jacob. TU comparison (in *quaestio*). P none.

61. *QG* 4.88 367.11 Marcus. MBL Gen 24:3. SBL Gen 12:1ff. FR allusion. TE lit. CSM as above — possible answer to *quaestio* rejected. TU background. P none.

62. *QG* 4.102 386.3 Marcus. MBL Gen 24:17. SBL Exod 16:16ff. FR allusion. TE (fig.). CSM in praise of restraint and measure, as seen in the distribution of manna. TU example. MOT thematic. P cf. *Her.* 191, *Post.* 139-142 (MBL).

63. *QG* 4.102 386.11 Marcus. MBL Gen 24:17. SBL Lev 12:8. FR allusion. TE (fig.). CSM in praise of restraint and measure, as seen in the injunction to sacrifice in accordance with the power of the hands. TU example. MOT thematic. P none (SBL not elsewhere utilized).

64. *QG* 4.110 394.9 Marcus. MBL Gen 24:22. SBL Lev 25:9. FR allusion. TE (fig./arithm.). CSM decad holy number of release. TU arithmology. P cf. *Congr.* 108, 113*, and above no. 54.

65. *QG* 4.110 394.13 Marcus. MBL Gen 24:22. SBL Exod 30:13-15. FR allusion. TE (fig./arithm.). CSM monad suited to Rebecca. TU arithmology. P cf. *Her.* 187.

66. *QG* 4.122 406.3 Marcus. MBL Gen 24:36. SBL Gen 16:15. FR allusion. TE lit. CSM why 'Sarah bore a son' and not 'Abraham begot'? -- because Abraham already had a son. TU background (for answer to *quaestio*). MOT verbal (ἔτεκεν). P none (but note *Virt.* 207).

67. *QG* 4.123 407.12 Marcus. MBL Gen 24:36. SBL Deut 33:6-7. FR quotation. TE fig. CSM Reuben and Judah illustrate relation learner and autodidact. TU comparison. MOT thematic. P none for this surprising allegory; for SBL cf. *Mut.* 210f.

68. *QG* 4.124 408.9 Marcus. MBL Gen 24:46. SBL Gen 18:6ff. FR allusion. TE (lit.). CSM Abraham and Sarah, like Rebecca, show exemplary haste. TU example. MOT verbal (σπεύδω). P cf. *Abr.* 108, *Post.* 140 (MBL).

69. *QG* 4.129 412.7 Marcus. MBL Gen 24:51. SBL Prov. 19:14. FR quotation. TE fig. CSM Rebecca suited to Isaac as woman suited to man, or rather virtue to reason. TU proof. MOT verbal (γυνή). P none.

70. *QG* 4.132 414.17 Marcus. MBL Gen 24:57. SBL Num. 30:3. FR quotation (slightly adapted). TE (fig.). CSM speech clear evidence, whereas thought always changing. TU proof. MOT verbal (στόμα). P none.

71. *QG* 4.138 419.16 Marcus. MBL Gen 24:62. SBL 1 Sam 9:9. FR allusion. TE (fig.). CSM seeing, contemplation and true prophecy. TU proof. MOT verbal (via synonym ὅρασις-βλέπων). P cf. *Migr.* 38, *Deus* 139, *Her.* 78, *De Deo* 2 (SBL standard proof text, MBL not elsewhere used).

72 *QG* 4.147 429.16 Marcus. MBL Gen 25:1. SBL Gen 1:31. FR quotation. TE (fig.). CSM Abraham's three wives symbolize 3 best senses — sight, hearing, smell —, as indicated by fact that these only attributed to God. TU proof. MOT thematic. P cf. *Migr.* 42, 135 (though emphasis differs).

73. *QG* 4.147 429.18 Marcus. MBL Gen 25:1. SBL Ps 68.34. FR quotation. TE fig. CSM see above. TU proof. MOT thematic. P none.

74. *QG* 4.147 429.19 Marcus. MBL Gen 25:1. SBL Gen 8:21. FR quotation. TE fig. CSM see above. TU proof. MOT thematic. P cf. *Congr.* 115 (though emphasis differs).

75. *QG* 4.147 430.1 Marcus. MBL Gen 25:1. SBL Gen 16:15. FR allusion. TE (fig.). CSM see above — Ishmael related to hearing. TU proof (via etymologies). MOT thematic. P common theme, e.g., at *Fug.* 208 (where Ishmael and Isaac compared).

76. *QG* 4.147 430.3 Marcus. MBL Gen 25:1. SBL Gen 21:6. FR allusion. TE (fig.). CSM see above — Isaac as 'laughter' related to light and sight. TU proof (via

etymology). MOT thematic. P etymology ubiquitous (e.g., *Cher.* 5), but connection with sight uncommon and doubtless *ad hoc.*

77. *QG* 4.151 433.16 Marcus. MBL Gen 25:7. SBL Num. 8:24-5. FR allusion. TE (fig./arithm.). CSM Abraham's 175 years = 7 x 25, and 25 is the age that the Levites begin their temple duties. TU arithmology. P cf. *Det.* 63-5 and above no. 17.

78. *QG* 4.169 455.13 Marcus. MBL Gen 25:29. SBL Gen 25:8. . . FR allusion. TE (fig.). CSM Esau's 'leaving of' quite different to that of the patriarchs. TU comparison (contrast). MOT verbal (ἐκλείπω). P cf. *Sacr.* 5, 81 (MBL), but applications differ.

79. *QG* 4.195i 71.17 Petit. MBL Gen 26:32-3. SBL Ps 18:8. FR quotation. TE (fig.). CSM soul confesses limits of her knowledge and by an oath invokes God's faithful testimony. TU proof. MOT thematic. P cf. *Spec.* 2.10, *Plant.* 82 (MBL), and see further below §4i.

80. *QG* 4.215 512.12 Marcus. MBL Gen 27:28. SBL Gen 1:1. FR allusion. TE (fig.). CSM the order of the blessings received by Jacob is the same as the cosmos received when it was created, i.e., first place to heaven, second place to earth. TU comparison. MOT verbal (οὐρανός, γῆ). P none specific (cp. *Leg.* 1.1).

81. *QG* 4.226 524.4 Marcus. MBL Gen 27:33. SBL Num. 17:20. TE (fig.). CSM before evil creeps in, the mind is blessed and sets forth unhampered on the royal highway. TU standard theme. MOT thematic. P common theme, cf. *Gig.* 64, *Deus* 159 etc., and see further below §4i.

82. *QG* 4.233 532.13 Marcus. MBL Gen Gen 27:38-39. SBL Exod 2:23-4. FR allusion. TE (fig.). CSM both Esau's and Israel's crying aloud indicate repentance and so usher in salvation and blessing. TU example. MOT verbal (ἀναβοάω). P cf. *Det.* 93 (similar MOT, this time from Gen 4:10, but context differs).

83. *QG* 4.244 549.2 Marcus. MBL Gen 28:7. SBL Deut 21:18ff. FR allusion. TE lit. CSM obedience to both parents (Jacob), to one of the two, or to neither. TU background. MOT thematic. P common exegetical theme, cf. *Ebr.* 14-95 (but MBL *not* used at 82), *Mut.* 206, *Spec.* 2.232f.; also *Congr.* 70 (MBL).

84. *QE* 1.1 3.7 Marcus. MBL Exod 12:2. SBL Gen 1:9-13. FR allusion. TE lit. CSM in creation fruits ready for man, as if vernal equinox. TU comparison. MOT thematic. P cf. above nos. 22 & 27.

85. *QE* 1.1 3.19 Marcus. MBL Exod 12:2. SBL Lev 23:10-11. FR allusion. TE (lit.). CSM that scripture regards vernal equinox at beginning of the cycle of months is shown by the offering of the sheaves as first fruits. TU proof. MOT thematic. P cf. *Spec.* 2.150*.

86. *QE* 1.2 7.13 Marcus. MBL Exod 12:3. SBL Exod 30:19 FR allusion. TE (fig.). CSM purity needs to be prepared before offering sacrifices. TU example. MOT thematic. P cf. *Mos.* 2.138.

87. *QE* 1.10 18.9 Marcus. MBL Exod 12:6. SBL Num 18:21ff. FR allusion. TE (lit.). CSM why do all the people sacrifice and not just the priests? TU background. MOT thematic. P cf. *Spec.* 1.79ff., and cp. *Spec.* 2.145-6, where similar *quaestio* implied.

88. *QE* 2.2 36.6 Marcus. MBL Exod 22:21. SBL Exod 3:7-10. FR allusion. TE (fig.). CSM Israel sojourned and mistreated in the land of Egypt. TU background. MOT thematic. P cf. *Mos.* 1.72.

89. *QE* 2.10 45.2 Marcus. MBL Exod 23:3. SBL Deut 1:17. FR quotation. TE (lit.). CSM poverty demands mercy, but justice must be impartial. TU proof (standard text). MOT verbal (κρίσις). P cf. esp. *Spec.* 4.71-2*, (also note *Ios.* 72); SBL also at *Her.* 157, *Somn.* 2.24.

90. *QE* 2.14 51.14 Marcus. MBL Exod 23:18. SBL Lev 2:11. FR allusion. TE fig. CSM no leaven to be used with a sacrifice, for it symbolizes sensuality. TU comparison. MOT thematic. P similar allegory at *Congr.* 169 (cp. *Spec.* 1.293); MBL only here.

91. *QE* 2.28 69.9 Marcus. MBL Exod 24:1. SBL Exod 20:21. FR allusion. TE (fig.). CSM consequences of drawing too near the divine fire, as happened to the prophetic mind. TU comparison. MOT verbal (μακρόθεν). P none precise (cf. *Post.* 13, *Migr.* 168, 201 etc., but no contrast).

92. *QE* 2.41 84.12 Marcus. MBL Exod 24:12. SBL Deut 10:5. FR allusion. TE (lit.). CSM stone tablets later placed in ark. TU background. MOT thematic. P none (*Fug.*180 based on other texts).

93. *QE* 2.46 91.4 Marcus. MBL Exod 24:16. SBL Gen 1. FR allusion. TE (fig./-arithm.). CSM six apportioned to creation of cosmos and election of the contemplative nation. TU arithmology (comparison). P none precise; cf. above no. 19.

94. *QE* 2.46 91.13 Marcus. MBL Exod 24:16. SBL Exod 2:1-2. FR allusion. TE (fig.). CSM Moses' second birth better than his first. TU comparison. MOT thematic. P none precise (cf. *Mos.* 1.5); on second birth cf. nos. 30-1.

95. *QE* 2.46 92.7 Marcus. MBL Exod 24:16. SBL Gen 2:7. FR allusion. TE (fig.). CSM Moses called up on 7th day, thus superior to moulded man created on 6th day (!). TU comparison. MOT thematic. P none precise (cf. above nos. 30-1).

96. *QE* 2.49 95.8 Marcus. MBL Exod 24:18. SBL Num 14:32f. FR allusion. TE (lit.). CSM Israelites 40 years in the desert, Moses 40 days on the mountain (so that he can intercede). TU background (for answer to *quaestio*). P none precise (cf. *Mos.*1.238).

97. *QE* 2.76 126.17 Marcus. MBL Exod 25:33. SBL Hos. 14:5. FR quotation. TE (fig.). CSM lilies on the candlestick symbolize Israel's time of prosperity. TU comparison/proof. MOT verbal (κρίνον). P none precise (on Israel's prosperity, or lack thereof, cf. *Mos.* 2.44). Note that Philo may also be thinking of Isa 35:1, the context of which (desert) is actually more suggestive of his exegesis.

98. *QE* 2.101 148.14 Marcus. MBL Exod 27:2. SBL Deut 14:4-5. FR allusion. TE (lit.). CSM horns of altar explained in relation to dietary laws. TU background. MOT thematic. P cf. *Spec.* 4.105.

99. *QE* 2.102 150.3 Marcus. MBL Exod 27:3. SBL Lev 23:9-14. FR allusion. TE (lit.). CSM altar vessels made of bronze because of the sacrifices made on it (bronze symbolizes earth, where fruits etc. come from). TU background. MOT thematic. P none precise (cf. *Mos.* 2.106ff.).

100 *QE* 2.108 157.11 Marcus. MBL Exod 28:7. SBL Gen 32:29. FR quotation. TE (fig.). CSM shoulder pieces symbolize two kinds of toil, as described in the case of Jacob. TU proof (?). MOT thematic. P cf. *Mut.*43-4 (where MBL might have been expected), Mos. 2.130 (MBL).

IV. Results

The evidence has been set before us and demands analysis. This will take place approximately in the sequence in which each item was described above.

A. *Instantiation and Distribution*

In the six, or — as they actually number — eight,[14] books of the *Quaestiones* a century of references to secondary biblical texts were located. We have, therefore, a 100 instances in a total of 646 questions. Moreover it must be borne in mind that when references to other biblical texts do occur, they often come in small clusters of two or three. In fact only 75 *quaestiones* contain such references, i.e., little more than 10% of the total. In absolute terms, therefore, the incidence is assuredly *low* . When, basing my remark purely on an impression, I spoke of secondary biblical references in the *Quaestiones* as 'almost never' occurring except in the case of 'rare exceptions',[15] this was probably going too far. After all a hundred instances were found. But when we compare Philo's practice in the Allegorical Commentary, the contrast is marked. Let us take, for example, the double treatise *De Gigantibus–Quod Deus Immutabilis Sit.* Though only about a tenth of the length of the entire *Quaestiones*, it contains no less than 46 secondary biblical texts.[16]

[14] Cf. Marcus 1953 1.x-xiii, Royse 1976-7.

[15] See note 7 above.

[16] These can easily be identified through a glance at my structural analyses at Runia 1984 241-4, 1987 (appendix 3).

Moreover the discussion of these texts is generally much more extensive than the short references we find in the *Quaestiones* . To this important contrast we shall return below.

The distribution of the references to secondary texts is as follows:

QG I	14
QG II	26
QG III	8
QG IVA (§§1-70)	9
QG IVB (§§71-154)	20
QG IVC (§§155-245)	6
QE I	4
QE II	13

There is some variation here. Exegesis of the biblical text dealing with Noah induces Philo to refer to more secondary texts than exposition of the relations between Isaac, Esau and Jacob, and the explanation of the symbolism of the tabernacle furnishings. There do not appear to be significant conclusions to be drawn here. I defer, for the moment, the important question of whether there is any correlation between secondary texts in the *Quaestiones* and the Allegorical Commentary when both are giving exegesis of the same main biblical text.

B. *Location of Secondary Texts*

If the secondary texts we have located in the *Quaestiones* are culled together, their provenance can be summarized as follows (see also the ordered list in the Appendix):

Genesis	38	(64)
Exodus	17	(27)
Leviticus	16	(11)
Numbers	9	(9)
Deuteronomy	12	(12)
non-Pentateuchal	8	(5)

The figures in brackets refer to columns of references listed in the *Index Biblique*. It emerges that, though in absolute terms texts from Genesis and Exodus are most frequent, comparatively Philo refers to the other Pentateuchal and non-Pentateuchal more often than usual. This is not surprising, for we are dealing here with *secondary* texts, brought in to illumine primary texts, which are always drawn from Genesis and Exodus. It is further worth observing that 18 secondary texts are drawn from Gen 1-3, a further confirmation of how vital these first three chapters of the Law for Philo's whole exposition of Mosaic thought.[17] To the subject of Philo's use of non-Pentateuch texts in *Quaestiones* we shall return below in sub-section h.

C. *Form of Reference*

As in the Allegorical Commentary Philo is fond of giving a literal quotation of the secondary text to which he refers. This occurred in 29 of the 100 cases, while in two further instances paraphrases of the biblical text were given (nos. 24, 29). In the remaining 69 he alludes to the text only. The choice between quotation and allusion depends primarily on what the purpose of the reference to secondary text is. For example in the 15 arithmological passages Philo alludes only, never quoting the secondary text.[18] When a secondary text is used as a proof-text, it is more likely to be quoted, because a quotation points out the verbal clues which make the point at issue clear to the reader (especially in the case of a verbal 'mode of transition', on which see below sub-section e).

In the citation of Isa 1:9 at *QG* 2.43 (no. 24), it is apparent that Philo gives a paraphrase, for he has substituted the words 'blind' and 'barren' for the 'Sodom' and 'Gomorrah' in the text. But in many other cases Philo's fidelity to the wording of the biblical text is difficult to check on account of the Armenian transmission. It has been shown that in the Allegorical Commentary he often deviates quite markedly from the LXX text in his citations of scripture, whether in order to 'improve' Mosaic Greek style or for other reasons.[19] Doubtless this will also have occurred on occasion in the 29 cases which I have above classed as 'quotations.'

---

[17] Cf. Runia 1986a, 525-6.

[18] But note that in the Allegorical Commentary secondary texts in arithmological contexts are quite often quoted; cf. the quotes at *Congr*. 95, 99, 106, 115.

[19] Cf. the careful analysis of all the biblical citations in *Gig.–Deus* in Nikiprowetzky 1983*b*, 91-118.

D. *Type of Exegesis*

Philo's procedure in the *Quaestiones* has been described by Goodenough in his introductory volume on Philo in the following terms:[20]

> The *Questions* was originally quite as important a work as any of Philo. The method is again commentary, but this time Philo discusses the text verse by verse, and usually under two heads, the literal meaning and the intellectual or mystical meaning. Each section is introduced by the 'question': 'What does it mean when it says' — and then a verse is quoted. . . . The literal meaning seems always the interpretation which would be used by a preacher addressing such an audience as did Philo in his sermons *On Blessings and Curses*. . . . The accompanying mystical commentary is an invaluable supplement which fills in many gaps in the Allegory.

Let us look at Philo's use of secondary texts in the light of this double exposition of both the literal and the figurative meaning (as I would prefer to call them), which is in such sharp contrast to what we encounter in the Allegorical Commentary. The secondary texts are located as follows (by 'announced' I mean that Philo expressly indicates he is giving that kind of exegesis):

in the *quaestio*	2
in announced literal exegesis	14
in implicit literal exegesis	18
in announced figurative exegesis	10
in implicit figurative exegesis	38
in arithmological passages	14
(in methodological discussions	4).

Two conclusions can be drawn. Firstly it is striking that in only about a quarter of the cases does Philo explicitly tell us what kind of exegesis he is giving (i.e., τὸ ῥητόν or τὸ πρὸς διάνοιαν). In a large number of

[20] Goodenough 1962, 49. Note that it is extremely doubtful whether we can describe any Philonic treatise as consisting of *sermons*.

cases, when he is not explicit, it is not easy to determine what kind of exegesis is being presented. The boundary between Abraham the historical patriarch and Abraham the prototype of the σοφός is in practice not as clearly demarcated as Philo's apparently rigid method might imply. Secondly it is evident that a higher proportion of secondary texts are found in passages of figurative exegesis than in passages of literal exegesis. This all the more the case if one recognizes that the arithmological passages also represent a form of figurative, i.e., symbolic, exegesis. Clearly Philo feels a greater need for supplementary explanation or elucidation as furnished through secondary texts when engaged in figurative or allegorical exegesis. It is true that more room is given to literal exegesis in the *Quaestiones* compared with his other writings; but it is the allegorical exegesis that remains the more important.

E. *Types of Usage*

In our century of instances there is a great diversity of usage of secondary texts, too great to allow discussion of every individual case. It will be best to try to capture these within the following typology.

(1) *Background*. In this type of usage Philo refers to a secondary text in order to furnish some background information necessary or useful for understanding the main text. This information is in most cases historical (e.g., the number of Abraham's servants (no. 52), Israel's hardship in Egypt (no. 85) or pertaining to the law (e.g., the dove as sacrificial animal (no. 23), the vessels of bronze (no. 99). In only one passage is philosophical background information supplied, on the nature of the blood-soul and its difference from the rational soul (nos. 32-3). Sixteen instances of this type of usage were located.

(2) *Example*. Often in answering the question to which the main text gives rise Philo finds it profitable to give an example which will shed light on his explanation. Such examples usually invoke well-known exegetical themes, such as the ascent and descent of the angels on Jacob's ladder and Moses's ascent and descent on Mount Sinai (nos. 55-6), or the case of Cain as the limit of wretchedness (no. 49). In no. 10, however, we find a rare reference to the seven years of plenty and want in Egypt for which there are no parallels in Philo's oeuvre. Seventeen secondary texts were found to be used for such exemplaristic purposes in the *Quaestiones*.

(3) *Comparison.* In a large number of instances Philo introduces an example which amounts to direct comparison between a figure or theme in the main biblical text and a corresponding figure or theme in the secondary text. These comparisons I have regarded as a separate type of usage. Enoch is compared with Moses and Elijah (nos. 8-9), Noah's ark is compared with the ark in the tabernacle (no. 15), Jacob's courtship is compared with Isaac's courtship (no. 60), and so on. Not surprisingly these comparisons are often suggested by verbal similarities in the two texts (see further below on modes of transition). Indeed Philo considers such comparisons to be deliberately intended by scripture (and not just the work of the exegete). For example at *QG* 2.66 (no. 35) we read, '(Scripture) likens Noah to that first moulded earthy man, for it uses the same expression of him, when he came out of the ark, as of the other...'. In three instances a contrast rather than a comparison is invoked (nos. 38, 59, 78). Note, also, that in three cases (nos. 40, 57, 60) the comparison is already present in the actual *quaestio* . In all 23 instances were found in which secondary texts were used for purposes of comparison.

(4) *Proof.* A fourth category of usage that is very common occurs when Philo invokes secondary texts in order to strengthen or confirm the exegesis which he has developed in order to answer the *quaestio.* To give one example: in no. 44 Philo deduces two circumcisions from Gen 17:10-11, a literal one of the flesh and an allegorical one of the mind; the citation of Deut 16:16 is meant to 'prove' that the reading of the double circumcision in this text can only be read figuratively. Philo often indicates that he has proof in mind by the way he introduces the reference to the secondary text: e.g., no. 70 '*wherefore* in another passage of the legislation (Moses) says...', no. 85 'and one may *make certain* of this from the sheaves of first fruits which (Scripture) commands. . .' Many of these 'proof-texts' occur at the end of a *quaestio*, with the obvious intent of rounding off a persuasive bit of exegesis (this is especially the case with the non-Pentateuchal texts, on which see below). We note also that a number of the comparisons mentioned in the previous category of usage also function as proof-texts (e.g., the contrast between Pharaoh and Abraham in no. 59, which is meant to bolster Philo's allegorical interpretation of the double invocation in Gen 24:3). Clearly our categories are somewhat fluid. On 24 occasions references to secondary texts were made for purposes of proof.

(5) *Arithmology*. A feature of the *Quaestiones* is that Philo pays much attention — more in fact than in the Allegorical Commentary — to important numbers in the biblical narrative. On 14 occasions secondary texts are used in arithmological contexts. In addition to the rather monotonous catalogues of arithmological lore based on the intrinsic nature of numbers,[21] Philo likes to give other examples of numerical importance drawn from scripture, and for this he has to refer to other biblical texts. The number 80, which Abraham bears when Ishmael is born (actually he is 86), is important for diverse arithmological reasons, but also because Moses was 80 when he began to be a divinely inspired legislator (no. 42, note that that a comparison is involved, but on arithmological grounds, cf. also no. 93). It is remarkable that 6 of the 14 instances focus in order the three numbers 7, 25 and 50 which Philo associates with the Levites (nos. 12, 16, 39, 43, 54, 77).

(6) *Standard texts and themes*. A small group of texts, 6 in number, have escaped our classification so far. In two passages (*QG* 1.55, 2.54, nos. 2-3, 28-9) Philo uses a pair of favorite texts to explain that scripture uses anthropomorphic language to speak about God for pedagogic purposes, but that it should not be taken as literally true. In no. 81 Philo alludes to one of his favorite exegetical themes, the royal highway that veers neither to right or to left. This can hardly be called an example or a proof text. It is more like a casual allusion. It is remarkable that such allusions are very rare in the *Quaestiones*. On no.41 see below subsection J.

(7) *The quaestio*. Finally it should be noted that in four cases the secondary text is alluded to (not quoted at any length) in the actual exegetical question as it is formulated at the beginning of the *quaestio*; cf. nos. 40, 57, 60, 66. In each case the question involves the direct comparison of the two texts.

There is an important conclusion to be drawn from the various categories of usage we have outlined. In every case the secondary texts are invoked in order to refract light on the main text and the *quaestio* to which it gives rise. They are kept wholly subordinate and are never given any independent treatment. For this reason the references to secondary texts, whether they are quoted or merely alluded to, are invariably very brief, and never amount to more than 2 or 3 lines at the most. Not a single exception to this will be found in the entire *Quaestiones*.

---

[21] These are collected in Staehle 1931.

F. *Modes of Transition.*

What are the factors that cause Philo to select the secondary texts he uses in the *Quaestiones*? Naturally there has to be a thematic connection between the main and the secondary text. But in my analyses of treatises in the Allegorical Commentary it emerged that the 'mode of transition' from primary to secondary texts is very often determined by *verbal* parallelisms in the two texts.[22] Is this also the case in the *Quaestiones* ?

The results of our enquiry were as follows: in the 78 relevant cases there were 26 instances in which verbal parallels played a role in Philo's section of the secondary text; in the other 52 cases the mode of transition was purely thematic. The ratio is thus one-third to two-thirds, which can be compared with a half–half ratio found in one treatise of the Allegorical Commentary.[23] Philo thus places somewhat less emphasis on verbal parallels in the *Quaestiones* than in the Allegorical Commentary, but they still play a highly significant role.

Now it might objected that I am exaggerating the role of verbal parallels in Philo's selection of secondary texts. After all Philo can be expected to compare the ark of Noah and the ark of the covenant, whether the κιβωτός occurs in both texts or not (cf. no.15). To this I would reply that Philo on more than one occasion points out that scripture uses parallel expressions to emphasize significant comparisons — e.g., in no. 30 ('this prayer [i.e., the one given to Noah] was granted to the man made in the image of God. . . . . But has it not been clearly shown *through these words* that he considers Noah. . . .') and no. 35 ('scripture likens Noah to that first moulded earthy man, for it *uses the same expression* of him . . . as of the other. . . . . '). In other words Philo is convinced that careful use of language is one of the primary means by which the coherence of scripture is effectuated, so that the exegete, by exploiting the parallels he discovers, is not just building his own interpretative construction, but is in fact uncovering layers of meaning actually present in scripture itself. In practical terms this means that the train of thought of many passages cannot be understood unless one has an eye for the verbal parallels Philo exploits. Why would Philo wish to compare Esau with the Patriarchs in *QG* 4.169 (no. 78), if it

[22] See above n. 5.

[23] Cf. 23 verbal and 22 thematic parallels in *Gig.–Deus* (based on the analyses referred to in n. 15).

were not for the fact that the verb ἐκλείπω was used for both. Note how in *QG* 4.132 (no. 70) Marcus, by using a translation of the *Hebrew* original of Num 30:3 ('comes forth from *thy lips*') and not of the LXX, needlessly obscures the fact that it is the word στόμα in the passage which makes it suitable as a proof-text for the rather audacious allegorical interpretation of the main biblical lemma which Philo presents.

G. *Parallels*

How does the evidence we have compiled relate to the rest of Philo's oeuvre? In looking at the parallels we could find for usage of secondary texts in other writings, it is important to recognize that not all parallels are of equal strength and relevance. I would suggest a three-fold division, which I will discuss one by one.

(1) *Strong parallels.* The most significant parallels to what we have found in the *Quaestiones* are those instances in which both the main and the secondary text occur together in another Philonic passage. These parallels I call 'strong' and have labelled with an asterisk. Only 10 such parallels were found (nos. 2, 3, 11, 37, 53-55, 64, 85, 89), of which all except the last two are located in the Allegorical Commentary. There is a strong parallel between *QG* 2.66 and and *Agr.* 20-5, for example, for in both passages a contrast is made between Cain and Noah on the basis of the differing words used to describe them in Gen 4:2 and 9:20 (ἐργαζόμενος τὴν γῆν, γεωργός). We note that in the *Agr.* passage more emphasis is placed on the pleasure-seeker, in the *QG* passage on the man of moderation — i.e., the main text exerts its influence on the direction that the exegesis takes.

(2) *Weaker parallels.* In a larger number of cases Philo uses secondary texts which belong to his standard exegetical repertoire, i.e., he uses them more than once elsewhere in his works in a way similar to what we find in the *Quaestiones* passage. Cf. nos. 4, 16-17, 21-3, 25, 28-9, 32-3, 45, 49, 51, 56, 71, 75-6, 81, 83-4 — 21 cases in all. An example is found in *QG* 2.29, where Philo broaches the theme of leprosy, namely the paradox that when the spot no longer spreads the sufferer is clean, a theme which he uses 3 times in the Allegorical Commentary (at great length in *Deus* 123-36). There are even more cases when it was possible to find at least one other parallel: nos.1, 6-7, 12-14, 36, 39, 41, 43-4, 46-8, 52, 59, 62, 65, 68, 72, 77, 79, 96-8, 90, 98 — 27 cases in all. A nice example is found in *QG* 4.10. The theme

of Abraham's host of servants is also used at *Det.*14, but for a quite different purpose, namely to show that the text should be read allegorically (whereas in *QG* we find a literal interpretation). In 7 instances we could find only vague parallels, which can hardly be called parallel in the true sense: nos. 5, 8, 19, 27, 74, 78, 82.

(3) *No parallels.* The largest group, however, consists of those passages for which no adequate parallels could be found at all: nos. 9-10, 15, 18, 20, 24, 26, 30-1, 34-5, 38, 40, 42, 50, 57-8, 60-1, 63, 66-7, 69-70, 77, 80, 91-7, 99-100 — 35 cases in all. For this high proportion of unparalleled material two partial explanations can be given. The *Quaestiones* give a verse-for-verse exegesis of large sections of Genesis and Exodus which are elsewhere not subjected to such close scrutiny. It is inevitable, therefore, that ideas will emerge here which are nowhere else to be found. A striking example occurs in nos. 92-6, in which exegesis of Exod 24:12-18 is given. For none of the passages involving secondary texts could adequate parallels be found, but this is less surprising when we realize that these verses are nowhere else commented on (as a glance at the *Index Biblique* shows). Secondly, Philo employs a lot more literal exegesis in the *Quaestiones*, and this also leads to much unparalleled material. Examples are questions on Noah's family (nos. 20, 40), the courtship procedures of the three patriarchs (nos. 60-1) and quite a few others.

But this is not the whole story. There are also highly interesting allegorical passages for which there are no parallels in the Allegorical Commentary, even in places where we might expect them, e.g., the allegory of Reuben and Judah (no. 67) and of the three wives of Abraham (nos. 72-6). Moreover there are at least 10 passages where ideas are put forward which are in contrast to what Philo presents elsewhere. In *QG* 1.32 Philo argues that the first men had acute senses because of their giant bodies (cf. also *QG* 1.92, 4.200); yet in *Gig.* 58 he denies in the strongest terms that the reference to giants should be taken literally at all.

The evidence on parallels for the secondary texts used in the *Quaestiones* thus leads to a two-pronged conclusion. On the one hand it is apparent that Philo is working with an integrated and largely coherent body of material. Otherwise the large number of parallels between the *Quaestiones* and other works could not be explained.[24] On the other hand

[24] I set aside here the thorny question of the extent to which Philo is indebted to a traditional body of exegetical material; cf. the essay of D. Hay elsewhere in this volume.

it is equally clear that the *Quaestiones* constitute an independent work with its own aims and methods, containing much interesting material which scholars have as yet barely started to quarry. But in this context there is a more specific question that must be asked.

H. *Relation to the Allegorical Commentary*

There are considerable sections of the Allegorical Commentary and the *Quaestiones* where the main biblical texts which are being interpreted run wholly parallel. The most important of these are:

Leg. 1.19 – 3.253*	*QG* 1.1-51
Cher.	*QG* 1.57-8
Sacr.	*QG* 1.59-60
*Det.***	*QG* 1.67-76
Post. 170-85	*QG* 1.78
Gig.-Deus	*QG* 1.89-99
Agr.-Sobr.	*QG* 2.66-7, 73-7
Her. 96-316	*QG* 3.1-16
Congr.	*QG* 3.18-25
Fug.	*QG* 3.26-36
Mut.	*QG* 3.39-43, 53-60

*and fr.p. 8 Harris from the lost 4th book

** note that *Det.* 132-53 is parallel to *QG* 4.99-106.

It is a remarkable lacuna in Philonic scholarship that no systematic analysis has ever been made of these parallel sections in the two exegetical series. What can we, anticipating this full-scale enquiry, derive from our results on Philo's use of secondary texts?

There is, needless to say, a vast difference in scale between the two series. Exegesis of a few verses (or even words) of the main biblical text can occupy a whole treatise of 50 pages text in the Allegorical Commentary, whereas in the *Quaestiones* Philo deals with them in the space of a few pages. But it is of paramount importance to realize the difference in scale is not usually caused by direct exposition of the main text, but by lengthy exegeses of secondary texts brought in relation to the main text. The obvious question is, therefore, whether the secondary texts sparsely spread throughout the *Quaestiones* are also used as such in the parallel sections of the Allegorical Commentary listed above. The results are very interesting and should be dealt with one by one:

nos. 2-3: Lev 23:9 and Deut 8:5 cited together at both *QG* 1.55 and fr. p.8 Harris in exegesis of Gen 3:22; but note that the subject matter is not the same, for the fragment deals with the *quaestio* posed in *QG* 1.54.
nos. 10-13: Of the four secondary texts only one, Exod 31:3, is used in *Gig.–Deus* ; in *QG* 1.99 *ad finem* there is a very oblique reference to the theme of the ὁδὸς βασιλική dealt with at great length in *Deus* 145ff., but I did not think this could be called usage of a secondary text.
nos. 35-7: Two of the secondary texts are not used in *Agr.–Plant.*, one is (Gen 4:2 at *Agr.* 20ff.).
no. 41: No allusions to Gen 12:1 at *Her.* 96-9 (but the secondary text is very subtle).
no. 43: No allusion to Lev 25 at *Mut.* 1-2 (where the secondary text is Num 18:26, also found in no. 46).
nos. 46-7: This is a highly interesting case, for at *Mut.* 190-1 both secondary texts (Gen 21:33 and Num. 18:26ff.) are used, but not in relation to 90, as in *QG* 3.56, but in relation to 100.

The conclusion is inescapable. Whatever the extent of the parallels between the *Quaestiones* and the Allegorical Commentary might be, the parallelism in selection and usage of secondary texts is minimal. There are, of course, many fewer secondary texts in *Quaestiones* than in the Allegorical Commentary, but it is surprising how few of the ones there are find use in the parallel sections. In fact there is only one unambiguous example, the reference to Bezalel in *QG* 1.91. This limited conclusion does not favour the hypothesis put forward by Sandmel that the *Quaestiones* are preparatory exegetical notebooks, in which Philo collected material that he would put to more effective use in later treatises.[25] It gives more support to the alternative view that the *Quaestiones* are an independent exegetical series, the purpose of which was not subordinated to the production of other works.[26]

Elsewhere in this volume A. Terian has presented a strong, and for the most part persuasive, arguments in favour of the chronological priority of the *Quaestiones* in relation to the Allegorical Commentary. One aspect of our investigation impinges on his study. Terian affirms

[25] Sandmel 1979, 82.
[26] Cf. Nikiprowetzky 1977, 202.

that in *Sacr.* 51 Philo with the words διὰ τῶν προτέρων βιβλίων cross-refers to *QG* 1.59 and 2.66 in order to answer the question of what is meant by τὸ γῆν ἐργάζεσθαι in Gen 4:2.[27] This is clearly not impossible. But the cross-reference does seem very far away. If the Allegorical Commentary and the *Quaestiones* are independent works, is it likely that Philo would choose to set aside this allegorically significant question and merely refer to a work written in quite a different period? If Terian had given closer attention to *QG* 2.66 he might have reached a more plausible, though equally speculative hypothesis. From our evidence it is apparent that in the answer to this *quaestio* Philo refers to no fewer than 3 secondary texts (or 4, if we include Gen 8:16). One of these is Gen 4:2, the main text in *Sacr.* 51. Another text is Gen 3:23, which says that God sent Adam out of paradise *to work the earth* (ἐργάζεσθαι τὴν γῆν). These are precisely the same terms used in Gen 4:2 of Cain (and compared with Noah in *QG* 2.66). Now Gen 3:23 in all probability occurred as a main biblical text in the lost fourth book of the *Legum Allegoriae* (where the parallel to *QG* 1.55 was also located), for this book dealt with Gen 3:19-23. I suggest, therefore, that the explanation of what is meant by 'tilling the soil' referred to in *Sacr.* 51 occurred in an exegesis of Gen 3:23 in the lost fourth book of the *Legum Allegoriae*.

I. *Non-Pentateuchal Secondary Texts*

No reader of Philo can help noticing that he concentrates almost exclusively on the text of the five books of Moses.[28] It was rather surprising to observe above, in sub-section (b), that eight of our 100 secondary texts are located outside the Pentateuch: two from the historical books (nos. 9, 71), two from the Psalms (73, 79), one from Proverbs (69), one from Hosea (97), and two from Isaiah (20, 24). A partial reason can be given for this surprisingly high representation. Analysis of Philo's use of Pentateuchal texts elsewhere in his works shows that they are almost invariably used as proof-texts, i.e., in order to add confirmatory material to the exegesis of another (Pentateuchal) text and not for their own sakes.[29] Now this is precisely the primary function of most of the secondary texts in the *Quaestiones*, so the non-Pentateuchal

[27] See the essay by Terian in this volume.
[28] A reason for this is suggested at Runia 1986*b* , 190; cf. also Amir 1983, 8, 91ff.
[29] Exceptions at *Cher.* 49-52, *Agr.* 50-4.

texts are perhaps for this reason more welcome than usual. It is at any rate noteworthy that all eight examples are used for purposes of proof or confirmatory comparisons, and that all but one are located at the end of the *quaestio*, the natural place for proof-texts to be found.

The one exception just mentioned is the citation of Ps 68:34 at *QG* 4.147, and there is another factor that makes this text somewhat puzzling Whenever Philo cites a non-Pentateuchal text, it typically contains a theme which Philo wishes to exploit, but for which there is no appropriate Pentateuchal text available. A good example is the 'lily text' cited at the end of *QE* 2.76 (no. 97). Nothing similar to this text can be found in the Pentateuch, and it allows Philo to round off his symbolic exegesis with an interesting (and confirmatory) observation. But why does Philo need a text from the Psalms to prove that the sense of hearing is (anthropomorphically) attributed to God? He could just have easily have used a text such as Exod 2:24, which is in fact cited at *QG* 4.233 (! — no. 82) and *Det*. 93. The only reason I can think of for this puzzling citation is that Philo has inherited the cluster of three proof-texts in *QG* 4.147 from traditional exegesis, and that he reproduces them here, even though one is contrary to his usual practice.

The task of a proof-text is to prove something, and in this regard there is one more puzzle. In *QG* 2.26 Philo ponders the question why scripture says that 'God remembered Noah and the beasts and the cattle', but fails to mention his wife and children. The answer given is that a harmonious household can be named after one person:[30]

> But when there is concord, one household is described after one eldest person, and all (the others) depend on him like the branches which grow out of a tree or like the fruits of a plant which do not fall off. And the prophet has said somewhere, "Look at Abraham your father and at Sarah who travailed with you (Isa 51:2)," which shows very clearly that there was (only) one root in respect of concord with the woman.

Surely at first sight the proof-text is close to nonsensical here, for it appears to mention *both* Abraham and Sarah, and *not* subsume the wife under her husband's name. The solution to this puzzle is fortunately

[30] Translation Marcus. The words 'travailed with you' in the quoted text are an evident mistranslation, as perceived by Mercier, who translated the last sentence as follows (1979, 237): 'Le prophète a dit aussi quelque part: «Contemplez Abraham, votre père, et Sara, qui vous a enfantés»; le fait que la souche était unique montre plus clairement la concorde avec la femme.' Aucher (text in Mercier) translates the last part: *quod nempe una erat stirps, ad mulierem versus concordiam patefacit.*

straightforward. All translators have cut off the quoted text too early. The full text of Isa 51:2 is:

> ἐμβλέψατε εἰς Αβρααμ τὸν πατέρα ὑμῶν καὶ εἰς Σαρραν τὴν ὠδίνουσαν ὑμᾶς· ὅτι εἷς ἦν, καὶ ἐκάλεσα αὐτὸν καὶ εὐλόγησα αὐτὸν καὶ ἠγάπησα αὐτὸν καὶ ἐπλήθυνα αὐτόν.

Although the last four verbs with their singular object help confirm Philo's point, he does not cite them. But he does cite the three earlier words, ὅτι εἷς ἦν, perhaps adding a noun (equivalent to *stirps* in the Armenian[31]) and a final comment (πρὸς γυναικὸς τὴν ὁμόνοιαν δηλῶν *vel sim.*). In this way the citation of Isa 51:2 as a proof-text does make sense.

J. *Comments on Individual Texts*

As was stated in the introductory section, it will not be possible to look at each individual passage, fascinating and rewarding though that would be. I will now make some comments on a few passages, enabling us to tie up some loose threads.

QG 2.17, 45, 56, 66 (nos. 19, 26, 30-1, 35). Philo is keen to compare Noah with Adam, for after the disaster of the flood, the earth commences as it were a 'second genesis'. But note the apparent inconsistency that in three texts Noah is compared to the moulded man, and in the other emphatically to the incorporeal man (*QG* 2.56). Moreover in *QG* 1.93 (no. 13) Philo locates the 'incorporeal man' in Gen 2:7, which is in flat contradiction to his exegesis elsewhere (cf. *Leg.* 1.31).[32] Philo makes no attempt to integrate these passages. His exegesis in the *Quaestiones* is highly atomistic, looking at the problem of the single text and not aiming at systematics.

QG 3.1 (no. 41). This is a curious example, which I hesitated to include and, as noted above, fits in with none of my 'categories of usage'.

---

31 The problem here is clearly the Armenian word rendered *stirps* by Aucher and "root" by Marcus. Does it represent a variant reading in the LXX text? But the Greek equivalent for this word is likely to be either ῥίζα (suggested by Marcus) or στέλεχος, neither of which can go with εἷς. It is of course possible that Philo paraphrases the last part of the text that he quotes. But it is essential to his meaning.

32 This text is not exploited by Tobin 1983 in his monograph analyzing Philo's exegesis of the texts dealing with the creation of man (the same applies to no. 95).

The verbal similarity between Gen 15:7 and 12:1 causes Philo to conflate the two texts. If one does not recognize the second text in the background, then the shift from 'giving' to 'revealing' is puzzling. This example is more like the explicatory use of secondary texts in the Allegorical Commentary than the illustrative or confirmatory usage prevalent in the *Quaestiones*.

QG 4.29 (nos. 55-6). Marcus points out that the main text and the two secondary texts occur together in *Somn.* 1.70-1. But the application of Exod 19:17 in that text is quite different to the theme of ascent and descent discussed here. Perhaps Exod 19:24 is uppermost in Philo's mind. But Moses does a lot of ascending and descending in Exodus, and it is possible that Philo's reference is rather general.

QG 4.195i (no. 79). This text only exists in a 4th century Latin translation. In *Plant.* 82 Philo uses Gen 26:32-33, the main text in *QG*, as a secondary text. Isaac calls the well 'oath' because it is τὸ πίστεως βεβαιοτάτης σύμβολον μαρτυρίαν θεοῦ περιεχούσης. It might be thought that here too Philo has Ps 18:8, the secondary text in *QG*, in mind. But the evidence of *Spec.* 2.10 militates against this suggestion, for there too Philo associates oath-taking with invoking God as witness, i.e., he sees a natural thematic connection which does not need to be set in motion by a text from the Psalms.

QG 4.226 (no. 81). The allusion to the exegetical theme of the royal highway is more overt than in *QG* 1.99 discussed above in subsection H. The question might be raised, however, as to what motivated Philo to introduce the theme precisely here, since there does not seem to be a direct thematic connection. It is possible that the mention of blessing in the main text reminded him of the blessing of Balaam, and hence of the royal road through Edom: cf. Num 24:9, *Mos.* 1.294.

V. Conclusion

In retrospect this article may have seemed a rather technical, even tedious, exercise, concentrating on the dry formal aspects of Philo's exegesis in the *Quaestiones* and neglecting the life that flows through its veins. Nevertheless our study has led to some valuable results, which can be summarized as follows.

1. The number of secondary texts to which Philo refers in the *Quaestiones* is *strictly limited.* This is in significant contrast to the Allegorical Commentary, where the detailed exegesis of secondary texts is essential to Philo's method.

2. The basic function of the secondary texts which Philo adduces is to *illustrate* or *confirm* his exegeses. For this reason the references are very brief, never exceeding a few lines. This is again quite different to his practice in the Allegorical Commentary, where exegesis of secondary texts very often has an explicatory rather than an illustrative task, and not seldom is as extensive as the treatment of the main text. For this reason I speak of secondary *texts* and not secondary *exegesis* in the title of this article.

3. In the majority of cases *thematic* considerations determine Philo's choice of secondary texts. Nevertheless in a third of our examples parallelisms in *wording* between the main and secondary texts could be discerned (verbal mode of transition).

4. The extensive number of *parallels* that could be found between our examples and other writings of Philo show that his corpus presents an integrated and largely coherent body of material. But one should not overlook the fact that 35 cases of secondary texts were found, for the usage of which no precise parallels are available. Moreover, when the *Quaestiones* and the Allegorical Commentary are directly compared, it emerged that there was practically no correlation in the choice of secondary texts when the two series expound the same main text. Clearly, in this regard at least, the *Quaestiones* do not have a preparatory character.

The *Quaestiones* form an independent and important segment of the *corpus Philonicum*, fully deserving to be studied for their own sake. If this article has shed some light on their method, and by so doing will stimulate scholars to investigate them further, it will have more than fulfilled its purpose.

APPENDIX

I append a list of our 100 instances of Philo's use of secondary texts, this time ordered according to the secondary texts themselves as they are located in the Bible. The numbers refer to the list in the text of the article.

SBL	*no.*	*text*	*Marcus*	*MBL*
Gen 1	4	*QG* 1.55	33.19	Gen 3:22
Gen 1	6	*QG* 1.64	39.7	Gen 4:7
Gen 1	19	*QG* 2.17	97.6	Gen 7:11
Gen 1	93	*QE* 2.56	91.4	Exod 24:16
Gen 1:1	22	*QG* 2.31	109.19	Gen 8:4
Gen 1:1	80	*QG* 4.215	512.12	Gen 27:28
Gen 1:9	36	*QG* 2.66	157.13	Gen 9:20
Gen 1:9-13	27	*QG* 2.47	128.5	Gen 8:14
Gen 1:27-28	30	*QG* 2.56	140.14	Gen 9:1-2
Gen 1:31	72	*QG* 4.147	429.16	Gen 25:1
Gen 2:5, 7	31	*QG* 2.56	142.2	Gen 9:1-2
Gen 2:6	38	*QG* 2.67	159.11	Gen 9:20
Gen 2:7	13	*QG* 1.93	62.6	Gen 6:6
Gen 2:7	32	*QG* 2.59	145.8	Gen 9:4
Gen 2:7	95	*QE* 2.46	92.7	Exod 24:16
Gen 2:9	5	*QG* 1.55	33.23	Gen 3:22
Gen 2:9	18	*QG* 2.12	87.16	Gen 7:2-3
Gen 3:23	35	*QG* 2.66	157.10	Gen 9:20
Gen 4:2	37	*QG* 2.66	158.5	Gen 9:20
Gen 4:13	49	*QG* 4.4	275.22	Gen 18:3
Gen 5:32, 6:10	40	*QG* 2.79	170.8	Gen 10:1
Gen 6:4	1	*QG* 1.32	19.25	Gen 3:1
Gen 6:9	26	*QG* 2.45	125.5	Gen 8:12
Gen 8:21	74	*QG* 4.147	429.19	Gen 25:1
Gen 12.1	41	*QG* 3.11	76.5	Gen 15:7
Gen 12:1ff.	61	*QG* 4.88	367.11	Gen 24:3
Gen 12:13	57	*QG* 4.60	340.4	Gen 20:2
Gen 14:14	52	*QG* 4.102	84.7	Gen 18:8
Gen 16:15	66	*QG* 4.122	406.3	Gen 24:36

Gen 16:15	75	*QG* 4.147	430.1	Gen 25:1
Gen 18:6ff.	68	*QG* 4.124	408.9	Gen 24:46
Gen 21:6	76	*QG* 4.147	430.3	Gen 25:1
Gen 21:33	47	*QG* 3.56	259.12	Gen 17:17
Gen 25:8. . .	78	*QG* 4.169	455.13	Gen 25:29
Gen 28:1	60	*QG* 4.88	367.1	Gen 24:3
Gen 28:11ff.	55	*QG* 4.29	304.14	Gen 18:33
Gen 32:29	100	*QE* 2.108	157.11	Exod 28:7
Gen 41	10	*QG* 1.89	56.6	Gen 6:1
Exod 2:1-2	94	*QE* 2.46	91.13	Exod 24:16
Exod 2:23-24	82	*QG* 4.233	532.13	Gen 27:38-39
Exod 3:7-10	88	*QE* 2.2	36.6	Exod 22:21
Exod 4:14	53	*QG* 4.16	290.8	Gen 18:12
Exod 5:2	59	*QG* 4.87	366.13	Gen 24:3
Exod 7:7	42	*QG* 3.38	225.17	Gen 16:16
Exod 12:2	25	*QG* 2.45	123.13	Gen 8:12
Exod 16:16ff.	62	*QG* 4.102	386.3	Gen 24:17
Exod 19:17-25?	56	*QG* 4.29	304.16	Gen 18:33
Exod 19:22	50	*QG* 4.4	275.25	Gen 18:3
Exod 20:21	91	*QE* 2.28	69.9	Exod 24:1
Exod 25:11	15	*QG* 2.4	72.4	Gen 6:14
Exod 26:33	58	*QG* 4.80	360.2	Gen 23:9
Exod 30:13-15	65	*QG* 4.110	395.13	Gen 24:22
Exod 30:19	86	*QE* 1.2	7.13	Exod 12:3
Exod 31:3	11	*QG* 1.90	57.2	Gen 6:3
Exod 33:13	51	*QG* 4.82	82.14	Gen 18:6-7
Lev 2:11	90	*QE* 2.14	51.14	Exod 23.18
Lev 5:7	23	*QG* 2.38	116.5	Gen 8:8
Lev 12:8	63	*QG* 4.102	386.11	Gen 24:17
Lev 13:15	17	*QG* 2.12	86.19	Gen 7:2-3
Lev 13:23	21	*QG* 2.29	108.7	Gen 8:2
Lev 17:11	33	*QG* 2.59	145.11	Gen 9:4
Lev 23:9	2	*QG* 1.55	32.27	Gen 3:22
Lev 23.9	28	*QG* 2.54	135.7	Gen 8:21
Lev 23:9-14	99	*QE* 2.102	150.3	Exod 27:3
Lev 23:10-11	84	*QE* 1.1	3.7	Exod 12:2
Lev 23:10-11	85	*QE* 1.1	3.19	Exod 12:2

Lev 25:4, 10	43	*QG* 3.39	228.3	Gen 17:1
Lev 25:4ff.	39	*QG* 2.78	170.3	Gen 9:28
Lev 25:8-17	16	*QG* 2.5	76.15	Gen 6.15-16
Lev 25:9	64	*QG* 4.110	394.9	Gen 24:22
Lev 25:10	54	*QG* 4.27	301.19	Gen 18:24-32
Num 8:24-25	77	*QG* 4.151	433.16	Gen 25:7
Num 14:9	14	*QG* 1.100	67.22	Gen 6:13
Num 14:32f.	96	*QE* 2.49	95.8	Exod 24:18
Num 17:20	81	*QG* 4.226	524.4	Gen 27:33
Num 18:21ff.	87	*QE* 1.10	18.9	Exod 12:6
Num 18:26ff.	46	*QG* 3.56	258.27	Gen 17:17
Num 30:3	70	*QG* 4.132	414.17	Gen 24:57
Num 35:10ff.	45	*QG* 3.52	252.14	Gen 17:14
Deut 1:17	89	*QE* 2.10	45.2	Exod 23:3
Deut 8:5	3	*QG* 1.55	33.1	Gen 3:22
Deut 8:5	29	*QG* 2.54	135.7	Gen 8:21
Deut 10:5	92	*QE* 2.41	84.12	Exod 24:12
Deut 10:16	44	*QG* 3.46	241.11	Gen 17:10-11
Deut 14:4-5	98	*QE* 2.101	148.14	Exod 27:2
Deut 16:16	48	*QG* 3.61	263.14	Gen 17:24-25
Deut 21:18ff.	83	*QG* 4.244	549.2	Gen 28:7
Deut 26:1-11	7	*QG* 1.64	39.27	Gen 4:7
Deut 32:49	34	*QG* 2.65	156.6	Gen 9:18-19
Deut 33:6-7	67	*QG* 4.123	407.12	Gen 24:36
Deut 34:5-6	8	*QG* 1.86	54.14	Gen 5:24
1 Sam 9:9	71	*QG* 4.138	419.16	Gen 24:62
2 Kgs 2:11-12	9	*QG* 1.86	54.16	Gen 5:24
Ps 18:8	79	*QG* 4.195i	71.17 Petit	Gen 26:32-3
Ps 68:34	73	*QG* 4.147	429.18	Gen 25:1
Prov 19:14	69	*QG* 4.129	412.7	Gen 24:51
Hos 14:5	97	*QE* 2.76	126.17	Exod 25:33
Isa 1:9	24	*QG* 2.43	122.6	Gen 8:11
Isa 51:2	20	*QG* 2.26	104.17	Gen 8:1

CHAPTER FIVE

REFERENCES TO OTHER EXEGETES

DAVID M. HAY

One of the pleasures of reading Philo is that one may pursue even a very limited line of inquiry and come upon fascinating phenomena. Such phenomena include those passages in the *Quaestiones* in which Philo refers to other exegetes. I wish to describe those references and then ask if they shed any light on the nature and purposes of the *Quaestiones* and on the relation of that work to Philo's other writings.

With regard to the word "exegete," I use the term here very broadly to mean "any person who is understood by Philo to maintain a particular interpretation of scripture." I by no means wish to suggest that all "exegetes" are scholars on Philo's level. As I use the term, an "exegete" might be an "ordinary man or woman in the street" — perhaps even a pagan in the street.[1] The only qualification for the title "exegete" as I shall employ the term is that the individual is known to maintain a particular line of interpretation of the Jewish scriptures.

In the table which follows, the information presented follows a code of abbreviations:

?/ = Philo's language ("someone *may* say that . . . ," etc.) suggests that the reference may be to a hypothetical rather than actual interpreter

/? = Philo's language leaves unclear the question whether the other exegetes mentioned in the passage are understood to maintain the specific exegetical opinion that follows their mention

des = some description of the other exegete(s) is presented by Philo

[1]Cf. Winston and Dillon 1983, 287.

indef = other exegetes are mentioned without being specifically described (e.g., "Some say. . . .")

mult = more than one group of exegetes is mentioned

L/C/A = literalist, critic (a literalist exegete who attacks the contents of scripture), allegorist

L/A = interpreters are both literalists and allegorists

lit = literalist interpretation credited to other exegete(s)

all = allegorical interpretation credited to other exegete(s)

cosmo/sac hist/eth/meta/psych(anat/war/pilg) = types of interpretations ascribed to other exegete(s): cosmological, sacred-historical, ethical, metaphysical, psychological (anatomy of the soul, war within the soul, pilgrimage of the soul toward God)

PAR-E = there is a passage in the rest of the Philonic corpus that comments on the same verse and refers to other exegetes

PAR-E? = there is room for doubt that the parallel passage contains a reference to other exegetes

I. Table of References

QG

1. 1.1—?/—indef—L—lit: cosmo—PAR-E
2. 1.5—?/indef—L—psych(anat)—PAR-E
3. 1.8—indef—L/A—lit—all: psych(anat)—PAR-E?
4. 1.10—des—mult—all: cosmo, psych (anat, pilg)—PAR-E
5. 1.18—des—C—lit
6. 1.32—indef—L—lit
7. 1.53—?/—indef—C—lit
8. 1.57—indef—A—all: cosmo—PAR-E?

9. 1.81—indef—L—lit: eth
10. 1.93—indef—L—lit: meta — PAR-E
11. 2.28—indef—L—lit
12. 2.58—indef—L—lit
13. 2.64—indef—L—lit
14. 2.79—des—L—lit
15. 3.3—des—C—lit—PAR-E?
16. 3.5—des—A: cosmo
17. 3.8—des—L—lit—A—all: eth *or* psych (pilg)—PAR-E
18. 3..11—des—A—all: cosmo—PAR-E
19. 3.13—indef—L—PAR-E
20. 3.43—des—C—lit—PAR-E
21. 3.48—des—A—all: psych (war)—PAR-E
22. 3.52—indef—L—lit
23. 3.53—des—C—lit—PAR-E
24. 4.2—des—mult—A—all: meta
25. 4.8—des—L—PAR-E?
26. 4.51—indef—L —lit/all: sac hist
27. 4.60—des—C—lit
28. 4.61—indef—C—lit
29. 4.64—indef—L—lit
30. 4.90—?/—L—lit
31. 4.91—?/—des—L—lit
32. 4.121—des—L—lit?
33. 4.123—/?—des—L—lit
34. 4.145—?/—des—mult—L/A—lit—all: psych (pilg)
35. 4.152—des—A—all: psych (war)
36. 4.167—des—A—all: psych (war)
37. 4.168—des—C—lit
38. 4.196—des—mult—L/A—lit—all: psych (pilg)

39. 4.200—indef—L—lit
40. 4.206—des—C—lit
41. 4.218—/?—des—A—all: psych (war)
42. 4.228—?/—indef—C—lit
43. 4.233—?/—indef—L—lit
44. 4.243—des—mult—L/A—all: psych (anat)

QE

45. 2.56—indef—A—all: cosmo
46. 2.71—des—A—all: psych (pilg)
47. 2.88—?/—indef—C—lit

II. Who They Were and What They Said

In nine of the forty-seven passages listed above, the references to other exegetes are hypothetical — i.e., Philo's language ("someone may say," etc.) permits the inference that these exegetes are unreal, invented for rhetorical purposes. But even if Philo does not know, or for some reason knows but does not wish to assert definitely, that some exegetes hold to a particular interpretation, his language suggests that exegetes exist who might maintain the interpretation so introduced. On the other hand, in thirty-eight cases Philo unambiguously affirms that there are interpreters who hold certain opinions.

For the most part, Philo refers to these exegetes as though they are contemporaries, introducing their ideas with "Some say" or other present-time expressions. In *QG* 3.48, however, he refers more than once to the justifications of circumcision propounded by "the ancients" and apparently means that they are the ones who symbolically explain the rite as excision of pleasure.[2] On the other hand, *QG* 4.167 speaks of allegorists who are "younger" and "recent."[3] In more astonishing

[2] It seems likely that Philo has the same "ancients" in mind when in *Spec.* 1.8 he speaks of "the old-time studies of divinely-gifted men who made deep research into the writings of Moses."

[3] Philo praises these exegetes; elsewhere, however, he applies "younger" to exegetes he regards as immature and unable to receive deeper interpretations (*Sacr.* 131; *Spec.* 3.134).

fashion, Philo speaks of the Greek philosopher Heraclitus as gaining or stealing from Moses his opinions on opposites and life in relation to death (*QG* 3.5; 4.152). Plainly Philo thinks of Heraclitus as one who read and interpreted the Pentateuch.[4] Thus Philo can in a sense think of persons of several centuries past as "fellow exegetes"!

Some sections in the *Quaestiones* mention both allegorists and literalists. Twenty-five of the passages contain references to literalists who are not critics. Eleven refer to critics, who are all also literalists. There are twenty-one references to allegorists (including references to five different groups of allegorists in *QG* 1.10 and to two in 4.2). Thus the proportion of references to literalists of all types to references to allegorists is 36:21, or about 7 to 4.

Philo regularly associates himself with allegorists, but he is willing on occasion to speak favorably of literalist opinions. He often reports a literalist interpretation without attacking it (e.g., *QG* 1.32, 81; 3.52; 4. 64, 121, 123, 145, 196). At other times he attacks literalist views (*QG* 1.1,93; 2.28, 64; 3.8; 4.91, 233; cf. 2.79). Philo can also attack the literal level of exegesis in general (*QG* 4.143), and a reproach he commonly makes against the critics is that they remain on that level (e.g., *QG* 3.43, 53). One scholar has recently maintained that Philo regards literal interpretations as deserving respect because they are the work of "divinely inspired men."[5] But Philo surely does not regard all literalists or literalistic interpretations as "inspired."[6]

The literalists had some interesting views about the greatness of biblical figures. Adam and Eve could understand snake language (*QG* 1.32). Both Abraham and Isaac were wealthy (*QG* 4.121, 123, 145). Isaac was physically huge (*QG* 4.200), pitied Esau (4.233) and suffered from only a temporary blindness (4.196). Related to this "historical" level of exegesis appear to be literalist perceptions of fixed time periods (*QG* 3.13) and a distinction between times of happiness and end-judgement indicated by the geographical locations of Paradise and Sodom (*QG* 4.51). Literalists were also interested in fine details of biblical genealogies (*QG* 1.81; 2.79).

A widespread interest in natural science (the physical world of the senses) seems reflected in the views of a number of exegetes, both

---

[4] Philo's references to Heraclitus are not uniformly hostile. See, e.g., *QG* 2.5; 4.1.

[5] Tobin 1983, 157.

[6] *Ibid.*, 158-62. The term θεσπέσιοι in *Spec* 1.8, 314 and *Migr*. 90 is nowhere applied by Philo to all literalists — or, for that matter, to all allegorists. Cf. Winston 1985, 559.

literalists and allegorists: the length of time creation required (*QG* 1.1); the earth as a source of life (*QG* 1.10), the seven planetary circles (*QG* 1.10), the sun as cause of the seasons (*QG* 1.10, 57), equinoxes and the four seasons (*QE* 2.71), divisions in the world (including the seasons — *QG* 3.5), the wind as cause of the flood's ceasing (*QG* 2.28 — an attempt to demythologize a miracle?), the rainbow (*QG* 2.64), the physical elements into which the body decomposes (*QG* 3.11). Perhaps connected with this concern for the material world is the view of some literalists that a biblical text seems to enjoin consumption of meat; Philo himself, without denouncing that interpretation, prefers to see in the text primary emphasis on the eating of herbs and an (allegorical) allusion to authority (*QG* 2.58).[7]

Not many of the literalist and allegorist passages emphasize ethical questions. One mentions a literalist who said Cain was omitted from the genealogy of Adam because of the foulness of his murder (*QG* 1.81). Philo associated himself with some allegorists who praised Abraham as a guardian of peace in his community (*QG* 3.8).

The nature of God is of concern in some of the passages. Some literalists think that God really changed His mind (*QG* 1.93).[8] Allegorists argue about how God can be one and yet appear as three (*QG* 4.2), and they appear to assert that the Logos plays on a prophet like a harp (*QG* 4.196).

Among the references to literalists who are not condemned as critics, some suggest perplexity over matters that might give rise to criticism of the scriptures: *QG* 3.52 (Why should infants suffer for their parents' failure to circumcise them?), *QG* 4.64 (How can ignorance and righteousness characterize the same action?), *QG* 4.90 (Why did Abraham's servant need an angelic companion?), and *QG* 4.91 (Did Abraham doubt?). A strong interest in defending circumcision is shown by some allegorists (*QG* 3.48).[9]

Of course Philo condemns the critics regularly as malicious and stupid, often affirming that they are incapable of allegorical insights into the scriptures (see, e.g., *QG* 3.3, 43; 4.168). They mock scripture for intimating that God gave animals as "helpers" to human beings in the

[7] Philo enthusiastically reports the sobriety of the Therapeutae in abstaining from wine and meat; he suggests that meat is dangerous because it arouses desire (*Contempl.* 73-74).

[8] Cf. Genesis Rabbah 27.4, where the reality of God's regret is assumed.

[9] In contrast to "extreme allegorizers" who evidently see no value in the physical rite: *Migr.* 92.

sense of creatures to be eaten (*QG* 1.18). They scoff at the idea that God made clothes from animal skins (*QG* 1.53).[10] They seemingly take special offense at scriptural passages that appear to speak of animal sacrifices (*QG* 3.3). They are amused when Moses suggests that great blessings are indicated in name changes like those of Abram to Abraham and Sarai to Sarah (*QG* 3.43, 53). They accuse Abraham of lying to Abimelech and betraying his own marriage (*QG* 4.60-61); and they call Jacob a crook (*QG* 4.206; cf. 4.228). They find ridiculous the Septuagint's rendering of a Hebrew cognate accusative (*QG* 4.168),[11] and they seem to think Moses was confused about the meaning of "one and many" (*QE* 2.88). Philo's anger toward such exegetes is obvious, and he implies that good exegesis is a product of sound faith and character as well as of technical competence and ability to see "beyond the literal."

Why does Philo bother reporting the views of the critics? We must assume he thought them important. Perhaps they were extremely important to some members of the Jewish community in Alexandria and Philo felt he had to denounce them.[12]

John Dillon has recently urged that some of the other exegetes mentioned by Philo, especially critics with Stoicizing tendencies, are imaginary "straw men," introduced to be knocked down. Likewise he thinks that the *aporiai* in Philonic commentaries, suggesting a tradition of hair-splitting criticism of Moses (which would include some of the questions introducing sections of the *Quaestiones*), are invented by Philo as a consequence of his actual dependence on a Middle Platonic literary tradition.[13] Dillon's conjectures may be correct, but they hinge on a questionable comparison with Platonist commentaries[14] and come down to a bare possibility that the only reports we have about these other exegetes — Philo's — are rhetorical fictions.

[10]Plutarch reports that some people regard all animal fur or skin as impure, and the Therapeutae wore linen apparently because they shared that view. See Winston 1981, 319, n. 24.

[11]Robertson 1934, 477-78, finds the cognate accusative common in both ancient Hebrew and Greek, but clearly the critics to whom Philo alludes consider this usage unacceptable. Cf. Smyth 1956, 355-57 and Conybeare and Stock 1980, §56.

[12]On the connection between the critics and apostasy, see Shroyer 1936, 277-282.

[13]Winston and Dillon 1983, 83-84. By contrast, Dillon thinks that the literalists Philo mentions are actual "orthodox rabbis" or pious Jews like the Therapeutae. He does not say why he thinks Philo would invent critics but not literalists to serve as targets for his criticism.

[14]See Runia 1986*a*, 503-505.

Some allegorists known to Philo were interested in developing non-literal interpretations of biblical references to sacrifices. *QG* 3.8 mentions without condemnation readers who take Abraham's sacrifice in Genesis 15 literally, but Philo adds that allegorists ("we disciples of Moses") interpret it symbolically of the man of virtue who restrains quarrels and promotes peace. In *QG* 2.71 Philo mentions allegorists who interpret a passage about libation bowls as meaning that virtuous souls dedicate their virtue to God — another instance of detecting moral symbolism in sacrificial language.

The allegorists were also notably interested in psychological allegory, stressing sometimes the various elements of human nature (*QG* 1.8, 10), sometimes the conflict between those elements (*QG* 3.48; 4.152, 167, 218), and sometimes the road of piety or the soul's pilgrimage toward God (*QG* 1.10, 3.8; 4.145; *QE* 2.71).[15] The literalists were also interested in the makeup of human nature.[16]

In general the classes of exegetes and the types of exegesis associated with them in the *Quaestiones* resemble those encountered in the rest of the Philonic corpus.[17]

III. Some Parallels between the *Quaestiones* and Other Philonic Writings

Of the forty-seven references to other exegetes in the *Quaestiones*, nine have significant parallels in other Philonic writings, which mention such exegetes in connection with the interpretation of the same biblical texts. In addition there are five other non-*Quaestiones* passages which possibly allude to other exegetes holding views similar to those mentioned in the *Quaestiones*.

On the other hand, there are interpretations offered in the *Quaestiones* that do not appear in the parallel passages of the Allegorical Commentary, and the reverse is also true. An example of the former is the report that some literalists explain Gen 24:67 in relation to Isaac's

[15]On these areas of psychology, see further Hay 1987, esp. 888-907.

[16]Tobin 1983, 158, contends that for Philo allegory basically means "allegory of the soul" — all other modes of exegesis are literal. He points out that in discussing the creation of man Philo reserves the term "allegory" for allegory of the soul (35, n. 23) This may be Philo's general tendency, and it may be entirely true for Philo's discussions of the creation of man, but we note his use of ἀλληγορέω in connection with a *cosmological* interpretation in *Cher*. 25.

[17]See Hay 1979-80 and 1980, and Mack 1984*b*, 242-43.

many houses (*QG* 4.145), an idea lacking in *Post.* 77-78. An illustration of the latter is the allegorical interpretation of Gen 15:16 presented in *Her.* 300-306 but conspicuously absent in *QG* 3.13. Sometimes, too, Philo mentions an exegetical view in both the *Quaestiones* and another treatise but connects it with other exegetes only in the former.

Most striking are those exegetical opinions which are linked with other exegetes in both the *Quaestiones* and other treatises. The other exegetes are just as likely to be real even if Philo mentions them only in the *Quaestiones*; and their influence on his thinking was presumably important even if he mentions them only once. And yet, if he in different passages mentions the same exegetes (or same type of exegetes, taking the same or similar lines of interpretation regarding the same texts), this suggests that he found them particularly important. Moreover, it offers another basis for assessing the relationship between the *Quaestiones* and the rest of Philo's writings.

In *QG* 1.1 Philo says that the suggestion of indefinite time in Gen 2:4 confutes persons who think the world came into being in a certain number of years. In *Leg.* 1.19-21 Philo says that Moses wrote this passage in order that

> you [the reader] may not suppose that the Deity makes anything in definite periods of time . . . There is an end, then, of the notion that the universe came into being in six days

Evidently Philo is thinking of other exegetes who take what in his judgment is a simplistic approach to cosmogony.

An interest in physical cosmology is shown by persons who interpret the sword of the cherubim (Gen 3:24) as the sun (*QG* 1.57). The same interpretation appears in *Cher* 25-26 alongside two others; there Philo says he prefers to think of the sword as a symbol of divine reason, but he first mentions two physical interpretations without, however, attributing them to other interpreters.

Physical allegory is reflected in the "opinion of many" (*QG* 3.11) that Abraham's going to his "fathers" (Gen 15:15) means the dissolution of the body into the elements. In *Her.* 275 Philo mentions people who take the "fathers" in this passage to mean the elements of earth, water, air, and fire although the soul "departs to find a father in ether." In the same passage he says there are exegetes who equate the "fathers" with astronomical bodies (the sun, moon, and stars). He mentions still other exegetes who think rather of "the archetypal ideas" in which the mind of the sage (Abraham) will find a new home after death. In *QG* 3.11 he says his own opinion is that the "fathers" are "incorporeal Logoi of the divine world."

Another Platonizing allegorization appears in *QG* 1.8. In answer to the question why the man formed of dust was placed in Paradise, but not the man made in God's image, Philo reports that some exegetes say that the former, as a sense-perceptible being, belonged in a physical garden, whereas the latter is "an intelligible and incorporeal species" (apparently a Platonic Form) and hence cannot be located spatially.[18] A parallel passage in the Allegorical Commentary (*Plant* 32-45) offers a somewhat similar interpretation, but connects mention of other exegetes ("men with their eyes opened") not directly with the two men created in Genesis 1-2 but with the trees in the Paradise Garden (§§36-37); and Philo also says here (without directly referring to other exegetes) that the man formed in the image of God "differs not a whit" from the symbolic and incorporeal "tree of life" (§44).

Fairly close to this is a series of non-literal interpretations of the "tree of life" presented in *QG* 1.10: while some interpreters regard it as a literal tree, others whom Philo knows interpret it as (a) the earth, (b) the seven planetary circles, (c) the sun, (d) government of the soul, (e) piety. The last is the view of "worthy and excellent men" — and Philo plainly prefers it. One parallel passage (*Leg.* 1.59) reports that some interpreters identify the tree as the human heart. Without mentioning other exegetes, *Opif.* 154 argues against a literal view of the tree and *Migr. 37* equates it with virtue.

Discussing the question of why God breathed into the face of the man formed of dust (*QG* 1.5), Philo mentions persons who say that "the head is the temple of the mind." Are these persons scriptural exegetes? At least a religious mindset is suggested by the term "temple." The parallel passages (*Leg.* 1.32-42; *Spec.* 4.123) suggest the same general interpretation of Gen 2:7 without mentioning other exegetes.

Apologetic interests are reflected in the series of justifications of circumcision in *QG* 3.48 and *Spec.* 1.3-9. In the former passage Philo is interpreting the basic commandment in the Torah (Gen 17:12) and refers to "ancients" who said it is a symbol of cutting off superfluous desires and implies "circumcision of the heart." They also commended

---

[18]The other exegetes mentioned in *QG* 1.8 seem to maintain a curious amalgam of literal interpretation regarding the "moulded man" and allegorical interpretation regarding the "man formed according to the divine image." On the connection of Philo's thinking about Gen 2:7 with wider hellenistic Jewish and "pre-Gnostic" traditions, see Pearson 1984, 322-330.

it as signifying the excision of arrogance. In the same passage he says "the ancients" also advocated it as a means of promoting fertility. (In this passage Philo does not make it clear if he thinks of "the ancients" as having explained the biblical text as well as the rite.) In *Spec.* 1.3-9 Philo, without directly referring to Gen 17:12, offers four justifications of circumcision as "handed down to us from the old-time studies of divinely-gifted men who made deep research into the writings of Moses." In this connection he mentions promotion of fertility (§7) and the similarity of the penis to the heart as the source of intellectual creativity (§6). In *Migr.* 92 he speaks of allegorists who regard the rite as a sign of cutting off pleasures and arrogance.

A similar interest in ritual of another kind is credited to exegetes who believe that Abraham sat over the sacrifice of birds and sought truth by studying their entrails (*QG* 3.8). In *Her.* 237-48 Philo says of the same biblical text (Gen 15:11) that the word "birds" clearly alludes to two types of thinking for "those who have eyes to see" — and from this we might deduce that he knows people who interpret the text as referring to literal birds.

Quite puzzling is a reference in *QG* 3.3 to "idle calumniators" who reject the scriptures and talk nonsense about them, claiming that Gen 15:9 speaks of nothing but a sacrificial victim. "And as for what happens to them, they say that this is an indication of chance and of opportunely-visible likenesses." Philo does not clearly indicate why these interpreters were critical of the biblical passage. Were they opposed in principle to animal sacrifice?[19] In *Her.* 102-112 and 123-27 Philo, without mentioning other exegetes, gives an allegorical interpretation of the same passage, and he seems to imply that a literal one is inappropriate.

Perhaps related to people who think the scriptures encourage augury are those who claim that Gen 15:16 ("the sins of the Amorites are not yet complete") affirms the power of fate. In *QG* 3.13 Philo reports without comment that "some say that by this expression Fate was introduced by Moses into his narrative." In *Her.*300-302 his words are more belligerent:

> Such words as these [Gen 15:16] give weaker minds a handle for supposing that Moses represents fate and necessity as the cause of all events. [But Moses]

[19]Note the suggestion in *Migr.* 92 that "extreme allegorists" might ignore the Temple. Philo's own view of Mosaic sacrifices was positive, but stressed the intentions of worshipers. See Wolfson 1947, 2.241-248; Nikiprowetzky 1967; and Hecht 1979-80.

> envisaged something else . . . Someone who is borne on the universe like a charioteer or pilot. . . .

Just as Philo repudiates ideas that Fate rather than God controls events, so he denounces the idea that God is changeable. He insists in *QG* 1.93 that Gen 6:6 does not mean, as some exegetes imagine, that God repented of having created humankind. He writes in a harsher vein in *Deus* 21-22 with regard to the same text:

> Perhaps some of those who are careless inquirers will suppose that . . . the Creator repented of the creation of men . . . . Those who think thus may be sure that they make the sins of the men of old time seem light and trivial through the vastness of their own godlessness. For what greater impiety could there be than to suppose that the Unchangeable changes?

Of the passages we are considering, those that speak most definitely of hostile critics are *QG* 3.43 and 53. These refer evidently to a single group of persons who ridicule the scriptural accounts of God's renaming Abram "Abraham" and Sarai "Sarah." Evidently these individuals say that a divine blessing consisting in the alteration of a few letters is worthless and contemptible. Philo says that they themselves are foolish and belong to the company of the "uncultivated, or rather of the uninitiated and of those who do not belong to the divine chorus." He calls their mockery impious and superficial because it ignores the allegorical sense of the name changes. Just as sharp are his words in *Mut.* 60-63, apparently about the same group of scoffers:

> quarrelsome and captious . . . people who wish to attach blame where it is not due . . . and wage war to the death against what is holy. . . . And this they do especially with the changes of names.

He goes on to describe an individual who scoffed in this manner and shortly thereafter committed suicide for trivial reasons, the "uncleanness" of his death being the penalty for his offense.

Lastly, we may mention two passages that speak of the need to conceal teachings and perhaps exegetical results from unworthy people. In both *QG* 4.8 and *Sacr.* 58-59 the ash-cakes of Gen 18:6-7 are interpreted to mean "secrecy" in the sense that knowledge of God and his Powers must be hidden from undeserving or "uninitiated" people. In what their unworthiness consists goes unstated in both Philonic passages; but perhaps both allude to literalists or critics of the Jewish scriptures (cf. *QE* 2.34). Be it noted, however, that Philo does not claim that other exegetes share his interpretation of the ash-cakes.

What might we conclude from these limited data about the relationships between the *Quaestiones* and the rest of the Philonic corpus? First, it seems clear that Philo mentions the same types of exegetes, ranging from allegorists to literalists and literalistic critics of scripture and Judaism, in the *Quaestiones* and in his other exegetical writings. Secondly, Philo's mention of the same views of other exegetes in the *Quaestiones* and in his other writings suggests that he viewed those opinions as particularly important, positively or negatively. Third, the significant differences in interpretations and references to other exegetes in the *Quaestiones* on the one hand and the Allegorical Commentary on the other suggest that the *Quaestiones* were not simply notes written in preparation for the composition of the latter.

On the other hand, the interpretations ascribed to other exegetes explicitly or implicitly in the *Quaestiones* and in some of the other treatises are often so similar that we must infer a relationship between theses works beyond their common authorship. Perhaps there was no great time gap between the composing of the *Quaestiones* and the other treatises. It may be that Philo had some kind of filing system that permitted him to readily consult or ponder the same interpretations of other exegetes on the same passages. Possibly, too, Philo was in frequent contact personally or through reading with the same exegetes whom he mentions in the *Quaestiones* and in the other treatises.

IV. Clues to the Origin and Purpose of the *Quaestiones*

Can the references to other exegetes shed light on the essential character of the *Quaestiones?*

One possible relationship between the other exegetes Philo mentions and the *Quaestiones* is that all the questions used at the beginning of the sections of the work are taken by Philo from those other interpreters. Thus the entire work could be seen as a set of answers to questions formulated by others, though Philo presumably found all the questions meaningful or at least sufficiently significant to deserve replies.[20] This hypothesis has the charm of simplicity, but there is no way to prove it.

Yet we can note that the views Philo attributes to other exegetes in the *Quaestiones* sometimes take the form of questions and that these questions sometimes restate the questions at the beginning of the sections in which they are found. Thus in *QG* 4.64, 90 and 91 the initial question

[20]Cf. Hay 1979-80, 64, n.8 and Tobin 1983, 172.

seems merely restated in the questions or comments ascribed to other exegetes. In such cases it seems likely that Philo intends to inform his readers[21] that he himself is not the originator of the question that guides the discussion of the particular section. Where Philo cites the views of critics, it seems most likely that the opening questions introducing the section derive from those critics or, at least, are a restatement of the point of contention. Finally, in most cases the opinions Philo attributes to other exegetes in the *Quaestiones* can most naturally be understood as answers to the initial questions of the sections; hence those questions themselves probably antedated Philo's discussion of them. This impression is strengthened when we observe that, among the forty-seven *Quaestiones* passages containing references to other exegetes, fully thirty-three begin by referring to the interpretations of other exegetes. So it is probable that the initial questions in those *Quaestiones* sections containing references to other exegetes were not first raised by Philo.

It is further noteworthy that in several cases references to other exegetes are presented without any comment by Philo. A striking case is *QG* 3.13, where he refers to exegetes who think Gen 15:16 speaks about the power of fate. Elsewhere (*Her* 300-306), as we have already seen, Philo sharply attacks that view; here he says nothing. Other examples may be found in *QG* 1.57; 4.51. Would Philo have left matters so unclear if he intended this work to be published or read to a general audience? These features make it easier to think that the *Quaestiones* are private notes or ones designed for limited circulation among fellow exegetical specialists, written either by Philo or by someone who heard him speak or teach.

The sheer frequency of the references to other exegetes in the *Quaestiones* is comparatively high. In the Loeb Classical Library edition there are 550 pages for the text of *QG* and 175 for that of *QE*. Together they include 47 passages containing references to other exegetes (there are 44 in *QG* alone). In the 1,260 pages of Greek text in volumes 1-5 (including all of the treatises in the Allegorical Commentary), there are 42 references to other exegetes. Is this greater frequency in the *Quaestiones* accidental? We may conjecture that Philo was stimulated or goaded into the writing of his books about the scriptures largely by the efforts past and present of other interpreters. When he came to compose his more careful discussion of ideas and texts, the Allegorical

---

[21]This suggests something about the readers Philo expects to have: they are interested in the exegetical problems he discusses but not so familiar as he with "the secondary literature" — i.e., they need to be informed about what other exegetes have said.

Commentary, he reduced the number of references to other exegetes because he believed it no longer necessary or useful to mention them so often. He mentions these other exegetes, as usual without naming them, to stake out positions of varying quality so as to clarify his own views, perhaps for himself as well as for others.

The anonymity of the references to other exegetes strongly suggests that Philo does not mention them to lend his own work greater authority. The fact that in the Allegorical Commentary he reduces the number of references to other exegetes (by comparison with the *Quaestiones*) is a clue that he felt no obligation to mention them and could easily dispense with doing so. All of this, in turn, suggests the strong possibility that even in the *Quaestiones* he has not referred to other exegetes as often as he might have — and that in turn raises the possibility that a number of questions and answers in sections of the *Quaestiones* which lack references to other exegetes actually were influenced by the opinions of other interpreters. We may particularly suspect this to be the case when, without referring to other exegetes, Philo presents a line of interpretation that fits well with interpretations he has ascribed to other exegetes elsewhere in the *Quaestiones*. For example, the interpretation of Enoch's translation as movement from a sensible form to "an incorporeal and intelligible form" (*QG* 1.86) strongly suggests influence from the Platonizing allegorists mentioned in *QG* 1.8. Stronger still is the similarity between *QG* 1.4 and 1.8, though only the latter passage explicitly speaks of other exegetes. It is obvious that there were others besides Philo who read Moses in the light of Platonic philosophy. How far they agreed or disagreed with Philo in nuances and general orientation cannot well be decided; nor can we speak of more than a possibility that Platonizing interpretations in the *Quaestiones* which lack overt reference to other exegetes may nonetheless have been influenced by them.[22]

Sandmel has argued on more general grounds that the *Quaestiones* "is mostly on the order of preliminary notes for treatises, some of which Philo wrote and others he planned but did not get around to."[23] On the

---

[22]Tobin 1983, 33, argues that *QG* 1.8 proves that the distinction between the intelligible, heavenly man and the earthly sense-perceptible man found in such passages as as *Opif.* 134-35 and *Leg.* 1.31-32 are the work of pre-Philonic interpreters. He further asserts that "all of the interpretations that lead up to and serve as a basis for that interpretation are pre-Philonic." This method of extrapolation is attractive, but it involves a weighing of probabilities and reliance on a criterion of consistency in ideas that may in some cases lead to exaggeration of the extent of pre-Philonic traditions. Cf. Hay 1979-80, 60.

[23]Sandmel 1979, 79.

narrow basis of my studies of the references to other exegetes in this work I am inclined to agree, but with two qualifications. First, we need not infer that the *Quaestiones* was completely written before Philo began work on the other treatises. The treatises in the Allegorical Commentary present interpretations that are sometimes different and often more "polished" than those in the *Quaestiones*. Probably, then, the composition of the *Quaestiones* preceded that of the corresponding sections in the Allegorical Commentary — though it is also possible that Philo went back and forth between the two, perhaps sometimes pulling together exegetical notes in the *Quaestiones* before settling down to composing a treatise in the Allegorical Commentary dealing with the same scriptural material.[24] A second qualification of Sandmel's position seems warranted as well. The *genre* of the *Quaestiones* is surely different from that of the other exegetical writings, but the genre is not obviously that of "preliminary notes for treatises." In the treatises which make up the Allegorical Commentary and the Exposition of the Law, Philo typically presents interpretations of biblical passages with a concern to define correct or acceptable interpretations, be they literal or allegorical. In the *Quaestiones* he seems less often concerned to distinguish good from bad interpretations and far more tolerant of literal interpretations and of literalists (although there are some sharply-phrased remarks about the superiority of allegorical exegesis — e.g., *QG* 2.79, 3.8, 4.145, 196) . Occasionally he is content to list a series of interpretations without indicating how far he agrees or disagrees with them. Quite often the *Quaestiones* mention interpretations never taken up or repudiated in the Allegorical Commentary.[25] We may conclude, therefore, that Philo in other exegetical writings often built on interpretations limned in the *Quaestiones*, but we need not infer that the latter were written simply as preliminary notes toward the composition of the former.

---

[24]A contrary view is argued on slender evidence by Marcus 1953, 11.x. He contends that the *Quaestiones* is subsequent to the Allegorical Commentary (although he admits that one work might be earlier than the other in some sections and later in others). Royse 1976-77, 49, argues persuasively that *De Opificio Mundi* made further commentary on Gen 1:1-2:4 unnecessary in both the *Quaestiones*, and the Allegorical Commentary. This is one indication that the latter two works were in some sense written in parallel.

[25]Sandmel's qualification of his own judgment that the *Quaestiones* contain notes for some treatises Philo "never got around to" fails to explain why extant treatises of the Allegorical Commentary dealing with the same passages covered in extant portions of the *Quaestiones* quite often do not take up all the seemingly interesting issues or ideas expressed in the in latter.

V. Conclusions

Philo does not think of himself as doing exegesis in a vacuum or even in an ivory tower, far removed from the serious ongoing religious decisions and challenges of Jews of his time. For him exegetical study and writing is a way of discovering religious truths to live by and unearthing errors that must be overcome. He conceives of exegesis as a kind of dialogical enterprise that involves many debate partners and opponents.

The very form of the *Quaestiones* suggests that Philo regarded himself as belonging to a community and succession of exegetes. The explicit references to questions and answers propounded by other interpreters make it clear that Philo takes their views seriously. Yet his failure to name any other exegete suggests that for him the questions and answers are to be evaluated with little regard for the identity of those who created them. The question-and-answer format is, however, no arbitrary literary convention. It reflects the activity of real exegetes who lived before or during Philo's lifetime. Hints of that format in the more complex works in the Allegorical Commentary[26] suggests that they, too, may have originated in the give-and-take of exegetical discussions with colleagues and students. Finally, the references to flesh-and-blood interpretive partners in the *Quaestiones* suggest that Philo wrote largely for the benefit of persons concerned not only about exegesis but also about living out their Jewish identity.

---

[26]See Nikiprowetzky 1983*a*, 53 and Borgen 1984*a*, 134-35.

CHAPTER 6

PHILO'S *QUAESTIONES:* PROLEGOMENA OR AFTERTHOUGHT?

GREGORY E. STERLING

The most neglected component of the Philonic corpus is the *Quaestiones et Solutiones in Genesim et in Exodum*. There are at least three factors which have contributed to this. First, the basic text is only extant in Armenian.[1] Fortunately, we also have about two hundred Greek fragments[2] and a partial fourth century Latin version;[3] nevertheless, on the whole we must rely on the literal and, apparently, faithful sixth century Armenian translation af the now lost Greek *Vorlage*.[4] Unfortunately, the version itself is beset with difficulties: it is clearly fragmentary;[5] its structural divisions and the references to the structure of the Greek text in the Greek fragments and Eusebius do not

[1]Aucher 1826. We continue to need a full critical edition of the Armenian which takes into consideration all the Greek fragments and the Latin translation.

[2]The most recent collection is Petit 1978, on which I depend in this paper. The last published identifications are those of Royse 1984. That there are textual variations between the Greek and Armenian is made clear by the first Greek fragment where the Armenian has *anorošewi* ("undetermined") and *anparoyr* ("uncircumscribed") for the ἀόριστον of the Greek.

[3]The Latin is *QG* 4.154-245. Fortunately we have a critical edition: Petit 1973.

[4]There is a general consensus regarding the wooden literalness of the Armenian translation. For references, see Hilgert's article in this volume; Marcus 1953, 1.vii-viii; and Bolognesi 1970, esp. a statement on p. 53: "Che pure la traduzione di quest' opera di Filone abbia gli stessi caratteri di fedeltà assoluta all'originale greco che si possono riscontrare nella versione dei trattati filoniani di cui possediamo il testo greco, e nelle altre versione armene della *yownaban dproc'*, risulta evidente dal confronto che si può stabilire tra il testo armeno e gli scarsi frammenti a noi giunti del testo greco." On the issue of the compatibility of the two languages see Rhodes 1972.

[5]This is unquestionably true with regard to *QE*. It may also be true of *QG*, but much less so. The evidence points to our possessing the six — whether there were more is unknown — books of *QG*. For details, see Royse 1976-77, esp. 49-63.

agree;[6] and finally, the extant of the original *Quaestiones* has been debated.[7] It is, therefore, not surprising that the bulk of the work on the *Quaestiones* until very recent years has been on textual matters. The second reason for neglect is that translations of the *Quaestiones* into modern languages did not appear until the second half of the twentieth century. The first was that of Ralph Marcus, who published his English translation in the Loeb Classical Library in 1953.[8] The third reason is that the abbreviated question-and-answer format of the *Quaestiones* has not compared favorably with the fully blossomed allegorical exegesis in the Allegorical Commentary.[9] Within the last decade the scope of Philonic scholarship has been broadened to include more work on the *Quaestiones*. This is due, in large part, to Valentin Nikiprowetzky, who has convincingly argued that the *quaestio et solutio* is a key Philonic exegetical technique,[10] and Abraham Terian, who has repeatedly stressed

[6]Cf. Eusebius, *HE* 2:18, which speaks of five books for *QE*, whereas the Armenian knows of only two. In *QG* the Armenian has four books, while it is certain that there were six in the Greek. The most significant current discussions of this problem are those of Royse 1976-77 and Lucchesi 1976.

[7]The evidence for believing that the work extended to Numbers or even Deuteronomy is a series of four references in one MS of the *Sacra Parallela* (Vaticanus gr. 1553) and *Spec.* 1.269. Goodenough took this so seriously that he wrote "If, as seems likely, the work went at least through Numbers, it was Philo's *magnum opus*, and can no more be neglected than the *magnum opus* of any other writer" (Goodenough 1962, 49). For a summary of the evidence together with more sober judgments, see Royse 1976-77, 42-43. He concludes, "In summary, then, there is no clear evidence that Philo wrote *Quaestiones* on Numbers, Leviticus, and Deuteronomy. In any case, such works, if they ever did exist, were not known to Eusebius, and not utilized (as far as is known) by the Armenian or Latin translators, by the exegetical chains on the Octateuch, which liberally cite from *QG* and *QE*, by Procopius, by the *Sacra Parallela* (with the possible but doubtful exception of the four texts in Vat. gr. 1553), or by other florilegia" (p. 43).

[8]Marcus 1953. To this we should now add Mercier 1979 and Mercier and Petit 1984, which offers Aucher's Latin translation and a French one based on the Armenian, but which takes into account the Greek fragments and the Latin translation. Cf. p. 21. So, for example, Mercier followed the Greek text in the first *quaestio* by rendering it "L'Expression 'quand ils furent créés' semble indiquer un temps indéterminé."

[9]A good parallel to this is the esteem in which the Gospel of Mark has been held. As long as Augustine's celebrated assessment held ("Maruc eum [i.e., Mattheum] subsecutus tanquam pedisequus et breviator eius videtur [*de Consensu Evangelistarum*, 1.2 (4)]), Mark was neglected. When, however, in the nineteenth century C. H. Weisse (1838) and H. J. Holtzmann (1863) established the priority of Mark, the places Matthew and Mark had in the world of biblical studies almost reversed.

[10]Especially in three studies: Nikiprowetzky 1973, 1977, and 1983*a*.

the chronological priority of the *Quaestiones*.[11] Yet even in contemporary work, we still do not have adequate analyses of the *Quaestiones* themselves. It is this gap which I would like to begin to close with this paper.

We will proceed by offering, first, an analytical description of *QG* I; second, a comparison of *QG* 1 with its counterparts in the Allegorical Commentary ; and, third, a statement of our conclusions. I chose *QG* 1 not only for its manageable-but-representative length, but also for the frequency with which it sets side by side literal and allegorical interpretations.

I. An Analytical Description of *QG* 1

A. *Quaestiones*

The format of the *Quaestiones* consists of two elements: questions probing specific points of the text followed by brief answers. Even a cursory reading of the work reveals that Philo is working with established exegetical formulae as he phrases his queries.[12] The most common question is *andēr*, διὰ τί,[13] "why." He uses it in 64 of the 100 questions.[14] The next most frequently used interrogative is *zinc' ē* or simply *zinc'*, τί ἐστιν,[15] "what is." The word appears in 31 of the 100 *quaestiones*.[16] In each instance the phrase is followed by a citation from Scripture which ranges from a word or a phrase to an entire verse. In four instances the quotation is succeeded by a reason for the question. In two of the four (*QG* 1.42, 55), anthropomorphic problems are the concern; in the other two (*QG* 1.51, 74), difficulties raised by the text prompt the queries.

The remaining interrogatives are much less frequent: in five questions Philo uses a form of the interrogative adjective: *ov* (4), *owm* (6), *o* (12), *oyc'* (54), and *oyk'* (88). Presumably the Greek underlying

[11]See his essay in this volume as well as Terian 1984.

[12]This was pointed out in Borgen and Skarsten 1976-77, 10.

[13]Based on the Greek fragment of *QG* 1.1.

[14]*QG* 1.1, 5, 6, 7, 8, 9, 10, 13, 14, 15, 17, 18, 19, 20, 21, 25, 26, 27, 28, 29, 30, 31, 33, 34, 35, 37, 41, 43, 44, 45, 46, 47, 48, 49, 50, 52, 53, 56, 57, 59, 60, 61, 66, 67, 68, 69, 71, 75, 76, 77, 78, 79, 80, 81, 83, 84, 85, 89, 91, 92, 94, 95, 96, 97.

[15]This is based on the Greek fragment to *QG* 1.51.

[16]*QG* 1.2, 3, 6, 10, 11, 16, 22, 23, 24, 25, 36, 38, 39, 40, 42, 51, 55, 62, 64, 65, 70, 72, 73, 74, 82, 86, 90, 93, 98, 99, 100.

these was a form of the interrogative pronoun τίς. In two questions he utilizes *iw* (4) and *ziard* (87) which likely render πῶς.[17] Once he employs *owsti*, πόθεν, "whence" (63) and once *t'e* , which could represent πότερον (32).

The fact that some of these formulae were used in other exegetical treatments in the Hellenistic world[18] leads us to ask how the questions arose. Was Philo simply employing known formulae to state his own questions, or is he answering questions at least some of which have already been raised by predecessors? Before responding to this, we need to understand the nature of our document. A careful reading of the text indicates that it is a verse-by-verse commentary. The following chart demonstrates this by listing the passage on which each question is based.

B. *The Genesis Text Discussed in Each* Quaestio

1. 2:4	26. 2:22	51. 3:19	76. 4:15
2. 2:5	27. 2:21	52. 3:20	77. 4:23
3. 2:6	28. 2:23	53. 3:21	78. 4:25
4. 2:7	29. 2:24	54. 3:22	79. 4:26
5. 2:7	30. 2:25	55. 3:22	80. 5:1
6. 2:8	31. 3:1	56. 3:23	81. 5:3
7. 2:8	32. 3:1	57. 3:24	82. 5:22
8. 2:8	33. 3:1	58. 4:1	83. 5:21-23
9. 2:9	34. 3:1	59. 4:2	84. 5:23
10. 2:9	35. 3:3	60. 4:3-4	85. 5:23-24
11. 2:9	36. 3:5	61. 4:4-5	86. 5:24
12. 2:10	37. 3:6	62. 4:4-5	87. 5:29
13. 2:14	38. 3:6	63. 4:5	88. 5:32
14. 2:15	39. 3:7	64. 4:7	89. 6:1
15. 2:16	40. 3:7	65. 4:7	90. 6:3
16. 2:17	41. 3:7	66. 4:7	91. 6:3
17. 2:18	42. 3:8	67. 4:8	92. 6:4
18. 2:19	43. 3:8	68. 4:9	93. 6:6
19. 2:19	44. 3:8	69. 4:9	94. 6:7
20. 2:19	45. 3:9	70. 4:10	95. 6:7

[17] *QG* 2.4, Greek fragment. I take this reference from Marcus 1933.
[18] Saul Lieberman has pointed out that "Why?" was ubiquitous in exegetical treatments of both the Hellenistic and rabbinic worlds (Lieberman 1950, 48).

21. 2:19	46. 3:12-13	71. 4:11	96. 6:8
22. 2:19	47. 3:14-17	72. 4:12	97. 6:9
23. 2:20	48. 3:14-15	73. 4:13	98. 6:11
24. 2:21	49. 3:16	74. 4:14	99. 6:12
25. 2:21-22	50. 3:17	75. 4:15	100. 6:13

There are only four gaps of any note: three of these deal with genealogies which are understandably omitted (Gen. 4:16-22;[19] 5:4-20; and 5:25-28, 30-31); the fourth is a surprising omission. Why did Philo fail to comment on Gen. 3:10: τὴν φωνήν σου ἤκουσα περιπατοῦντος ἐν τῷ παραδείσῳ? Perhaps this was not considered as glaring an anthropomorphism as it appears to be. In any event, it is clear the the *Quaestiones* are designed to be a running commentary.

But who raised the issues dealt with in this commentary? Another way of posing this question is to ask first what are the exegetical concerns expressed by the questions and answers? Of the 100 questions dealt with in *QG* 1, 41 deal with philosophical issues,[20] while 59 wrestle with issues posed by the text itself. We may subdivide the latter into questions asking for clarification[21] and those dealing with difficulties. I would categorize the problems as follows:

ἄλογος:	3, 32, 53, 66, 76
Anthropomorphisms:	21, 42, 45, 55, 68, 69, 93, 95
Unexplained Assumption:	63
Contradictions in the text:	14, 74
Order of the text:	18, 59, 61

It is probable that Philo noticed some of these in his own careful reading. However, it is certain that several of these categories preceded Philo. We know that Demetrius addressed exegetical issues in the *quaestio et solutio* format as early as the third century B.C.E.[22] and that

[19]It is, nevertheless, somewhat puzzling why we have nothing about some of the statements in this text — e.g., the affirmation of Ιουβαλ in v. 21: οὗτος ἦν ὁ καταδείξας ψαλτήριον καὶ κιθάραν. Philo does deal with this unit of text in *De Posteritate*.

[20]*QG* 1.1, 2, 4, 6, 8, 10, 11, 12, 13, 19, 24, 25, 31, 37, 38, 39, 40, 41, 46, 48, 49, 50, 54, 56, 57, 60, 64, 75, 77, 78, 79, 80, 82, 83, 84, 85, 86, 87, 88, 91, 100.

[21]*QG* 1.5, 7, 9, 15, 16, 17, 20, 22, 23, 26, 27, 28, 29, 30, 33, 34, 35, 36, 43, 44, 47, 51, 52, 58, 62, 65, 67, 70, 71, 72, 73, 81, 89, 90, 92, 94, 96, 97, 98, 99.

[22]Cf. Holladay 1983. See F 2 and 5.

Aristobulus wrestled with anthropomorphic issues in the second century B.C.E. In as recently published dissertation, Thomas Tobin has convincingly argued that Philo took over treatments of anti-anthropomorphic interpretations.[23] This would suggest that in at least this area Philo was simply raising known issues.

A second and more direct approach to this line of investigation is to note the explicit statements referring to others at the outset of the answers. So, for example, in *QG* 1.53 Philo says: "Some may ridicule the text. . . ." There can be no doubt that it is this ridicule of other individuals which has prompted some questions.[24]

It thus appears that Philo intended to write a verse-by-verse commentary by presenting questions to the text couched in standard formulae. The main thrust of these *quaestiones* was to allow Philo the opportunity to explicate the text not only literally but also philosophically. Embedded within this process was an apologetic concern in which Philo took over questions already in the exegetical tradition in order to give his work a sense of completeness.

C. *Solutiones*

The second member of each exegetical unit is the *solutio*. The most arresting dimension of these answers is the role which literal and allegorical exegesis play. There are three types of answers. The first and most prevalent is the strictly literal: fifty-one out of 100 answers move only on this level.[25] The second category consists of the twenty-four *solutiones* which offer only allegorical responses.[26] Within this group as a sub-category are four of Philo's Neo-Pythagorean

[23]Tobin 1983, esp. pp. 36-55. Tobin does not think Philo is directly dependent on Aristobulus but on anti-anthropomorphic interpretations which developed in the first half of the first century B.C.E. (p. 54).

[24]David Hay correctly points this out in his essay in this volume. I have classified this under the rubric ἄλογος. This was a standard ground for objection in both Greek and rabbinic sources. Cf. Lieberman 1950, 64-67.

[25]When I use the term "literal" here, I do not exclude texts which may deal with a philosophical concern. What I mean are those texts which are attempting to grapple with statements in Philo's bible which do not resort to allegorical exegesis. In *QG* 1 they are: §§1, 3, 5, 14, 15, 16, 17, 18, 20, 22, 23, 24, 26, 27, 28, 29, 30, 32, 33, 34, 35, 36, 42, 43, 55, 58 (?), 59, 60, 61, 62, 63, 64, 65, 66, 67, 68, 69, 70, 71, 72, 73, 74, 76 (?), 81, 89, 92, 93, 96, 97 (?), 98, 99.

[26]*QG* 1.2, 4, 8, 19, 38, 40 (?), 50, 51, 54, 56, 57, 75, 77 (?), 78, 79, 80, 83, 84, 85, 86, 88, 90, 91, 100.

arithmological texts.[27] The third and final group of twenty-five present both the meaning *ad litteram* as well as *ad mentum*. Here Philo nearly exhausts his vocabulary to mark the step from ἡ ῥητὴ ἀπόδοσις to ἀλληγορία: "symbolically, symbolical, symbol" (*QG* 1.6, 7, 13, 31, 39, 41, 44, 49, 82, 87, 95);[28] "allegorically, allegorize, allegorical, allegory" (*QG* 1.10, 11, 12, 37, 45, 47, 94); "deeper meaning" (*QG* 1.46, 48, 53); "metaphorically"(*QG* 1.52) "philosophically" (*QG* 1.9); "typifies" (*QG* 1.21); "figurative" (*QG* 1.25). Such bridge-formulae were common in at least Neoplatonic commentaries (especially Proclus).[29]

Of more importance is the relationship which is presented between the two-levels of meaning. In nineteen cases, there does not appear to be any tension between them: *QG* 1.6, 7, 9, 21, 25, 37, 41, 44, 45, 46, 47, 48, 49, 52, 53, 82, 87, 94, 95). Twice Philo expresses preference for the allegorical over the literal (*QG* 1.13, 31). In only four instances does he appear to reject the literal, and even then he does so in a way that not close the door on it completely (*QG* 1.10, 11, 12, 39).

This analysis suggests that Philo is attempting to present possible exegetical options for the text by citing variegated views. He is obviously pleased with the polyvalent nature of the biblical text and refrains from casting a decisive vote for either one or the other levels of meaning. What is surprising — from the perspective of the remainder of the Philonic corpus — is the amount of attention given to ἡ ῥητὴ ἐξήγησις: it is present in 75 percent of the *solutiones* in comparison with ἡ ἀλληγορία, which figures in 49 percent.

II. The *Quaestiones* and the *Allegorical Commentary*

A. *The Relationship*

The relationship of the *Quaestiones* to the Allegorical Commentary is of crucial concern for a proper comprehension of the Philonic corpus.

[27]*QG* 1.75, 77, 83, 91. The key to understanding Philo's arithmology is *Leg* . 1.4: βούλεται οὖν τά τε θνητὰ γένη καὶ πάλιν αὖ τὰ ἄφθαρτα κατὰ τοὺς οἰκείους ἐπιδεῖξαι συστάντα ἀριθμούς . . . . A very helpful discussion of this area is provided by Moehring 1978. One point of importance is that Philo's arithmology was fully developed by the time he wrote the *Quaestiones*. The most elaborate treatment of the hebdomad in the Philonic corpus is in *QE* 2.68 (see Moehring, 212-13). The Greek citation and all other quotations from the Allegorical Commentary are from PCW.

[28]The English is from Marcus 1953.

[29]Cf. Dillon 1983.

It is to the great merit of Nikiprowetzky that he demonstrated the centrality of the *quaestio* and *solutio* for an understanding of the Allegorical Commentary in a convincing manner.[30] Although a firm judgment is not possible, it appears to this writer that one major source of influence on Philo's procedure is betrayed in his description of the Therapeutae. In *Contempl.* 75-78, he describes at length the process of instruction at a banquet. ὁ πρόεδρος αὐτῶν . . . ζητεῖ τι τῶν ἐν τοῖς ἱεροῖς γράμμασιν ἢ καὶ ὑπ' ἄλλου προταθὲν ἐπιλύεται (*Contempl.* 75). Philo then describes the actual process of exposition: αἱ δὲ ἐξηγήσεις τῶν ἱερῶν γραμμάτων γίνονται δι' ὑπονοιῶν ἐν ἀλληγορίαις (§78). He explains: ἅπασα γὰρ ἡ νομοθεσία δοκεῖ τοῖς ἀνδράσι τούτοις ἐοικέναι ζῴῳ καὶ σῶμα μὲν ἔχειν τὰς ῥητὰς διατάξεις, ψυχὴν δὲ τὸν ἐναποκείμενον ταῖς λέξεσιν ἀόρατον νοῦν. It would be difficult to write a more fitting summary of the Philonic corpus. Although it is undoubtedly true that Philo has surreptitiously slipped some of his own ideals of exegesis into this description, nonetheless it remains probable that the Therapeutae did in fact practice exegesis along the line Philo indicated.[31] Whether the Therapeutae exercised any influence on the form of his exegesis, the *quaestio* and *solutio* stand as a — if not the — major hermeneutical device of Philo.

A second link which joins the *Quaestiones* to the Allegorical Commentary and Exposition of the Laws[32] is the presence of two-tiered exegesis in all of them. The following chart indicates passages in the Philonic corpus which begin with a literal exposition and then move into an allegorical one:

---

[30]He wrote: "En effet, l'obscurité de l'analyse et l'atomisation du texte sont le résultat du fait que l'on a négligé le fil conducteur, la trame véritable, la forme essentielle et, si l'on nous passe l'expression, la cellule mère des développements exégétiques philoniens, à savoir la *quaestio* suivie de sa *solutio*" (Nikiprowetzky 1983*a*, 8). The effect of his work can be seen in David Runia's remark that Nikiprowetzky's point is generally accepted by Philo scholars (Runia 1987, 11). See also Borgen and Skarsten 1976-77, 9.

[31]This is supported by the fact that the other group who captured Philo's attention were the Essenes, whose *pesher* method was portrayed in allegorical terms by Philo. See *Prob.* 80-82, where he wrote τὰ γὰρ πλεῖστα διὰ συμβόλων ἀρχαιοτρόπῳ ζηλώσει παρ' αὐτοῖς φιλοσοφεῖται.

[32]For a recent survey of the treatises in each of these categories, see Borgen 1984*b*.

Treatise	Subject	Literal	Allegorical
Conf.	Babel	1-13	14-198
Mut.	Name Changes	60-62	62-80
Somn. 1	Pledges	92-101	102-114
Somn. 1	Toughness of Jacob	120-126	127-132
Somn. 2	Joseph's Dream	110-115	115-134
Abr.	Migrations	60-67	68-88
Abr.	Abraham and Sarah in Egypt	89-98	99-106
Abr.	Hospitality of Abraham	107-118	119-132
Abr.	Sodom and Gomorrah	133-146	147-166
Abr.	Offering of Isaac	167-199	200-204
Abr.	Separation of Abraham and Lot	208-216	217-224
Abr.	Genesis 14	225-235	236-244
Jos.	Selling of Joseph	1-27	28-36
Jos.	Joseph and Potiphar's Wife	37-57	58-79
Jos.	Interpreting Dreams	80-124	125-156
Mos. 2	High Priest's Apparel	109-116	117-135
Spec. 1	Circumcision	1-7	8-11
Spec. 1	No Other Gods	21-22	23-31
Spec. 1	Priests' Bodies	80	80-81
Spec. 1	Altar	285-286	287-288
Spec. 2	Oaths	24-28	29-31
Spec. 2	Passover	145-46, 148-49	147
Spec. 2	Leaven	182-183	184-185
Spec. 3	Woman Seizing Man's Genitals	175-177	178-180
Spec. 4	Clean and Unclean	106	107-109
Spec. 4	Clean and Unclean	110-111	112
Spec. 4	Clean and Unclean	113	113-115
Spec. 4	Boundary Stones	149	149-150

There are several observations which emerge from this chart. First, it is clear that the bifid exegesis of the *Quaestiones* is a common pattern in Philo. Second, this pattern is much more prevalent in the Exposition of the laws than in the *Allegoriae*. This is what we would expect since Philo was clear in his insistence that the laws be kept literally, even though he preferred to accent the inner or hidden concept.[33] Third, it seems to me that this is the technique which explains the basic structure of both *De Abrahamo* and *De Iosepho*.[34]

B. *The Chronological Order*

Once we recognize that both the basic format and the exegetical pattern of the *Quaestiones* are endemic to the remaining exegetical treatises of Philo, we are compelled to ask which has priority.[35] When Marcus issued his translation in 1953, he argued that there were three texts in the *Quaestiones* which referred back to the Allegorical Commentary (*QG* 2.4; *QE* 2.34, 113).[36] This judgment followed the assessment of L. Cohn, who likewise thought they were later than the *Allegoriae*.[37] Their verdict has not, however, gone unchallenged. Samuel Sandmel,[38] Nikiprowetzky,[39] and, most notably, Terian[40] have all maintained the priority of the *Quaestiones*.[41] To date the arguments have centered either on statements in the text referring to other works[42] or on the general impression that the *Quaestiones* are a first draft of what emerges in a more polished form in *Allegoriae*.[43] It seems to me that the line of investigation would be more fruitful if we moved to a comparison between the *Quaestiones* and Allegorical Commentary. There are three

[33]The *locus classicus* is *Migr*. 89-93.

[34]Each of these treatises appears to consist of independent exegetical units utilizing this pattern which have been linked together in the process of providing an exposition of the whole narrative.

[35]For very helpful summaries of the published opinions, see Nikiprowetzky 1977, 231-34, n. 216 and Nikiprowetzky 1983*a*, 67-9, n. 1.

[36]See Marcus 1983, 1:x, n. a.

[37]Cohn 1899, 391.

[38]Sandmel 1954, 249 and 1979, 79.

[39]He has, like Sandmel, made this point repeatedly. See Nikiprowetzky 1973, 323; 1977, 235, n. 216; 1983*a*, 8, 53.

[40]See his essay in this volume.

[41]At the Philo consultation at the national SBL meeting on 24 November 1985, there was a general consensus among the participants that the *Quaestiones* were prior.

[42]See Terian's essay in this volume and Nikiprowetzky 1977, 331-32.

[43]So Nikiprowetzky. Cf. also Winston 1981, 6-7: "These treatises are generally less sophisticated than Philo's other exegetical works and give the appearance of being rough compilations of raw material (neither Genesis nor Exodus is completely covered) to be utilized in future writings."

specific areas in which I believe productive research can and should be done.

(1) *The Order.* It is generally recognized that the main biblical texts cited by Philo in the *Allegoriae* furnish the structural basis and continuity of the exegetical treatment.[44] Philo selects various phrases or verses from the text, *lemmata*, upon which the commentary is based. Each individual unit is a κεφάλαιον. The question we would like to raise is: Can we discover any correspondence between the order of the κεφάλαια in the *Allegoriae* and the *Quaestiones*? In order to answer this, I am providing the following chart which allows us to glance at the κεφάλαια in the Allegorical Commentary and the appropriate *quaestio* in *QG* 1. In addition, I have indicated the fundamental correspondence of the contents by inserting references in italics. Only initial citations are entered in the center column.[45]

Treatise	Genesis Text	*QG* 1
Leg. 1.1	2:1	
Leg. 1.2-16	2:2	
Leg. 1.17-18	2:3	
Leg. 1.19-20	2:4	1
Leg. 1.21-27	2:4-5	2
Leg. 1.28-30	2:6	3
Leg. 1.31-42	2:7	4-5
31-32		*4*
33-42		*5*
Leg. 1.43-55	2:8	6-8
43-45		*6*
46		*7*
53-55		*8*

[44]Cf. Runia 1987, 10-11.

[45]I realize that the extent of κεφάλαια is open to debate. I have simply attempted to divide the text on the basis of biblical citations; considering the introduction of a text from the main narrative which had not previously been cited as the introduction of a new "chapter." Further, I do not mean to imply that the contents of the *Allegoriae* fully parallel those of the *Quaestiones*. It is very obvious that the *Allegoriae* are much fuller. The basis for Philo's expansion of exposition is currently under debate. One of the major participants in this dialogue is Burton Mack, who argues that Philo used the *chreia* technique in *Sacr.* 1-10 (Mack 1984*a*). His work is very provocative, but still *sub judice*.

Leg. 1.56-62	2:9	9-11
56-58		*9*
59-60		*10*
61-62		*11*
Leg. 1.63-87	2:10-14	12-13
63-84		*12*
85-87		*13*
Leg. 1. 88-89	2:15	14
Leg. 1.90-108	2:16-17	15-16
(90)101-104		*15*
105-108		*16*
Leg. 2.1-8	2:18	17
Leg. 2.9-18	2:19	18-23
9-11		*18*
12-13		*19*
14-15		*20*
		21
16-18		*22*
		23
Leg. 2.19-39	2:21	24-27
19-20		*27*
21-24		*25*
25-30		*24*
31-39		
		26
Leg. 2.40-48	2:22-23	28
Leg. 2.49-52	2:24	29
Leg. 2.53-108	2:25, 3:1	30-31
53-70		*30*
71-108		*31*
		32-43
Leg. 3.1-48	3:8	44
Leg. 3.49-55	3:9	45
Leg. 3.56-58	3:12	46
Leg. 3.59-64	3:13	46
Leg. 3.65-106	3:14	47
Leg. 3.107-113	3:14	48
Leg. 3.114-160	3:14	48
Leg. 3.161-181	3:14	48
Leg. 3.182-187	3:15	48

Leg. 3.188-199	3:15	
Leg. 3.200-219	3:16	49
Leg. 3.220-245	3:16	49
Leg. 3.246-247	3:17	50
Leg. 3.248-250	3:18	50
Leg. 3.251	3:18	50
Leg. 3.252-253	3:19	51-56
Cher. 1.30	3:24	57
Cher. 40-130	4:1-2	58
40-124		
124-130		*58*
Sacr.1-10	4:2	
Sacr.11-51	4:2	59, 61
Sacr. 52-139	4:3	60-66
Det.1-56	4:8	67
Det. 57-68	4:9	68-69
57-60		*68*
61-68		*69*
Det. 69-95	4:10	70
Det. 96-99	4:11	71
Det. 100-103	4:11	
Det. 104-118	4:12	
Det. 119-140	4:12	72
Det. 141-149	4:13	73
Det. 150-162	4:14	73
Det. 163-166	4:14, 16	74
Det. 167-176	4:15	75
Det. 177-178	4:15	76
Post. 1-32	4:16	
Post. 33-65	4:17	
Post. 66-74	4:18	
Post. 75-82	4:19	
Post. 83-99	4:20	
Post. 100-113	4:21	
Post. 114-123	4:22	
		77
Post. 124-185	4:25	78
(*Praem. 10-14*)		79
		80-81
(*Praem. 15-21*)		82

		83-86
(*Praem. 22-23*)		87
		88
Gig. 1-5	6:1	89
Gig. 6-18	6:2	
Gig. 19-55	6:3	90
Gig. 55-57	6:3	91
Gig. 58-67	6:4	92
Deus. 1-19	6:4	
Deus. 20-85	6:5-7	93-95
20-50		*93*
		94
51-85		*95*
Deus. 86-116	6:8	96
Deus. 117-121	6:9	97
Deus. 122-139	6:11	98
Deus. 140-183	6:12	99
		100

The selection of the same texts is not, in and of itself, all that remarkable. Since both the *Quaestiones* and the *Allegoriae* are essentially verse-by-verse commentaries, one expects to find a common pattern.[46] What is noteworthy is that the two follow a common order. Even when the Allegorical Commentary deals with issues covered by several *quaestiones*, it does so in the same order. (There are, of course, exceptions.) We can now be reasonably certain that the *Quaestiones* are either a distillation of the *Allegoriae* or a prolegomena to it. Their brevity and simplicity point to the latter.

(2) *Solutiones* in the *Allegoriae*. What moves our *a priori* hunches to firm conclusions is the presence of *solutiones* in the *Allegoriae* for the *quaestiones* of the *Quaestiones*! In some instances the *quaestio* is itself raised. In most, however, the *quaestio* is simply presupposed. The following examples will illustrate this phenomenon.[47]

[46]It is striking that both treatments ignore Gen 3:10. That text is cited only incidentally at *Leg*. 3.54.

[47]The translations are taken from the PLCL.

Quaestio: *QG* 1.1

Why, when he (Moses) considers and reflects on the creation of the world, does he say, "This is the book of the coming into being of heaven and earth when they came into being?"

Solutio: *Leg.* 1.19-20

"Book" is Moses' name for the Reason of God, in which have been inscribed and engraved the formation af all else. But that you may not suppose that the Deity makes anything in definite periods of time, but may know that to mortal kind the process of creation is unobserved, undescried, incomprehensible, he adds, "When it came into being," not defining "when" by a determining limit, for the things that come into being under the hand of the First Cause come into being with no determining limit. There is an end, then, of the notion that the universe came into being in six days.

Quaestio : *QG* 1.2

What is the meaning of the words, "And God made the green thing of the field before it came into being on the earth, and every green grass before it grew"?

Solutio: *Leg.* 1.22-24

What he means is something of this sort. As before the particular and individual mind there subsists a certain original as an archetype and pattern of it, and again before the particular sense-perception, a certain original of sense-perception related to the particular as a seal making impression is to the form which it makes; just so, before the individual objects of intellectual perception came into being, there was existing as a genus the 'intellectually-perceptible' itself, by participation in which the name has been given to the members of the genus; and before the individual objects of sense-perception came into existence, there was existing as a genus 'sensibly-perceptible' itself, by sharing in whose being all other objects of sense have become such. "Green of the field," then, is what he terms the "intellectually-perceptible" of the mind; for as in a field the green things spring up and bloom, even so the 'intellectually-perceptible' is a growth springing from the mind. Before, then, the particular 'intellectually-perceptible' came into being, the Creator produces the solely abstract 'intellectually-perceptible,' as a generic existence. This he rightly calls, "all," for the particular 'intellectually-perceptible,' being a fragment, is not all, but the generic is so, being a full whole. "And all the grass of the field" he says, "before it sprang up," that is to say, before the particular objects of sense sprang up, there existed by the Maker's forethought the generic 'sensibly-perceptible,' and that it is that he again calls "all." Natural enough is his comparison of the 'sensibly-perceptible' to grass. For as grass is the food of a creature devoid of reason, so has the 'sensibly-perceptible' been assigned to the unreasoning part of the soul. Else why, after saying before "green of the field," does he go on to say, "and all grass," as if it were impossible for green of the field to come up as grass? The fact is, 'the green of the field" is the 'intellectually-perceptible,' an outgrowth of the mind, but the "grass" is the 'sensibly-perceptible,' it in turn being a growth of the unreasoning part of the soul.

Quaestio: *QG* 1.4

Who is the "moulded" man? And how does he differ from him who is (made) "in accordance with the image (of God)"?

Solutio: Leg. 1.31-32

"And God formed the man by taking clay from the earth, and breathed into his face a breath of life, and the man became a living soul." (Gen. ii.7). There are two types of men; the one a heavenly man, the other an earthly. The heavenly man, being made after the image of God, is altogether without part or lot in corruptible and terrestrial substance; but the earthly one was compacted out of the matter scattered here and there, which Moses calls "clay." For this reason he says that the heavenly man was not moulded, but was stamped with the image of God; while the earthly is a moulded work of the Artificer, but not His offspring. We must account the man made out of the earth to be mind mingling with, but not yet blended with, body. But this earthlike mind is in reality also corruptible, were not God to breathe into it a power of real life; when He does so, it does not any more undergo moulding, but becomes a soul, not an inefficient and imperfectly formed soul, but one endowed with mind and actually alive; for he says "man became a living soul."

Quaestio: *QG* 1.6

Why is God said to have "planted Paradise" and for whom? And what is Paradise?

Solutio: *Leg.* 1.45

[1][48] Well, then, God sows and plants earthly excellence for the race of mortals as a copy and reproduction of the heavenly.

[2] For pitying our race and noting that it is compact of a rich abundance of ills, He caused earthly excellence to strike root, to bring succor and aid to the diseases of the soul.

[3] It is, as I said before, a copy of the heavenly and archetypal excellence, to which Moses gives many names. Virtue is figuratively called 'pleasaunce'. . . .

To avoid being misled by a few examples, I worked through *Leg.* 1 and obtained the results summarized in the chart below. I have put into

[48]Divisions (with numbers) are added to *Leg.* 1.45 to bring out the passage's relation to the three questions of *QG* 1.6.

italics the text in *Legum Allegoriae* which restates the same question so as to call attention to it.

Quaestio in *QG*	Solutio in *Leg.* 1
1	19-20
2	22-24
3	
4	31-32
5	*33*, 39-41
6	45
7	46
8	53
9	56-57
10	59
11	
12	63
13	85
14	
15	101
16	105

It will be immediately noted that in three instances *Legum Allegoriae* fails to provide a response to the *quaestio* in *QG*. In each instance this is due to the shift in exegesis as a result of the more thorough allegorical treatment in the *Legum Allegoriae*.[49] What is more impressive (and which the chart does not indicate) is that in eleven of the remaining thirteen examples the *solutio* stands either immediately after the citation of the biblical text or very close to it.[50] It, therefore, appears that the *Quaestiones* were the ἀφορμή of the *Allegoriae*.

(3) *Differences in Treatment*. The final heuristic procedure is to compare the *Quaestiones* and *Allegoriae* where they overlap, particularly in those instances where they differ. Our task is to ask whether we can discover any rationale for the disagreements. Once we have done this we will be in a position to decide about the movement of the exegesis, i.e.,

[49]For question #3, see *Leg*. 1.28-30; for #11 see §§61-62; and for #14 see §§88-89.

[50]The two exceptions are questions 5 and 7.

from the *Quaestiones* to the *Allegoriae* or vice versa. Three examples will illustrate this procedure.[51]

Quaestio: *QG* 1.8

Why does he place the moulded man in Paradise, but not the man who was made in his image?

QG	*Leg. 1.53-55*
Some, believing Paradise to be a Garden, have said that since the moulded man is sense-perceptible, he therefore rightly goes to a sense-perceptible place. But the man made in His image is intelligible and invisible, and is in the class of incorporeal species. But I would say that Paradise should be thought a symbol of wisdom. For the earth-formed man is a mixture, and consists of soul and body, and is in need of teaching and instruction, desiring, in accordance with the laws of philosophy, that he may be happy. But he who was made in His image is in need of nothing, but is self-hearing and self-taught and self-instructed by nature.	Speaking here of the man whom God moulded, it merely says that He 'placed him in the garden.' Who then is it of whom it says later on 'The Lord God took the man whom He had made, and placed him in the garden to till it and to guard it' (Gen ii.15)? It would seem then that this is a different man, the one that was made after the image and archetype, so that two men are introduced into the garden, the one a moulded being, the other 'after the image.' The one then that was made according to the original has his sphere not only in the planting of virtues, but is also their tiller and guardian, and that means that he is mindful of all that he heard and practised in his training; but the 'moulded' man neither tills the virtues nor guards them, but is only introduced to the truths by the rich bounty of God, presently to be an exile from virtue. For this reason in describing the man whom God only places in the garden, Moses uses the word 'moulded,' but of the man whom He appoints both tiller and guardian he

[51]All English translations from PLCL.

> speaks not as 'moulded,' but he says 'whom He had made'; and the one He receives, and the other He casts out. And He confers on him whom He receives three gifts, which constitute natural ability, facility in apprehending, persistence in doing, tenacity in keeping. Facility in apprehending is the placing in the garden, persistence in doing is the practice of noble deeds, tenacity in keeping the guarding and retaining in the memory of the holy precepts. But the 'moulded' mind neither keeps in mind nor carries out in action the things that are noble, but has facility in apprehending them and no more than this. Accordingly after being placed in the garden he soon runs away and is cast out.

QG 1.8 implies that God set the man he ἔπλασεν in the garden, but that the man κατ' εἰκόνα had no need of the garden. *Leg.* 1.53-55, on the other hand, suggests that both were set in the garden. This is due to the variant reading in Philo's text of Gen. 2:15 where he reads ἐποίησε instead of ἔπλασεν, as in the LXX.[52] In *Leg.* 1.31 and 90, Philo has introduced the distinction between the "heavenly man" (Gen. 1:27) and the "earthly man" (Gen. 2:7). In 1.31 he wrote: διὸ τὸν μὲν οὐράνιόν φησιν οὐ πεπλάσθαι, κατ' εἰκόνα δὲ τετυπῶσθαι θεοῦ, τὸν δὲ γήϊνον πλάσμα, ἀλλ' οὐ γέννημα, εἶναι τοῦ τεχνίτου. It is this distinction between ὁ ἄνθρωπος ὅν ἔπλασεν and ὁ ἄνθρωπος ὅν ἐποίησεν that lies at the heart of the exposition of the *Legum Allegoriae*.[53]

---

[52]Philo betrays no awareness of the particular implications of this term in *QG* 1.14, where he deals with Gen 2:15. On the subject of Philo's text, see Katz 1950. Regrettably, Katz does not deal specifically with this passage.

[53]Tobin 1983, 102-34, provides a very important discussion of the double creation of man. I am in agreement that the double creation was due to an attempt to explain the two separate creation stories and that Platonism was the catalyst for the procedure. I am not, however, fully convinced that this was pre-Philonic, as Tobin suggests. The reason for

We are now left with two choices. We may either argue that Philo changed his mind about the reading of Gen. 2:15 and consequently dropped his allegorical treatment of the "heavenly man" in the garden, or that he sharpened his allegorical pencil after writing the *Quaestiones* and included the more sophisticated treatment in *Legum Allegoriae*. The latter is much more likely given the centrality of the point in *Legum Allegoriae*. *In nuce*, for Philo the former would be retrogression; the latter an advance.

The second example is Philo's identification of the four rivers of Gen. 2:10-14. The treatments may be summarized as follows:

River	*QG* 1.11	*Leg*.1.63-73
Pishon	φρόνησις	φρόνησις
Gihon	σωφροσύνη	ἀνδρεία
Tigris	ἀνδρεία	σωφροσύνη
Euphrates	δικαιοσύνη	δικαιοσύνη

It is very clear that a change has taken place in Philo's scheme of identification. The question is why? In *QG* we are not offered any explanation for the ordering of the virtues; however, in *Leg*. 1.70-71 we are. In §71 he explained: οὕτως καὶ τῶν ἀρετῶν πρώτη μὲν ἡ περὶ τὸ πρῶτον μέρος τῆς ψυχῆς, ὃ δὴ λογικόν ἐστι, καὶ τοῦ σώματος διατρίβουσα κεφαλὴν φρόνησις, δευτέρα δὲ ἀνδρεία, explaining: ὅτι περὶ τὸ δεύτερον μέρος ψυχῆς μὲν θυμόν, σώματος δὲ τὰ στέρνα φωλεύει. He continues: τρίτη δὲ σωφροσύνη, ὅτι περὶ τὸ ἦτρον, ὃ δὴ τρίτον ἐστὶ τοῦ σώματος, καὶ περὶ τὸ ἐπιθυμητικόν, ὃ τρίτην εἴληχε χώραν ἐν ψυχῇ, πραγματεύεται. It is difficult for me to imagine why, once Philo has made this neat identification of the virtues in a descending order with the parts of the body (hence soul), he would drop it or, even more, alter it. It is clear that *QG* is a rough draft.

Quaestio: QG 1.25

What is the "side" which He took from the earth-born man; and why did He mould the side into a woman?

---

my hesitation here is the difference in Philo's treatments between *QG* and *Legum Allegoriae*. Did he learn or formulate the exegesis of the latter between the writing of the two documents? Either way, I believe my argument stands.

QG

The literal sense is clear. For by a certain symbolical use of 'part' it is called a half of the whole, as both man and woman, being sections of Nature, become equal in one harmony of genus, which is called man. But in the figurative sense, man is a symbol of mind, and his side is a single sense-faculty. And the sense-perception of a very changeable reason is symbolized by woman. Some speak of prowess and strength as 'side,' whence they call a fighting athlete with strong sides a powerful man. Accordingly the lawgiver says that woman was made from the side of man, intimating that woman is a half of man's body. For this we also have evidence in the constitution of of the body, its common parts, movements, faculties, mental vigour, and excellence. For all things are seen as if in double proportion. Inasmuch as the moulding of the male is more perfect than, and double, that of the female, it requires only half the time, namely forty days; whereas the imperfect woman, who is, so to speak, a half-section of man, requires twice as many days, namely eighty. So that there is a change in the doubling of the time of man's nature (or natural growth), in accordance with the peculiarity of woman. For when the nature of the body and soul of something is of double measure, such as man's, then the forming

Leg. 2.19-24

These words in their literal sense are of the nature of a myth. For how could anyone admit that a woman, or a human being at all, came into existence out of a man's side? And what was there to hinder the First Cause from creating woman, as He created man, out of the earth? For not only was the Maker the same Being, but the material too, out of which every particular kind was fashioned, was practically unlimited. And why, when there were so many parts to choose from, did He form the woman not from some other part but from the side? And which side did he take? For we may assume that only two are indicated, as there is in fact nothing to suggest a large number of them. Did he take the left or the right side? If He filled up with flesh (the place of) the one which He took, are we to suppose that the one which He left was *not* made of flesh? Truly our sides are twin in all their parts and are made of flesh. What then are we to say? 'Sides' is a term of ordinary life for 'strength.' To say that a man has 'sides' is equivalent to saying that he is strong, we say of a powerful athlete 'he has stout sides,' and to say that a singer has 'sides' is as much as to say that he has great lung power in singing. Having said this, we must go on to remark that the mind when as yet unclothed and unconfined by the body. (and it is of the mind when not so confined that he is speaking) has many powers. It has the power of holding

and moulding of that thing is in half-measure. But when the nature of the body and the construction of something is in half-measure, such as woman's, then the moulding and forming of that thing is in double measure.

together, of growing, of conscious life, of thought, and countless other powers, varying both in species and genus. Lifeless things, like stones and blocks of wood, share with all others the power of holding together, of which the bones in us, which are not unlike stones, partake. 'Growth' extends to plants, and there are parts in us such as our nails and hair, resembling plants; 'growth' is coherence capable of moving itself. Conscious life is the power to grow, with the additional power of receiving impressions and being the subject of impulses. This is shared also by creatures without reason. Once more, the power of thinking is peculiar to the mind, and while shared, it may well be, by beings more akin to God, is, so far as mortal beings are concerned, peculiar to man. This power or faculty is twofold. We are rational beings, on the one hand as being partakers of mind, and on the other as being capable of discourse. Well, there is also another power or faculty in the soul, closely akin to these, namely that of receiving sense-impressions, and it is of this that the prophet is speaking. For his immediate concern is just this, to indicate the origin of active sense-perception. And logical sequence leads him to do so.

There are two major variations in these accounts. First, in *QG* Philo accepts the literal meaning, while in *Leg.* 2 he explicitly rejects it. Second, in *QG* he offers two explanations for "side": one, it is "a single sense-faculty" — hence woman is "sense-perception"; two, "some" have suggested that "side" is "strength." In *Leg.* 2, Philo drops the reference to "some" and offers αἱδυνάμεις as his own explanation. This, however, is not proffered as one of two options, since the two options mentioned in *QG* are integrated into a single position in *Leg*. 2: sense perception is a power! How are we to explain this? It looks as though Philo has woven the two options of *QG* into a coherent exposition in *Legum Allegoriae.*

III. Conclusions

Any assessment of a Philonic treatise must begin with the recognition that Philo was first and foremost a biblical exegete.[54] The issue with *Quaestiones* is for what or whom was Philo an exegete? Marcus and Royse have persuasively argued that the book divisions of the Greek text correspond to the *sedarim* of the Babylonian lectionary system.[55] This might seem to justify the terse assessment of the *Quaestiones* by Colpe as "nicht wissenschaftlich, sondern katechetisch gemeint sind."[56] But are the *Quaestiones* that simple? It is true that they lack — as we have seen — the polish and sophistication of the *Allegoriae*. Yet it is just as true that the basics for the *Allegoriae* are already present in the *Quaestiones*.[57] So, for example, the primary allegorical identifications have already been assigned.[58] It is likewise unacceptable to claim that the *quaestio et solutio* method is reserved for catechesis since it is fundamental to the entire Philonic corpus[59] and a

[54]Cf. Nikiprowetzky 1977, 181, who summarizes the various options (documentary analysis, the homiletic theory, and the exegetical school) and concludes: "Lorsque nous affirmons que les écrits de Philon qui concernent la Bible sont un commentaire de l'Ecriture, nous entendons avec Völker que Philon doit être considéré avant tout comme un exégète qui n'exprime ses idées qu'en fonction du texte scripturaire. Il ne se propose pas de développer un système, mais il veut communiquer le sens profond de la Loi mosaïque qu'il suit verset par verset en gardant devant les yeux le texte sur lequel il travaille." The entire final chapter of his book is devoted to this issue. Here is another point of consensus, according to Runia 1987, 10.

[55]Marcus 1953, 1: xiii-xiv and Royse 1976-77, 48-63. On the lectionary system see Mann 1971 and Perrot 1973.

[56]Colpe 1961.

[57]So also Nikiprowetzky 1977, 234, n. 216: "La plupart des doctrines de Philon se recontrent en effet dans les *Quaestiones* et sous une forme que l'on ne saurait en justice qualifier de simplifiée."

[58]Man is given a mind, woman is identified as sense perception, and the serpent as sensual pleasure. There are instances where the *Allegoriae* offer allegorical interpretations where the *Quaestiones* do not — see, e.g., *Leg* 1.28 (*QG*1.3) and *Det*. 32 (*QG* 1.67).

[59]So Borgen 1984*b*, 242.

known form of writing a commentary.[60] Is it not just as likely that Philo simply accepted the lectionary divisions which he had in his bible as suitable and recognized ones?

I believe that the chances of standing on *terra firma* are better if we attempt to explain the *raison d'être* of the *Quaestiones* on the basis of what we know about them within the Philonic corpus. We have argued that the *Allegoriae* were developed from the *Quaestiones*. This would confirm Sandmel's suggestion that the *Quaestiones* "are preliminary notes on the basis of which Philo in part got around to composing treatises and in part did not."[61]

This is likewise the best explanation for Philo's cataloguing of views and concern to present both the opinions of those who interpreted the text literally and those who interpreted it allegorically. At the risk of oversimplification, I would suggest that the literal school of exegesis[62] allowed Philo to keep one foot planted securely within Judaism, while the allegorical school offered him the opportunity to set his other foot in the world of Hellenism.[63] In many ways, Harry Wolfson's comment may still stand: "It was Philo's purpose, therefore, to combine the traditional with the allegorical method, preventing the former from becoming hostile toward the latter and guarding the latter against breaking itself loose from the former."[64] Philo, quite obviously, had no trouble with a multivalent text.

Yet this still does not explain why the literal dominates the allegorical in the *Quaestiones*, while the reverse is the case in the *Allegoriae*. Here there are three possibilities: a significant shift took place in Philo's thought, they were written for different audiences,[65] or

---

[60]Cf. Marcus 1953, 1:ix.

[61]Sandmel 1954, 249 and 1979, 79.

[62]On this see Shroyer 1936. He summarized Philo's view of the literalists thus: "We feel sure that he is in agreement as far as they go with his fellows in Judaism who follow only the 'literal meaning.' In these literal presentations we may find the elements that go to make up the religion of these people who are Literalists and no more. And this religion was also the 'minimum' religion of the allegorical mystics of Philo's own group, to be surpassed by them, but not abandoned." See also Hay 1980 and his essay in this volume. S. Belkin has repeatedly tried to link Philo with midrash (Belkin 1960 and 1964. Cf. also Stein 1931.

[63]That Philo knew and used Greek allegory has been demonstrated by Dillon 1979-80 and Amir 1984. On Philo's allegory, see further Stein 1929 and Christiansen 1967. On his references to other allegorists, see Hay 1979-80.

[64]Wolfson 1947, 1:57.

[65]*Ibid.*, 1:122.

Philo's intentions were different for each work.[66] The problem with the first alternative is that the *Allegoriae* do not assume an anti-literal stance. The second option tends to move in the direction of a catechetical work. It therefore is best to ascribe the difference in emphasis to the fact that in the *Quaestiones* Philo wanted to present all the options, whereas in the Allegorical Commentary he wrote from a definite perspective.

This thesis, that the *Quaestiones* are the Prolegomena to the *Allegoriae*, means that the *Quaestiones* must be given a significant role in the interpretation of the *Allegoriae*. Students of Philo now need to do with these two appendages of the Philonic corpus what New Testament scholars have done with the synoptic gospels. We need to discover the ways in which the *Quaestiones* generated the expositions of the *Allegoriae*. I am convinced that such a procedure would enable us to understand better not only Philo's hermeneutics but his message as well.

---

[66]Nikiprowetzky 1977, 234, n. 216: "Il n'est pas certain, à bien considérer les choses, et même il est peu probable que l'attitude de Philon à l'égard du sens littéral diffère dans le *Commentaire* et dans les *Quaestiones*. Dans les *Quaestiones* qui, nous le répétons, ne sont pas orientées selon un point de vue spécial, à la façon du *Commentaire*, Philon s'efforce d'accueillir toutes les exégèses capables d'apporter des éclaircissements au texte biblique dont, dans la mesure du possible, elles «sauvent les apparences» en justifiant le sens littéral."

CHAPTER SEVEN

FROM GRAMMAR TO DISCOURSE: A STUDY OF THE *QUAESTIONES IN GENESIM* IN RELATION TO THE TREATISES

ANITA MÉASSON AND JACQUES CAZEAUX

Editor's note:

The following article is the result of a joint research project by its two authors. They are fully in agreement on the content and the ideas of the entire presentation. It will be useful, however, for the reader to know that the preface, the section on *QG* 1-3, the brief pages on *QG* 5-6 and the conclusion are primarily the work of Jacques Cazeaux, while the extensive analysis of *QG* 4 is primarily the work of Anita Méasson. The entire article was translated from a French manuscript by Dr. Jeannine Hammond, Associate Professor of French at Coe College. The translation was checked and approved by Professors Méasson and Cazeaux.

I. Preface

The *Quaestiones* themselves are not the object of this study. We will not look in depth at the richness of their teachings, nor will we make a detailed comparison of Philo's "ideas" in the *QG* with the notions, either similar or different, that are found in the Treatises. Instead, we intend to show the distance which separates the two "literary genres" of the Questions[1] on the one hand and the fully developed Treatises on the other.

After a period of being relatively forgotten, the *Quaestiones* are back in fashion. To speak clearly and to clarify my position, I think that the new popularity of the *Quaestiones* is like the popularity of theories which give a privileged place to an esoteric teaching of Plato, a teaching regarded as more certain and more Platonic than the Dialogues. Keeping

[1]In this article the term "Question" (capitalized) refers to an individual question together with Philo's "answer" in the *QG*. The term "Treatise" denotes one of Philo's exegetical treatises containing material related in content to *QG*.

everything in proportion, the same may be said about Philo. For us, the "true" Philo is the author of the Treatises, because the Treatises are finished works, "discourses" which have movement, whereas the Questions, even the richest and most beautiful of them, remain inert — the difference is a bit like that between grammar and the style of a masterpiece. The method of study which we apply to the Treatises is of no use with the *Quaestiones*. Perhaps not all the Questions are the work of Philo, at least in their redaction. They can be grouped into several series.[2] They are rarely linked one to another, even when a common theme establishes a sort of unified horizon among several of them, for example the "idea" that Noah's Ark symbolizes the human body (*QG* 2.1-8). They are more or less organized within themselves, but never with the sort of dynamic quality which gives force and movement to the Treatises. Last of all, they are closed, in the sense that it is very rare to find Questions which refer to another biblical text; and, even when that does occur, no dialectic holds these sister-texts together in a firm, evolving way. No Question has the intentionality of a page of a Treatise. But, reciprocally, it is inadequate to consider a Treatise as formed of a series of Questions; that would seem to be the opposite of Philonic technique. It is as if Philo started out with "note cards" resembling the Questions, intending to animate them and give them life, newness, and invention, as a director does who animates and makes use of actors, their costumes, their physiognomies, and their voices. They are nothing before the play is set in motion. Thus, we will often repeat, the similarity of the "concepts" or "ideas" found in the Questions and the Treatises is only a very small part of Philo's creation. And it must be added that the "allegories," the transformations of biblical names or the cosmological, psychological, and moral interpretations which Philo proposes in the Questions and which then reappear in identical form in the Treatises do not appear to us to be a cause for rejoicing, allowing us to say that Philo is constant, consistent with himself, or, on the other hand, variable. No one knows the chronology of Philo's works in either relative or absolute terms, and therefore we cannot settle the question of the relationship between the *Quaestiones* and the Treatises. It is simply from a "logical" point of view, using the criteria of complexity and movement, that we can say that the Questions are "anterior" to the

[2]According to the degree of elaboration, the textual length itself, or the fact that certain ones do not begin, as do the majority, with the simple "What is meant. . . ?" but already are in a form that introduces a paradox: "Why does God speak like a man, saying: Having gone down, I will see . . . ?" (*QG* 4.24).

Treatises. It is their literary "genre" which differentiates them; and it is possible to conceive of Philo composing a "chapter" of the *De Migratione Abrahami* in the morning, and, in the evening, writing a batch of Questions (I have intentionally chosen an example where comparison is impossible, since no Questions deal with Chapter 12 of Genesis . . .).

On the other hand, we will not make an exhaustive study of all the Questions. We will limit ourselves, first of all, to the *QG*. We intend to study two of the Books in some depth, proposing a complementary point of view: first, a study of Book 1 will make the vitality of the corresponding Treatises stand out; then, a study of Book 4 will show the *QG* in a better light. Our study will go a bit beyond these two works taken as samples; and we think that the reader of the *Quaestiones* in their entirety will realize that we have touched upon the essential points of a comparison which would be too tedious to do for the entire length of the text.[3] It would seem that the intellectual panorama of the *Quaestiones* is coherent enough in its elements, and from this basis it is possible to admit their homogeneity. We therefore feel that it is possible to discuss this work using samplings from it.

Let us add that the Armenian language gives an additional, insurmountable opacity to the *Quaestiones* in general. Most Philo scholars do not know Armenian, and just how well do specialists in Armenian know Philo? An additional problem: should one use one's knowledge of the Philo who writes in Greek to interpret the Armenian? And does one not risk straying from the task of translation into the realm of commentary, forcing a harmonization of the whole? This problem has no solution. Between this work of Philo and us there is clearly a barrier, like a piece of frosted windowpane; we can catch silhouettes, but the sharp lines of the profiles escape us — as they must have escaped the Armenians whose rough, wooden translation differs so markedly from the precision of Philo's Greek.

Finally, the prejudice that Philo is first and foremost an "allegorist" can be harmful to the correct perception of the possible relations between the *Quaestiones* and the Treatises. For us, the "allegories" are the elements, the raw textual material used for the construction of a dialectical discourse. Every Philonist knows that, as one moves from one Treatise to another, important variations or nuances can affect the

[3]A paradox: the Philo team asked me to have a study of a Philonic work translated so that my analytical method would be more accessible; but here I am dealing with the *Quaestiones*, a work which lacks dialectic and which therefore is more closely related to comparative methods or literary history . . . .

"allegory" of Joseph or of some biblical phrase. In contrast, the fixity of the allegorical interpretations dealing with Isaac,[4] for example, which are always related to Joy, Nature, and the End, does not constitute a sort of "theologoumenon" — an acquisition or a self-contained meaning of Philonic discourse; it is in each Treatise, in each specific location in the text that we must observe the thrust, the place, and the precise role played by this "allegory" which is the most constant of them all, noting that it is conditioned by its position in the total section, which could be a "chapter,"[5] a page, or, eventually, a whole Treatise. Philo's philosophical variations should be judged from the same point of view; their use in a specific location, their provisory intention which is nevertheless proportioned to the total work, the real architectonic structure — these are the only criteria to use. The allegory provides raw material, as do the "ideas," the special transformations of proper names, and all the other elements of discourse. Philo did not create "allegory"; he did not even give it a privileged position; he inserted it into an intellectual construction which encompasses allegory, philosophy, and the symbols which constitute in his work the High and the Low, the One and the Many, all the panorama of the "soul" — this "I," royal and common, which is the focal point of the discourse and its movement. This movement will therefore remain our criterion in the differentiation of the "literary genres," Question or Treatise; the Questions, in fact, are characterized by inertia. Yet, paradoxically, we will conclude that the Questions, while inferior, are not insignificant.[6]

II A. Profile of *QG*1[7]

QG 2.1 is the only passage in *QG* which calls attention to the beginning of a "chapter." In it, Philo announces that Noah's Ark symbolizes the body and that the details of the famous episode will prove it. In Book 1, the Questions are presented without any indication of unity or internal grouping. We are therefore going to consider them

---

[4]Let us note at once that the Triad of Abraham-Jacob-Isaac is far from holding the decisive place in the *Quaestiones* that it does in the Treatises.

[5]I have given this name to the units of medium length which make up a Treatise.

[6]We do not here take into account the point of view of the historian of ideas or the heroic historian of Philonic thought, both of whom will find much information in the *Quaestiones*.

[7]The following discussion of *QG* 1-3 is by J. Cazeaux.

here in the order in which they appear, discussing the text of each and then comparing them with the Treatises dealing with the same biblical texts.

(1) *QG* 1 takes us from Gen 2:4 to 6:13.

(2) There are no commentaries on Gen 2:12; 3:2,4,10-11; 4:6,16-22: 5:2,4-21,25-28,30-32a: 6:2,5,10. The reason for these omissions is not clear. They may be merely accidental, or it may be that Philo refuses to repeat himself (5:32b = 6:10, and Philo omits 6:10).

(3) The form of the questions is not absolutely constant. In most cases, they correspond to a Greek Τί; or Διὰ τί; But these two formulae seem to be equivalent. The majority of questions are straightforward: "What is the meaning of 'God made every green thing . . .'?" (*QG* 1.2). A certain number are elaborate and suggest an interpretation or a consciousness of paradox: "Why, reflecting on the creation of the world, does he (Moses) say 'This is the book of the genesis of heaven and earth. . . '?" (Question 1). The Questions of this type are *QG* 1.1, 4, 8, 13-15, 18-19, 21, 27-28, 32-35, 37, 42-47, 50-51, 55-56, 58-62, 66, 68-69, 76-77, 81-83, 94, and 97. For example, the Question of *QG* 1.43 is presented in this way: "Why, when they hid themselves from the face of God, was not the woman, who ate the forbidden fruit first, mentioned first rather than the man? (Scripture) says 'Adam and his wife hid themselves.'" But the relative complexity of such a question does not preface a more elaborate answer than does the simple "Why does he say . . . ?" From this point of view, one can say that the *Quaestiones* proceed in the opposite direction from the Treatises. In the Treatises, the interpretation of a biblical phrase sends the reader and the author to other texts; it is the "answer" which implies an overarching view of the biblical text. In the *Quaestiones* (at least in those with this greater complexity), the overarching view is used in the Question, but the "answer" does not benefit in any way. It remains targeted on the specific text and almost never makes reference to another biblical passage.

(4) The answers do not demonstrate an identical pattern. However, one can note that, like the more elaborate questions, they participate in the διαίρεσις, usually in the form of a dichotomy. Still, several kinds of "division" are to be found. Bipartite distinctions may be found in answers which distinguish (a) between two interpretations or (b) between two meanings. The interpretations may be distinguished as correct or incorrect (1,10,11,18), as acceptable or better (8, 12, 57), as literal or closer to "the nature of things" (6, 11, 13, 25, 31, [39], 44-49, 52-53, 88, 94-95, 97). The meanings can be defined by order ("first . . . next . . .

furthermore. . . ." -- 2, 3, 5, 7, [15], 21, 27, 30, 32, 34-36, 41, 51-52, 54, 84-85, 96) or as two potential meanings present within the biblical text (4, 9, 14, 16, 19, 22-23, 26, 28-29, 42-43, 54-56, 59-65, 70, 78, 81-82, 90, 92). The remaining answers show no "division": 17, 33, 40, 50, 58, 66-69, 71, 73-75, 77, 79-80, 82, 90, 92.

This obsession with dichotomy, of form (levels of meaning) or of substance (psychological division between reason and the senses; metaphysical division between ideal and empirical; moral division between just and corrupt), is obviously the feature which most closely ties the *QG* to the Treatises. But this similarity is as deceiving as that of two beings who breathe the same air, but of whom one has white skin and the other black, without other similarities. . . .

(5) The majority of the answers are flat, in the exact sense that they are laid out according to the "division," without surprises, without reference to other things, not even to other biblical texts. They are an organizing mechanism, using alternating terms. This is the source of the diminished character of many of the answers. One can, however, observe:

(a) A tendency to inflate arithmological subjects:[8] *QG* 1.77, 83, 87 and 91 develop numerical speculations more generously; but they remain linear, without the least dialectic (the measurements of the Ark, in *QG* 2, will be the pretext for the same kind of elaborations).

(b) Only once (*QG* 1.82) is there a suggestion of an overarching interpretation. In *QG* 1.76b-77 the author reminds us that Cain was the beneficiary of "mercy" and that the arrival of Enoch brings us into the era of "penitence". Mercy and penitence thus form a metaphysical-moral pair or totality. The pair "God"-"Lord" is suggested, but this unifying vision has no effect on the surrounding passages.

(c) A few answers do go a little deeper than the others, reaching beyond the level of definitions or static orderings:

QG 1.42, 55, and 95 present investigations of the problem of biblical anthropomorphisms in relation to the question of whether God *repented* his creation of man. Various data in the Bible are discussed somewhat in the style of the *Quod Deus*, but clearly without the in-depth quality of that Treatise.

QG 1.99 presents a more sustained examination of the biblical text "All flesh corrupted His way to Him (God) on the earth." Apparently (the beginning is obscure) the author is analyzing in succession three

---

[8]*QG* 1.43 and 61 could be included here.

main terms. "Flesh" refers to "man" (a word which in principle refers to the spirit); can "flesh" be an active element capable of an action? "Corrupt" — here it is the bringing together of "flesh" and the active verb "to corrupt" which poses the problem. Finally, the term "his" refers back to God. Perhaps this page is a précis or sketch of a dialectic; but if that is so, nothing really filters through, and charity is needed to imagine it in the background.

QG 1.40, another obscure text, seems to imply an elaborate understanding of the Philonic concept of "nudity," such as that found in *Leg*. 2.53-64 and *Fug*. 188-193. Curiously, *Leg*. 2.64, which also discusses the nudity of Adam and his wife, does not treat it at all in the manner of *QG* 1.40.

From the Questions in *QG* 1 one might painstakingly reconstruct the Philonic panorama and the "pages," as it were, of his mental Dictionary. Among the many concepts that appear in the *QG* are the distinctions between "Man" and "man," between Ideas and the world, between "mercy" and "lordship" (the concept, so to speak, of the division of the divinity), between two "lives" (the inversion of "first-born" and "youngest"), between the wretchedness of sensible existence and the intellectualist parable of salvation, between the immediate sense of the Scriptural text and the deeper level of intelligibility to which one must move.[9] But the proportions of these concepts and especially their "motricity" remain ungraspable here. The *Quaestiones* are a gold mine for the historian of thought; but, it must be clearly stated, the Philonist really has nothing to gain from *QG* 1, even in the Questions which speak to the passages of Genesis which are absent from the Treatises (for example, *QG* 1.32-42 concerns Gen 3:1 - end, a text not discussed at the conclusion of *Leg*. 2). Obscurity (accidental, due to the Armenian language), the absence of a unified method and especially the insularity of each question-and-answer: this Book reminds one of scattered debris or the results of a child's game in which the paternal manuscript has been used as a toy.

However, from a more positive perspective, the principle itself has a certain grandeur. What we have is probably a "catechism," offering a minimum of correspondences between the Literal and the Meaning in order to obviate large errors or malicious efforts.

(6) Finally, as I have said, the order in which these questions-and-answers are written down indicates that each is independent of the others.

[9]Including the "visible gods" of *Aet*. 20 (cf. *QG* 1.42, 54).

Except for the connection between "mercy" and "repentance" (*QG* 1.76b-77 and 82), no unifying principle other than the reference to the letter of the biblical text and the universal procedure of the "division" is present to help us break through the mysterious or scandalous shell. Unless one stays merely at the level of what the text says (the presence of a specific concept in both texts), a comparison of *QG* 1 with the corresponding Treatises will very quickly teach the reader all that can be learned. Choosing at random and at a purely material level, since I am comparing here the length of the exegeses, let us state, for example, that *QG* 1.72, based on these words, "You shall be groaning and trembling on the earth" (Gen 4:13), is composed of four lines, whereas the *Quod Deus* will extend the commentary from §119 to §140; in the same way, *QG* 1.85 is the counterpart of *Abr.* 17-26. Nevertheless, at the risk of fatiguing the reader, let us compare these texts:[10]

II B. The Treatises and *QG* 1[11]

Genesis	QG 1	Treatises
2:4	1	*Leg.* 1.19-21
2:5	2	*Opif.* 129-30; *Leg.* 1.21-27!
2:6	3	*Opif.* 133b; *Leg.* 1.28-30
2:7	4-5	*Opif.*135; *Leg.* 1.31-32,39; *Plant.* 18-19
2:8	6-8	*Leg.* 1.43-55!
2:9	9-11	*Leg.* 1.56-62
2:10	12	*Leg.* 1.63-84!
2:11,13-14	13	*Leg.* 1.85-87
2:12*	---	
2:15	14	*Leg.* 1.88-89
2:16-17	15	*Leg.* 1.89-100!

[10]The insularity of the *Quaestiones* jumps out at us. Plato's *Timaeus* 92 C is invoked in *QG* 1.6; Pythagoras, in *QG* 1.17; Homer's *Il.*12.239 and *Od.*20.242 in *QG* 1.24 and *Od.* 12.118 in *QG* 1.76. References to other scriptural books are even rarer: the only true one is *QG* 1.100 (Num 14:9). *QG* 1.67, 88 anticipate very slightly the text they begin to explicate. That is all.

[11]In the table a single asterisk indicates an "omission" in *QG* as it follows the text of Genesis. A double asterisk (**) indicates a passage of Genesis that is totally ignored in the commentaries of Philo available to us. An exclamation mark ("!") calls attention to the length of the exegesis in certain passages of the Treatises -- often several pages.

2:17	16	*Leg*. 1.105-108
2:18	17	*Leg*. 2.1-9!
2:18-19	18	*Leg*. 2.10-11
2:19	19-22	*Leg*. 2.11b-18
2:20	23	—
2:21	24	*Leg*. 2.19, 26-34!
2:21-22	25	*Leg*. 2.19-21,35-37 (*inclusio*)!
2:22	26-27	*Leg*. 2.20 (*sic*)
2:23	28	*Leg*. 2.40-48
2:24	29	*Leg*. 2.49-52!
2:25	30	*Leg*. 2.53-70!
3:1	31-34	*Leg*. 2.71-108!!
3.2**	—	—
3:3	35	—
3:4*	—	
3:5	36	—
3:6	37-38	—
3:7	39-41	—
3:8	42-44	*Leg*. 3.1-48!
3:9	45	*Leg*. 3.51-56
3:10-11*	—	
3:12-13	46	*Leg*. 3.56-64
3:14-17	47	—
3:14-15	48	*Leg*. 3.65-199!
3:16	49	*Leg*. 3.200-221!
3:17-19	50-51	*Leg*. 3.222-253!
3:20	52	—
3:21	53	—
3:22	54-55	—
3:23	56	—
3:24	57	*Cher*. 21-39!
4:1	58	*Cher*. 125-130
4:2	59	*Sacr*. 11-45a!
4:3-4	60	*Sacr*. 52-71! and 72-139!
4:4-5	61-62	—
4:5	63	—
4:6**	—	—
4:7	64-66	*Agr*. 127-146!; *Sobr*. 50; *Mut*. 195

4:8	67	*Det.* 1-46!
4:9	68-69	*Det.* 57-68!
4:10	70	*Det.* 79-95!
4:11	71	*Det.* 96-103
4:12	72	*Det.* 119-140!
4:13	73	*Det.* 142
4:14	74	*Det.* 164-166
4:15	75-76	*Det.* 167-178
4:16-22*	—	
4:23-24	77	*Det.* 50-51
4:25	78	*Post.* 124-185
4:26	79	*Abr.* 7-16
5:1	80	*Det.* 139; *Abr.* 9-11
5:2**	—	—
5:3	81	(*Post.* 42, 45)
5:4-21*	—	
5:22*	82	*Abr.* 17-26
5:21-22	83	—
5:23	84	—
5:24	85-86	*Abr.* 17-26, 35; *Post.* 43
5:25-28*	—	
5:29	87	(*Det.* 122-124a); *Congr.* 90-120!
5:30-31**	—	—
5:32b	88	*Sobr.* 31-44, 52, 67-68
6:1	89	*Gig.* 1-5
6:2*	—	
6:3*	90-91	*Gig.* 22-23, 56-57
6:4	92	*Gig.* passim
6:5*	—	
6:6	93	*Deus* 31-32
6:7	94-95	*Deus* 47-48, 51-69! and 70b-72
6:8	96	*Deus* 70-74 (86-) 104-116!
6:9	97	*Deus* 117-121
6:10*	—	
6:11	98	*Deus* 122-139!
6:12	99	*Deus* 140-183!!!
6:13	100	—

Thus the one hundred Questions of *QG* 1 extend over a little less than five chapters of Genesis. They "correspond to" the following seven Treatises: *Legum Allegoriae* 1-3, *De Cherubim*, *De Sacrificiis*, *Quod Deterius*, *De Posteritate Caini*, *De Gigantibus* and *Quod Deus Sit Immutabilis*. They contain the commentary on some biblical passages untreated in the other works that we have by Philo, the longest of these additional commentaries being that which covers Gen 3:1-7. But the disproportion between the *QG* and the Treatises, even in terms of quantity, is immense. Although the entire first half of *QG* 1 speaks to the same material as does the *Legum Allegoriae* (which is a lot from one point of view and very little from another), the *De Cherubim* must be content with the modest space available in *QG* 1.57-58; and the *De Gigantibus* with *QG* 1.89-92, which is only a little longer.

Obviously, however, the main difference is qualitative. To demonstrate this does not require a lengthy and wastefully-detailed comparison which might exhaust both the reader and the writer. Even if (as is not the case) all the concepts, etymologies and symbolic "transformations" could be found in the *QG*, there would be no more resemblance between them and the Treatises than between the painter's palette and the finished painting. The palette may be of interest for the history of art materials but not for the comprehension and appreciation of painting.

It is not, as V. Nikiprowetzky seems to suggest,[12] only a difference of degree, length, and complexity that separates the literary genre of the Treatises from that of the *Quaestiones*. It is a difference of kind. There is no more information given in the Treatises, but their relation to the *Quaestiones* is like that of a functioning light bulb to a bare filament. There is no organization in the *QG*, and it is at that point that the Treatises begin. We will not compare all the parallel passages in detail. But I will speak briefly about the careful organization of the *Legum Allegoriae*; then I will take its first "chapter" and compare it to the parallel *QG*; and, finally, I will do a double comparison: first, of *QG* 1.47-48 with *Leg.* 3.65-199 (primarily *Leg.* 3.75-104), and, secondly, of the same *Leg.* 3.75-104 with *Deus* 104-110. The rationale will become apparent.

---

[12]E.g., in his study of *De Gigantibus* and *Quod Deus* in Winston and Dillon 1983, 5-75.

A. *The Structure of* Leg. 1

The fundamental principle is simple. The biblical text of Genesis offers a series of repetitions. Hardly is the Creation finished at the end of Chapter 1 than Genesis 2 repeats the main ideas and sets forth a second version of the creation of man; even the sentences themselves are redundant. Philo has made use of this cascading system. With the help of the *Timaeus* and of Platonism in the widest sense, he interprets the doublets and the repetitions as an order descending from the Idea to the empirical. There is in God the Idea of ideas, the Logos; and in this latter there is the intelligible idea of the intellect and the intelligible idea of the realm of the senses. From "Image" to "image,"[13] can be found a graduated, descending sequence, in which empirical reality travels away from the Source and thus in the direction of density, obscurity, danger and evil. This schema is fully laid out in the *Legum Allegoriae*. Scholars have wondered what connection this work might have with the *De Opificio*. But the complexity of this metaphysical "entropy," descending from the Idea to pleasure, from the One to the multiple, suffices to explain the back-and-forth structure of its organization. Moreover, the model of the *Timaeus* invited Philo to take the *De Opificio* up to the "woman" and the "serpent," by an anticipation that the redundancies of the biblical text render plausible. At this point, let us take note of the fact that there is thus a controlling "idea" in the *Legum Allegoriae*, an idea that is completely grasped; but this idea plays no guiding role in the *QG*, even if it surfaces there sporadically (see *QG* 1.2).

The hinges or transitions from one plane to another are put in place in *Leg*. 1.21, where Philo speaks of Intelligence and Sensible Existence, both of them ideal, and intelligible — which is proven, in Philo's opinion, by the adjunction of "all," an infallible indicator of totality and therefore of unity and of the ideality which is close to the One (see the exegeses of *Leg*. 1.23 and 24). Then we move to *Leg*. 1.28, where the ideal ἀντίδοσις is foreshadowed; and next to *Leg*. 1.31, where the notion of "dispersion" prepares us for that of the multiple and where, therefore, we approach the movement from the Idea to the empirical universe. In

[13]Man was created "in the image of the Image." This expression of a mirror of a mirror (Gen 1:27) shows clearly for Philo what the allegorist can deduce from the rhythm and repetition of sentences. The result is a double authorization to find within Genesis 1 and 2 a series of levels or boxes within boxes, reminiscent of the Russian toy doll.

Leg. 1.32 Philo notes that this is still a movement *in fieri*, one not yet completed, which thus accommodates a new stage, as if Philo wanted both to account for all the repetitions in the Bible and to delineate carefully the different levels of reality. *Leg*. 1.31 is completed by *Leg*. 1.53; in it, with the appearance of empirical man, a first duality appears. We have thus followed the descent from "Man" to "man," meaning corruptible man. A complication should be noted here. In *Leg*. 1.43, Philo encountered the biblical phrase concerning the garden of Eden with its trees; and a second biblical passage refers to trees again. Philo interprets the first biblical text as a position of ideal Wisdom, and the second text as the passage toward "specific virtues," empirical and partaking of plurality (*Leg*. 1.43 is further developed in *Leg*. 1.56-62). In these pages, Philo establishes a double line of "entropy": that of humanity and that of divine providence. To "Man" corresponds "Wisdom"; and to "man" correspond the virtues, which are multiple but still participate in the divine, mercifully providing a way for man to climb back up. Empirical man needs to be helped, for multiplicity and participation immediately connote evil for Philo — even before the test, so to speak, which we call "the fall." Why? Because Philo does not speculate as a geneticist or as a paleontologist, even a religious one. His point of departure is real man, alive, and he sees in the biblical story of creation a sort of spectral analysis; he sees in the sequential narrative simultaneously judgment and hope. Thus, in *Leg*. 1.34-35 and 45-47, moral considerations are already present.[14] Most importantly, this is the source of Philo's very great care to affirm the nobility of the empirical state; if "Man" enjoys "Wisdom," "man" is the beneficiary of "all trees" (*Leg*. 1.56); and it is this quality of completeness, this "all," even if it is distributed among a number of virtues, which interests Philo.

It interests him so much that the entire conclusion of *Leg. 1*, while discussing the biblical text which speaks of the Four Rivers (*Leg*. 1.63-87) or the commandment about Adam's food (*Leg*. 1.89-108), proposes a moral tableau that is marvelous, happy, positive, where everything fits together, is complementary and forms a totality and redemption; thus *Leg*. 1.85 suggests that, if the description of the Rivers is to be read symbolically, it should be seen as a ἐπανόρθωσις and not as a simple

[14]At a biblical society meeting I tried to investigate the dialectic of *Leg*. 1.60-62. Philo is more interested in the end of the world than in its origin. See Cazeaux 1987*b*, 350-353. This "entropy" is, finally, positive, instead of being a dwindling away: the End draws everything towards it, including the exegesis. As a result, there is a very vigorous movement in the *Legum Allegoriae* — a dynamism lacking in the *Quaestiones*.

moral description. And, simply from the point of view of the general arrangement, which is our interest here, one must observe the admirable composition of *Leg*. 1.63-87 which speaks about these Rivers. *Leg*. 1.65 explains the origin of the Four Rivers in relationship to the unified Logos. *Leg*. 1.66-72 proposes a first allegory: *Leg*. 1.66-69 interprets the first three Rivers; *Leg*. 1.70-71 presents a synthesis, and *Leg*. 1.72-73 crowns them with the fourth river, the Euphrates, a reflection of perfection and, thus, an echo of the First Logos. A second allegory dealing with the same things appears in *Leg*. 1.74-87: here we find new etymologies, new readings, and especially the massive introduction of the history of Israel and different biblical quotations. Let us note that only the first River of Eden, the Pishon, is mentioned here, but that it makes possible a dazzling synthesis in which Isaac, the true cultus, and final humility (end of *Leg*. 1.84), which delivers from fatal pride, take on the sonorous names of Moses, Judah and Issachar, along with the sacerdotal vestment. Worship is the end of man, and, once more, redemption is assured. Finally, *Leg*. 1.85-87 again regroups the Four Rivers seen as the four cardinal Virtues under the gaze, immobile and banal as a result of its sublimity, of Justice — the Euphrates. . . .

This simple summary suffices. Of little importance is the fact that the Four Rivers differ in order and meaning in *QG* 1.12-13. It is the construction of *Leg*. 1.63-87 which makes the true difference. A governing idea exists in the *Legum Allegoriae* which takes upon itself and even transfigures the sequence of the words of Genesis, so that the caesurae at the end of phrases become simple respiration points, rhythmically breaking up a single discourse. The "entropy" itself, which from the beginning is seen to control the exegesis, has not continued to descend or be static. The ending provided by Israel or the High Priest is such that, even if the "matter" of Creation has become less elevated and diminished, its divine "form" remains and redeems.

In the same way, in the "coda" of *Leg*. 1 (88-108), Philo is careful to present an integrated commentary on the biblical verses about the commandment or the prohibition dealing with the trees of Eden. Anticipating twice, first the passage in which Adam names the animals (*Leg*. 1.91), and then the tragic ending of the test (*Leg*. 1.105), Philo gives us an overview, which is a first synthesis. Next, he extends the commandment, or the divine prohibition, to the Law, giving the example of the hinge-commandment on the subject of the respect due to "father and mother" (*Leg*. 1.99). Here can be sensed an exegesis which is reminiscent of that of *Her*. 167-173, on the happy asymmetry of the

Decalogue.[15] For the Jew, it is therefore the Torah which closes this first collection of interpretations, after the discussion of the cultus in *Leg.* 1.63-87. The synthesis around these two figures at the end, the turning away from the mystery of the Beginning, the emphatic appearance of the Israel of God — all this allows Philo to stress the interrelatedness of "philosophy," which seems to dominate the first part of the book, and true "theology," which is to say the example of the Patriarchs and the history of Israel. Even without entering into an examination of the secondary "chapters" and the "dialectics" of *Leg.* 1, we can clearly see the many differences between it and the literary genre of the *QG*. Such differences render any possible connections so equivocal that they are useless. Instead of "entropy" unifying the whole, it is, when all is said and done, the powerful Idea of Israel "in the image of the Image" which controls the redaction of *Leg.* 1.

B. *The Beginning of* Leg. 1

It would be too easy, in fact, to take the last "chapters" of *Leg.* 1 and contrast them with the corresponding portions of *QG*. The opening section of *Legum Allegoriae*, on the other hand, could at first glance appear to be related to *QG*. The more "philosophical" aspect, Philo's care to indicate the cascading effect of entities and of biblical phrases, the more rapid succession of these phrases and their interpretations, the almost complete absence of exterior reference, all these things form a sort of presumption of similarity. In fact, *QG* 1 begins with Gen 2:4, "This is the book of the coming into being of heaven and earth, when they were created," which corresponds to *Leg.* 1.19. It is curious that the commentary given by *Leg.* 1.19 is almost as brief as *QG* 1.1, since all the other exegeses of the Treatise are much more developed than those of the *QG*.

QG 1.1 and *Leg.* 1.19 look alike and are different. Both allegories are rapid and emphasize that divine action has nothing to do with time; this is the source of their resemblance. But *QG* 1.1 seems to consider the term "book" to mean the Bible itself, that is, the story of the creation; while *Leg.* 1.19 interprets it as "Logos," a quite important difference — not only because Logos is more imposing, but especially because in this way Philo shows that it dominates the exegetical pattern of a creation moving from the Idea to the empirical. *QG* 1.1 remains static, limited to

[15]See Cazeaux 1983, 279-81.

a sort of summary "catechism,"[16] whereas *Leg*. 1.19-20 forces us to master a whole larger than itself.

Leg. 1.19-20 is connected to what comes before and what comes after. Thus, *Leg*. 1.19 contains the expression "This perfect Logos which possesses a movement conforming to the Hebdomad. . . ." Through the use of this word "Hebdomad" the phrase of Gen 2:4 is closely attached to the first account of creation, and in particular to vv.1-3 which immediately precede it, and at the same time to *Leg*. 1.8-18, which deals with the Hebdomad.

In the same way, *Leg*. 1.19, which discovers the Logos in the expression "book," cannot be isolated from *Leg*. 1.21, which recalls this interpretation and then suggests a new one, Logos being also the meaning of "Day." Since this Day is "of great light and great brightness" (same *Leg*. 1.21), we are also obliged to recall *Leg*. 1.18, in which Philo emphasized the "light" of the Seventh Day.[17] Thus, *Leg*. 1.19-20 is woven into a continuous cloth. And that is not all.

In *Leg*. 1.19, Philo reexamines the expression "the Heaven and the earth," which had already shown up in *Leg*. 1 and in v. 1. Here, as before, he interprets Heaven as the world of Ideas and earth as the world of the senses. In this way, he creates an *inclusio* from *Leg*. 1.1 to *Leg*. 1.19-20. A coherent "chapter" is thus created, filled with allegories which interpret successively the values of the "Six" (*Leg*. 1.3-5), and then of the "Seven" (*Leg*. 1.8-18). To indicate the unity of the "chapter" even more clearly, Philo has placed, at the beginning and at the end, an identical reflection on how blasphemous it would be to assign a "time" to Creation (*Leg*. 1.2 and 20).

Finally, Philo's literary conscience goes even further. This introduction to the *Legum Allegoriae* in effect announces what we have been able to read into it above. Through his commentary on the Hebdomad Philo clearly indicates the kind of redemption which brings into harmony Heaven and earth, the Idea and the empirical world — since the astral world, the human body, the arts, and all the realm of the

---

[16]I have chosen this expression deliberately because I will use it later in a definition of the *Quaestiones*.

[17]Probably Philo connects the Seventh Day or Sabbath to the First Day, when the light shines brilliantly. The Logos is the heir of both Days (see *Leg* 1.15). The organization of *Leg* 1.1-20 is seen even more clearly, since *QG* 1 begins exactly where this organization leads . . . . We do not possess the anterior Questions, but I am not therefore proceeding by an *a silentio* argument: Question 1 is not at all tied to the Questions that follow it — like them it is isolated and impoverished.

senses participate happily in the "Seven" and, precisely, draw divine light from them (*Leg*. 1.9a, for the clear statement, and *Leg*. 1.8-18, for its development). Such is the program of Book 1.

Compared to that, although the *QG* make use of arithmology (to which the longer Questions owe much), we will read in them nothing which imitates, announces or summarizes the rhetorical organization of the *Legum Allegoriae*, even if one were to assume that the same concepts and exegetical procedures (arithmology, the box-within-a-box conception of reality, division, etc.) were present in both of them, which in fact is not the case.

A Note on the Parallelism of Notions in QG 1.1-16 *and* Leg. 1-3

Such parallels are rare. If we consider the details of the interpretation, the following Questions have some similarities to *Leg*. 1-3.

QG 1.1, 2 (which can also be found to resemble *Opif*. 129-130), 5, 6 (see similarities also in the *Opif*. 154), 15,16,19,20 (with notable divergences), 25 (in part), 45 (the whole text), 48 (in the middle), 49 (the end), 50 (the end), and 51.

The parallel between Question 51 and *Leg*. 3.251-253 is notable on two counts: first of all, the two texts are really quite close to each other; secondly, it should be pointed out that we are dealing with the last page of the *Legum Allegoriae*. Now, it has occurred to me that the most elaborate of the Questions in *QG* 1 correspond to the end or to the beginning of one of the Treatises which comment on the same passages of Genesis. This phenomenon, if it could be proven, could be of use to historians of Philo. It would bear upon the way the Philonic exegeses are "cut up," before the redaction of the *Legum Allegoriae* — *De Cherubim* — *De Sacrificiis*, etc., as well as upon the *QG* themselves. I have said "before," but I mean from a logical point of view, as though Philo were influenced by the existence of "series," liturgical or others. These more elaborate questions are farther on: they are *QG* 1.42, 54, 60, 76, and 78.

Most of the time, therefore, the Questions are noticeably different from the interpretations found in the Treatises. Here I am only speaking of "notions," leaving aside the never-resolved puzzles of the method of exegesis, of discourse, and of organization in these Questions. The most curious case, since it is a matter of well-organized interpretations, is that of the Four Rivers of Eden (*QG* 1.12-13, seen beside *Leg*. 1.63-84 !).

Let us add that when Questions 26 and 28-29 speak of Eve, they are more "feminist" than *Leg.* 1.40-52.

Finally, may I be permitted once again to underline the fact that it is not the similarity or difference of "concepts," of philosophy, of psychology, or of interpretations, which permit a true comparison of the two series of interpretations, and that it is even less true to say that the Treatises[18] belong to the same literary genre.

C. *The Remainder of the* Legum Allegoriae *and the "Chapter" of* Leg. 3.75-104 *Compared with* QG 1.47-48

(1) Leg. *2*

This passage begins with Gen 2:18, that is, directly following *Leg.* 1, which ends with the commentary on Gen 2:17. It is divided almost exactly[19] in two parts: the first (*Leg.* 2.1-52) is characterized by the more "philosophical" aspect of the exegesis, stressing psychology and moral considerations, and by a larger quantity of interpreted biblical text (Gen 2:18-24, occasionally with a very rapid cadence); the second (*Leg.* 2.53-108), on the other hand, is centered on two single words in succession: "nudity" (*Leg.* 2.53-70) and "serpent" (*Leg.* 2.71-108). It is remarkable that, starting with *Leg.* 2 and 3, the *De Cherubim* and the other Treatises up to the *De Posteritate Caini* (to speak only of those Treatises which parallel *QG* 1) all set up their commentaries according to this system, centering on and working at length with one word or with one biblical phrase. Simply from a "quantitative" view of the exegesis, the *Legum Allegoriae* gets heavier as it moves from Book 1 to Book 3. This density begins in the middle of Book 2, but we should not forget that Book 3 is about as full, by itself, as Books 1 and 2 together. This system is compatible with that of Book 1, which moves, as we have said, from "philosophy" toward a reflection, in increasing depth, on the history of Israel. Note that the second part of *Leg.* 2 is also characterized by this emphasis on the history of Israel and by appeals to other inspired texts. The notions of "nudity" and "the serpent" provide an opportunity each time to oppose the two figures of an antithetical

[18]One could not say, e.g., that *QG* 1.32-42 take the place of the commentary (on the temptation and fall of the first man and woman) that is missing between Books 2 and 3 of *Legum Allegoriae*.

[19]The first part contains 360 lines; the second, 412.

couple: good nudity versus bad[20] and maleficent serpent versus the serpent of benediction. There exists a chiasmus, according to the indications of goodness or evil. Thus we end with the serpent of Dan and its positive interpretation; and redemption, already set forth in Book 1, as we have suggested, returns once again to rescue us from the anguish that "passion" and "sensation" might provoke in us.

The first part of *Leg.* 2 is more complex, and its dialectic is more subtle than that of the second part. This is not the place to demonstrate the coherence of *Leg.* 2.1-52. We will limit ourselves to pointing out a few guiding threads. First of all, the "entropy" of Book 1 continues its effects, but it is discussed more discretely (e.g., *Leg.* 2.13 and 22). Next, and as a consequence of this ontological descent, we see that Philo is constantly preoccupied with the relationship between "act" and "potentiality"[21] (note the real linking of *Leg.* 2.19-23, 37-38a, and 40-43). This philosophical device leads up to a conclusion, one which takes those unfamiliar with Philo by surprise; we come to a halt on the danger resulting from the illusion which spirit itself and sensibility, its companion, sustain in supposing they have power to act independently of God. This blasphemy, which, as Philo often reminds us, is the most terrible one of all,[22] will have as its exact antidote, counterpart or redemption, the paradoxical exegesis of the serpent of Dan, at the end of the second part of *Leg.* 2. In this way the first part concludes with a glimpse of a crime (already avoided, moreover, by both Leah and Levi respectively, *Leg.* 2.47-48, and 51-52), before the second part develops more fully the theme of risk or rather of decision, which defines Book 2 conjointly with "help" and redemption, which was already the spiritual framework of *Leg.* 1. But, to be sure, the global coherence of *Leg.* 2 and the interconnections it has with Books 1 and 3 are to be seen in the details. For example, one could[23] analyze closely the discussion of "nudity" (*Leg.* 2.53-64); one could clarify Philo's conscious rhetoric, the passage from "three" to "two" nudities, their evident opposition, the paradoxes which guide, in both cases, the unwinding of the commentary (thus, Nadab and Abihu are both naked and enveloped in their own clothes, as if it were necessary to hide their nudity, which is about the

[20]An artifice allows Philo to distinguish three types of nudity but, finally, to set in opposition only two, the good and the bad. Thus the system of "pairs," which he will use extensively, is introduced.

[21]Which explains the strange references to "natural orders" in *Leg.* 2.22-23.

[22]See, e.g., *Cher.* 57-130 (esp. 57-64).

[23]See Cazeaux 1983, 585-591.

same as to suppress it). One could also show the intermediary role of *Leg.* 2.65-70 between nudity and serpent and at least point out that the ultimate blasphemy is here once again precisely evoked (*Leg.* 2.68b); it is a stage between the turning away of spirit and sensibility from their illusion (*Leg.* 2.46-48) on one hand, and, on the other, the healthy humility of the horseman of Dan, discussed at the end of Book 2 (*Leg.* 2.97-105).

Let us repeat our constant refrain: one will not find the smallest hint of a similar intention in *QG* 1.17-42. The point of contact appears in Question 25, in the middle, where "side" is translated as "strength," exactly as in *Leg.* 2.21; but, in essential contrast to this passage of the Treatise, Question 25 continues with the literal and banal idea of the comparative strengths of the man and the woman; and nothing really shows through afterward of the difficult cohabitation of "act" and "potentiality." The interpretation of the verb in "He built (her) in the form of a woman" could continue the similarity in detail, but it does not; *QG* 1.26 celebrates the useful role of a woman as manager of the household, whereas *Leg.* 2.38-39 insists logically on the woman's submission and passivity, in conformity with her nature as "potentiality." The decisive interpretation of Adam's verbal recognition of his wife, "bone of his bones . . . he called her woman," is totally different in *QG* 1.28 and *Leg.* 2.40-48, which contains an intentional orientation toward temptation, danger, and choice.[24] Thus, whether the details are alike or profoundly different, the result is the same; the Questions remain locked into themselves, "poor" in the sense that they have no movement and form no constellation. The complexity itself of *Leg.* 2, even in *Leg.* 2.53-108, its most simple part (I have not had the time to speak here about the "dialectics" of which it is composed), gives the reader the idea of an art, of a deliberate science of discourse — unless the reader opts

[24]In these pages I have proposed a rapid reading of *Leg.* 2, as I have already done for Book 1. I will not pursue the demonstration, but the reader can perceive there is an organization, a dominating idea, an intention. I do not really care whether or not the concepts or even the rather defined vision which I propose here is established or not; a different dialectic (recognized by a reader who sees the movement better than I do) would still bring us to the same sure conclusion: that intention is lacking in the *Quaestiones*. As in a theater, the scenery can be the same, totally or in part; the play changes. What is there to say if it is almost wholly redone? From my viewpoint, to which I stubbornly cling in all my readings of Philo, what matters is the play.

for the easy and simplistic representation of Philo as a delirious, word-crazy preacher.[25]

(2) Leg. *3*

Even before talking about the construction of Book 3 or discussing the "chapter" on divine liberty (*Leg.* 3.75-106), I would like to show the radical difference which separates a Treatise from the *Quaestiones*, using a precise and "remarkable" example, as they say in geometry. It is one of those Philonic "places" par excellence. The "place" (the pun already exists in Philo!): God asks Adam, "Where are you?" *QG* 1.45 gives two interpretations, of which the second is the more profound: one should understand the phrase as an exclamation — "Where has your sin put you, unhappy man?" It seems that, when he addresses Adam, God also includes man's capacities and therefore also sense-perception, symbolized by woman. In a rare and notable coincidence, the two arguments of *QG* 1.45 are also found in *Leg.* 3.49-50 and afterwards in 52 (in reverse order and separated by a new interpretation — *Leg.* 3.51). It should be pointed out that the *Legum Allegoriae* adds a reference here at the beginning of the allegory to the "change" (τροπή) which man undergoes and will undergo in the future. This theme of change is, as we have said,[26] one of the points of equilibrium of *Leg.* 2. And therefore, in spite of the material similarity of *QG* 1.45 to the Treatise, we immediately see that only in the Treatise does Philo control, remember, and organize his material. On the other hand, the allegories of "place" in *Leg.* 3.49-55 progress in such a way that they ascend, concluding with the notion of *exile*, which is connected to the idea that God is everywhere. This is the very same thing we see in *Leg.* 3.1-11, as Philo himself expressly points out (*Leg.* 3.54b). The subtlety of Philonic rhetoric often makes it extremely hard to uncover his methods and techniques completely, but all these clues should remind Philonists to be humble: *there is* coherence — a movement *does* exist. Attempts to

[25]Let us note an element of equilibrium in the whole of *Leg.* 2: God is presented here, at the beginning, as the Unique One; further on human beings are presented as choosers and, therefore, in contrast to God, variable, subject to τροπαί. This theme of changeability is treated twice in *Legum Allegoriae*, first in 2.31-34 and then in 2.83-87 — two passages which are about equidistant, one from the beginning, the other from the end of the book. We also note the middle position of 2.88-93, comparing the serpent-rod in the hand of Moses with the serpents of Eve and Dan.

[26]See the preceding footnote.

describe Philo's methods may vary, be reworked, or even fail, but the art remains, the artist remains, and the unity remains — hidden as are the truth and unity of the Sacred Book that the allegory is designed to reveal.

(a) *A Brief Overview of* Leg. *3*

Book 3 of the *Legum Allegoriae* is clearly much more intricate than the first two Books. It is almost as long as both of them together. It takes as its text the three punishments inflicted by God — on the serpent, the woman, and the man. The text concerning the serpent takes up the most space (*Leg.* 3.65-199), and the beginning (*Leg.* 3.1-64) is only just a little longer than the end (*Leg.* 3.200-253). The unity of Book 3 is indicated by a double *inclusio*: the "midwives" of *Leg.* 3.2-3 return in *Leg.* 3.243, and the theme of "flight" considered as a moral attitude inferior to resistance (*Leg.* 3.14-15) also returns at the end (*Leg.* 3.242).

Let us look at the central part, concerning the serpent-pleasure (*Leg.* 3.65-199). It also is divided into two sections. *Leg.* 3.65-106 forms a dialectic of seven examples of positive "predestination." I shall return to this point. Philo here discusses the curses that strike the serpent, but in a *formal* way: why does God punish without first listening to the guilty one? *Leg.* 3.107-199 discusses the curses of the serpent as regards *content*, with a careful study of each word. One could say that these two sections illustrate the two major types of allegory in the Treatises. The first constructs a figure of enlarged *chiasmus*; the second develops a sort of *tree*, as I will clarify later on.

On the other hand, it should be noted that Philo transforms the theme of the curse into contrary developments: instead of showing misfortune, he exploits the good side of things each time; and the serpent is forgotten, overshadowed by the wise men who gained mastery over pleasure. Moreover, each wise man is followed by a greater wise man, as for example *Aaron* is succeeded by *Moses*, and *the Hebrews* (nourished with the Manna-Logos) are succeeded by *Jacob* (nourished by God Himself). This is what I mean when I speak of a *tree:* a sort of sketch outlines itself in the reader's imagination, in which a branch divides and climbs even higher. Finally, let us point out that this system of development by *a fortiori*, which fills *Leg.* 3.118-199, had begun in *Leg.* 3.88, that is, in the second half of the "dialectic" of *Leg.* 3.65-106, which has the effect of giving an additional unity to the entire exegesis of

Book 3. Finally,[27] let us note the reference point role that philosophical reflection plays in this Book. By philosophical reflection I mean the reference to a psychological framework established long before: the creation of man and then woman, without overlooking the creation of the animals, shows the necessity of the difficult interplay in human beings between intellect and sensibility. Note that exegesis is much more important in Book 3 than is explicit philosophy (if one may be permitted to advance such a formula, which has no definitive sense, given the extent to which Philo joins descriptive psychology and moral guidance drawn from the Bible. . .). But if we do not count the conclusion (*Leg.* 3.246-253), which translates directly and in anthropological terms the last words of God to Adam on the subject of thorns, grasses, and the return to the dust of the earth, there are three rather long passages where the exegete leaves the biblical figures in order to discuss once again the psychological schema of intellect helped or ruined by sensibility. Note that these three passages (*Leg.* 3.56-64; 107-113, and 182-189) are all about the same length and, especially, that they frame the two major developments of Book 3: the first introduces the "dialectic" of *Leg.* 3.65-106; the second inaugurates the detailed exegesis of the curses, or rather separates it from the preceding section;[28] the third brings the work to an end.[29]

This rapid review of Book 3 should suffice to convince the reader that Philo has left nothing to chance and, at the same time, to make clear that it is not possible to follow the linking of the simple Questions in the *Legum Allegoriae*. Here, in a somewhat rapid fashion, in a sort of photographic *zoom*, is the dialectical sequence of the characters whom God chose before their merits.

---

[27]I cannot enter into detail here about the repetition of words and themes which assure the cohesion of Book 3 or of the unity of Books 1, 2, and 3. Let us remember that Book 1 begins with the significantly-related numbers 6 and 7 and that Book 2 begins with a meditation on the One.

[28]If one looks more closely, in effect, one sees that *Leg.*3.107-117, which begins the detailed reading bearing on the content of the curses inflicted on the serpent, nevertheless stays on the level of psychological generalities, in such a way that the true development by exegesis only begins with *Leg.* 3.118. This detail would be of some importance, if I could take time to analyze Book 3 here.

[29]Note the *inclusio:* pleasure is an "enemy of the senses themselves," says *Leg.* 3.111; and this idea is repeated in *Leg.* 3.182, the beginning of the last curse.

(b) *The Dialectic of* Leg. *3.65-106*

The serpent is condemned in advance and without being heard. Philo will show that, for better or worse, in both senses, God is evidently free and sovereign. This thesis will be proven in *Leg.* 3.75-106, using a series of patriarchal figures: Noah, Melchizedek, Abraham, Isaac, Jacob, Ephraim and Moses after Bezalel. I had to "complicate" the last example, Moses-Bezalel, because the development occupies a much larger space (*Leg.* 3.95-103) and because it is shaped by a sustained comparison between the "shadow" which belongs to Bezalel and the perfection which surrounds Moses; but I could have already "complicated" the presentation of Jacob and of Ephraim, because they also are examples of *couples* of oppositions, whereas Noah, Melchizedek and Abraham, and also Isaac are presented alone by themselves. That is a device, a movement[30] which is easily observed and, as such, exemplary. Philo's intention is not to line up "proofs" by accumulation, but, using these living proofs, to reveal a movement — within the soul, but here above all in God. . . . Let us state immediately that the center is immobile perfection: Isaac is clearly the example-figure of it (*Leg.* 3.85-87). Around him, six units are distributed, three on either side: three individuals (Noah, Melchizedek and Abraham) and three pairs (Jacob over against Esau, Ephraim preferred to Manasseh as memory is to simple recall, and Moses collaborating with Bezalel and bringing the divine shadow (that is to say, Bezalel) to divine perfection (Moses himself). One can see that the "pairs" differ variously: Esau is evil; Manasseh is subordinate; Bezalel already introduces us into divine regions, and for that reason the pair Moses-Bezalel is not presented in the same way as the two others, which are presented in a straightforward manner: "(The Bible) says that Jacob and Esau . . ."(*Leg.* 3.88) and "Joseph had his two sons approach — the elder, Manasseh, and the younger, Ephraim . . ." (*Leg.* 3.90). In contrast, Bezalel is described first and then the comparison with Moses comes to light. Also, they are not brothers like the others. Finally, their relationship rises into new mystical heights. This system does not exclude other relationships. Thus, the fundamental Triad of Abraham, Isaac, and Jacob continues to stand *in the middle* of this constellation. On the other hand, there is chiasmus or symmetry among the six models surrounding the immobile Isaac. It is in regard to the first *and* the last,

[30]Certain scholars are looking for the "movement" in Philo. Here is a sample. . . .

that is, Noah and then Bezalel-Moses, that Philo speaks of the recognition of God as "Principle, Cause"; it is with reference to Melchizedek *and* Ephraim that he speaks of "elevation," (ὕψιστος, in *Leg*. 3.82, and ὑψωθήσεται, in *Leg*. 3.90). In both cases, Philo notes their value in relationship to the *cultus*, priesthood for the one, sacrifice for the other (it is through a quite "arbitrary" exegesis that *Leg*. 3.94 passes from Ephraim to the story of Numbers 9!). Last of all, Abraham and Jacob have in common the political theme of "liberty": Abraham is promised a Πόλις, Jacob rules over the "slave" Esau. Thus, there is not only expansion and ascent from Noah to Moses (the whole under the "supervision" of the presence of eternity, represented by Isaac, in the center), but there is a response from one series to the another. In this way, the interpretation offers us a unified world.[31]

But where is all this leading? Towards a conversion in God. In effect, this complicated device was introduced by the idea that God made all things, "good and bad natures" (*Leg*. 3.75-76). But, in the process of ascending toward Moses and of considering his access to "God," in the precise sense Philo uses (that is, in terms of knowing the First Power, that of Creation and Providence, of "Goodness" [already, when speaking of Noah, the subject of the first portrait in the gallery, whose picture hangs directly opposite that of Moses — *Leg*. 3.78b]) — as a result of this ascent we see that only Providence remains, dispensing "good" only. The reserve of evils is found to be shut — "sealed." Such is the extraordinary implication of *Leg*. 3.104-106, which, in the form of a prayer, brings the contemplation of Moses to an end. In God there is a sort of movement: the righteous person must come to understand that the two Powers, Creative Goodness and Lordship, are finally resolved into just one, Goodness. As a counterweight to the "entropy" which draws the creature down (*Leg*. 1), an opposite movement is seen here — a movement within God, or rather in the sage's perception of God.

Note that right before the prayer of §§105-107, §104 repeats the theoretical formula of §75 on the subject of the "two natures, placed in the becoming, fashioned and turned on the lathe by God. . . ." This is done so that the ultimate anagoge of the prayer (with the prayer of Moses in the background, behind Philo's prayer) marks the fulfillment, but as a free gift and not as the obligatory expression of Wisdom, even the wisdom of a Moses. This reflex of Philo's theology is normative in his

[31] I have not mentioned a number of other connections, both within and outside the seven biblical figures.

work: the "End" is given, in no sense won. In contrast to Pandora and the Zeus of the *Il.* 24.527, the God of Philo decides to close the reserve of evils.

(c) *A Double Return to the* Quaestiones...

Although I have made this detour through the *Legum Allegoriae*, it is not my intent to speak of its contents. But the "simplicity" of the *Quaestiones* cannot really stand out unless the complexity of the Treatises themselves is verified, and verified in more depth than general references could afford. Philo's extreme attention to detail in the Treatises is an indicator of the great distance between the two literary genres. It happens that this "chapter" which I have singled out in *Leg.* 3 provides us with an interesting little item to investigate — with a touch of humor of my own.

In a passage devoted to Jacob at the end of *Leg.* 3.89 we find a phrase which, for once, seems to me to contain a corruption:

> For it is according to nature that in the eyes of God the one who is base and unreasonable is a slave, while the one who is honest, reasonable and good will have authority and liberty — and that without waiting for both to be full-grown in soul, but even in a state of indecision. For it is with one appearance that a simple breath of virtue manifests power and sovereignty, above even liberty, and it is, on the other hand, the first manifestation (γένεσις) of wickedness which enslaves the reasoning faculty, even if the offspring has not yet fully developed.

In my opinion, it is particularly in the final section that corruption of the text has set in. One should read δουλεύει, "is the slave of," instead of δουλοῖ, "makes a slave of, enslaves." The parallelism of the phrase which has unfolded to this point makes clear that what is being discussed are *the two sides* of a natural hierarchy, respected by nature *from the outset*: Good is, from the outset, a master; evil, a slave. The word for reciprocity, ἔμπαλιν, was probably understood very early as announcing an inversion of roles, when instead it indicates a complementarity of the system in relationship to time. But, in addition to the parallelism of the phrase taken as a unit and the ordinary theory of Philo, one of the *Quaestiones in Genesim* (4.157), on the same text of Genesis 25:23 — Rebecca receiving the oracle concerning her twins — can confirm for us that the end of *Leg.* 3.89 has undergone some textual damage. Here is this Question-Answer in its entirety:

What does it mean: "To her who asked, (the Lord) said: "Two nations are in your womb and two peoples (issued) from your womb will separate and one people will clearly surpass one people and the elder will serve the younger"? (Genesis 25:23).

This statement makes four things known. The first, which is the most astonishing: He did not say that two children were in the womb, but instead of children he said nations. And it is clear that he is alluding not to their names but to the nations which were to come into being from each of them, for they were to appear later as the ancestors of very great nations.

And the second thing, the most useful and helpful: There will be no mixing, but separation between the two peoples issued from them (separation between peoples on the level of appearances, but in reality separation between prudence and imprudence). For the same reason, having previously mentioned nations, at the end, he speaks of peoples, so named as an indication of reason and intellect. And the separation of opposed concepts is very useful, since one of them desires wickedness and the other, virtue.

And the third thing, the most just: It is that equals should not be mixed with and ranked with those who are not their equals. From whence he has very well said, "one people will clearly surpass one people." For, necessarily, among these two, one will surpass and increase, and the other will become lower and decrease. And "will clearly surpass" in its turn (is to be understood) thus: the good man (shall surpass) the bad, and the righteous the unrighteous; he who is humble and temperate (will surpass) the intemperate. For one of them is heavenly and worthy of the divine light, and the other is connected to the earth and corruptible and is like shadows.

And the fourth thing, the most true: that "the elder will serve the younger." For evil is older in time, since from our earliest age, it has grown with us, while the youngest is virtue, which is barely acquired by us at the last and belatedly, when the numerous excesses of the passions have already tightened and relaxed their intensity. For it is then that the intellect begins to judge and discriminate and to obtain sovereign rule. And these things are said to us, for who does not know that heaven has no share or mixture or part of evil? And the same is true of all the sense-perceptible gods who turn around it, for all of them are good and the most perfect of all in virtue. But in this world, prudence (and) wisdom are older than imprudence and folly, and justice is older than injustice and than each of the other opposite dispositions. In the human race, however, it is the opposite. For this good, as I have said, is born last and is the youngest; but its opposite, imprudence, has been established in us almost from childhood and grows up with us. Nevertheless, the youngest, by the laws of nature, is ruler over the elder.

Only the fourth point interests us for the moment. In it, we see very clearly that, though appearing first in time, evil is subordinate to good in an absolute sense, and the notion of "slavery" only appears in that absolute ranking. And[32] it is that sense which *Leg.* 3.89 should retain.

[32]Although the other allusions to Gen 25:23 do not develop it, they imply the same doctrine, which is often expressed in Philo's works (*Sacr.* 4, 42; *Congr.* 129).

We can therefore reconstitute the conclusion: "For it is with one appearance that a simple breath of virtue manifests power and sovereignty, above even liberty, and it is, reciprocally, the first manifestation of wickedness which *is the slave of* the reasoning faculty, even if its offspring (of evil) has not yet fully developed."

But let us not be ungrateful to *QG* 4.157. Whatever we may make of its value as a cross-reference, it is interesting in and of itself. In effect, it is one of the most organized of the Questions. It is not yet dialectical, but the sequence of its four interpretations suggests a ranking by stages: the first is directed by "astonishment"; the second evolves in the order of the "useful"; the third is related to "justice," since each of the two parties, the good and the bad, receives appropriate treatment; the fourth, finally, advances to "truth." That, of course, is probably a progression of the Platonic type. But there remains an aspect which is interesting to consider: each of the four interpretations studies one of the phrases of the lemma of Gen 25:23. And therefore the ascending order of the indices — astonishment, utility, justice and truth — is imposed by the progress of the biblical text itself. The Bible contains in its phrasing a movement, a pedagogy, an anagoge; and the arrangement of the answer conveys that effect. We have there, it would seem, a very inventive awareness of the inner character of the relationship between text and exegesis. One will also note that the four successive interpretations are linked together well: in the first, "children" is simply translated as "nations"; in the second, Philo interprets the textual shift from "nations" to "peoples" and notes the difference between these terms; in the third, we see that this "difference" leads to the idea of "domination" by one of the two parties. Without saying that the younger will rule, Philo now introduces a distinction between the heavenly origin of one and the earthly origin of the other. Finally, the fourth interpretation builds on the notion of the celestial origin of virtue to demonstrate the paradoxical superiority of the younger over the elder.[33]

Chance led us to consider *QG* 4.157, but it is practically unique in the whole corpus of the *Quaestiones*. Some other Questions allegorize the different words in a biblical phrase in succession, but without offering a similar linkage pattern. Examples include *QG* 2.11,12,16,42 (already more integrated); 3.1 (one of the more interesting in which to study the unity of the biblical text and the exegesis),10,27; and *QE* 2.7,13,33,68 (very elaborate, however). We find two Questions which

---

[33] Also see *QG* 3.55, etc.; 4.51, end. . . .

are somewhat close to the one we have examined: *QG* 3.57 on Ishmael, and *QG* 4.8 on the three measures of flour and the ash-cakes of which Abram speaks when Angels come to Mamre. But even there, it does not seem that Philo proceeds very clearly. The organization of all these Questions contrasts, moreover, with many others. This fact and the existence of questions which are already paradoxes or inchoate interpretations (perhaps one of the most deliberate being *QG* 4.140, "What are the meditations of Isaac, and why did he go out to meditate in the field toward daybreak and *why is the one with whom (he conversed) not revealed?*" — where the last question is dictated by the very beautiful unfolding of the answer) tend to make us think that the corpus of the *Quaestiones* is not fully homogeneous.[34]

(d) Leg. *3.65-106 and* Deus *104-110*

Finally, it is necessary to respond to an objection: one could in effect say that Philo in the *Quaestiones* is giving brief notes which do not allow time for a "dialectic," which is a complex movement, while, in the Treatises he suffers from no time constraints. It is true that the long discussion of *Leg.* 3.65-199 takes all the time it needs, while *QG* 1.48 treats the same biblical text on the cursing of the serpent in only a few lines. This disparity is obviously enormous. But it is really the literary genre and the intellectual orientation which are far apart. Actually, a given page of another Treatise may well, in an equally rapid manner, sketch a true "dialectic," about which one could say that it is the matrix or the condensation of the long pages of *Leg.* 3.65-106, which I have just analyzed above. Thus, for example, *Deus* 104-110.

The reader will remember that *Leg.* 3.65-106 takes the occasion of the cursing of the serpent to speak of the sovereign liberty of God: from Noah to Moses, Philo progresses along a ladder which follows both the historical order and the mystical order; we remember that this Moses, the highest rung in the ladder, is discussed using an *a fortiori* line of reasoning which situates him higher than all the others; we also remember that the patient maneuvering of Philo is intended to diminish the force, so to speak, of the Power of Lordship in order to give strength to the idea of a single Power, that of Creative Goodness. From Noah to Moses, from two Powers to the single concept Goodness — such is the

[34]This problem does not concern me directly in this article, which is devoted to comparing the linkages in the Questions with those in the Treatises.

"dialectic" which has been patiently organized and developed in a leisurely fashion.

Deus 104-110[35] does not take the story of the creation as a point of departure but instead uses the second point of origin, which is Noah. Note that Philo leads us from Noah to Moses and that he does it by means of a "dialectic." As is evident, this dialectic is handled within a short space and does not make the detour past all the biblical figures exhibited in *Leg*. 3.65-106. Instead, it takes the shortcut of a reflection on "merit," but it arrives at the same destination: the excellence of Moses makes him the contemporary of Goodness alone, which is to say of the Supreme Being himself.

First let us look at the text of *Deus* 104-110:

> 104. What is meant by the words: Noah found favor with the Lord God ? We must ask ourselves that question. Does that mean that he "obtained favor" or that "he was thought worthy of favor"? But this first interpretation seems improbable: for what more was accorded to him than was accorded to all creatures? All of them, both the complex and the simple and elementary, all have been judged worthy of favor.
>
> 105. The second expresses the idea better: the Cause has decreed worthy of good things those who have not defaced with base practices the divine coin they have within them which bears the stamp of God — their spirit, which is of sacred worth. And yet perhaps that explanation is still not the true one.
>
> 106. For how great must we suppose him to be whom God will judge worthy of favor? Hardly, I think, could the whole universe aspire to such favor, and yet the universe is the first, the greatest, and the most perfect of God's works.
>
> 107. It is better to accept this explanation: that if he is a being of investigation and of great knowledge, the man of worth is able, in all the areas of his investigation, to find this principle of the highest truth: that the favor of God is all things: earth, water, air, fire, sun, stars, heaven, and all animals and plants. But God has bestowed no gift of favor on Himself, for He does not need it, but He has given the favor of the world to the world, to its parts in themselves and among them all, the favor of the parts; and then the parts to the Whole.
>
> 108. It is not therefore because He has decreed them worthy of favor that He has liberally given good things to the Whole and to the parts. Looking to his eternal Goodness, He decided that to be beneficent was incumbent on His blessed and happy Nature. So that if anyone should ask me what motived the creation of the world, I will answer what Moses has taught, that it was the Goodness of the Existent, that Goodness which is the oldest of the Powers, which is the Source of favors.
>
> 109. But at the same time we must not forget that, if Noah was, according to the words (of the Bible), well pleasing to the Powers of the Existent, "to the Lord and to God" (Genesis 6:8), Moses was pleasing to Him whom the Powers

---

[35]Please see my reading of the Cycle of Noah in Cazeaux 1989.

attend, the One who is conceived by the mind as independent of them, in the mode of existence only (and not of essence). These words come from the Face of God: "You have found favor with Me" (Exodus 33:17) in which words He shows Himself as Him who has none other with Him.

110. It is thus that the Existent, the One, Himself alone, judges the superior wisdom of Moses as worthy of favor: the wisdom which reproduces its image is secondary, more specialized through the Powers, subjects (of the Being) where He is "Lord and God," ruler and bestower of good things.

Philo begins with a Question[36] which studies the synthetic locution "to find grace." Then he provides a series of three possible interpretations, three hypotheses, which progress in depth of meaning. The first implies that Noah benefits from a "special favor"(*Deus* 104); but Philo sets it aside in the name of the *universal* favor given the Creation. The second hypothesis is already more valid: through his virtue, Noah would have merited the favor of God if it were not true that God so surpasses the merit of any creature that even the Universe, first-born and so perfect, has no merit before Him (*Deus* 105-106). Finally, the third hypothesis comes: Philo breaks down the synthetic locution "to find grace" into this, an analytical form, "he found *that* all is grace." This third hypothesis is said to be "preferable." And, as a Philonic sign of its superiority, this hypothesis receives as much space as the first two hypotheses together (*Deus* 107-108). In addition, it gives birth to an unexpected elaboration. The name of Moses, pronounced at the end of *Deus* 108, indicated as the Scribe of God, is taken seriously: Noah received the favor of the Two Powers, since the Bible states clearly that he "found grace before the *Lord God*"; while Moses, on the other hand, found grace "before Me," a formula in which this divine 'Εγώ designates pure Being, above and beyond the Two Powers (*Deus* 109-110). We have arrived at perfection, but at the price of a distortion. Philo has proceeded in a paradoxical fashion: *Deus* 109-110 compares Noah to Moses, shifting suddenly again to the synthetic meaning of "to find

[36]Of the same type, textually, as all the Questions. Note that *Deus* 104-110 is the beginning of a greater grouping, *Deus* 104-121, and that, on the other hand, *Deus* 104-121 forms a second exegesis of the same words of Genesis 6:8, "Noah found grace before the Lord God." Finally, *QG* 1.96, which corresponds precisely to this biblical text, stays attached to the literal meaning and has no dialectical aspect in it. . . . It emphasizes that Noah has a first grace, *as do all men;* but Philo adds that Moses also has a *unique merit,* that of gratitude. Here one can sense the beginning of a resemblance to *Deus* 104, but at an extreme distance. One must understand that this gratitude consists, for Moses, in his confession that "all is grace," as the third hypothesis of *Deus* 107-108 will say. Everything happens as if *QG* 1.96 were in its turn bound to allegory by the *Quod Deus*!

grace." Note that in the first part of *Deus* 109, Philo tranquilly begins, "If Noah had the good will of the Powers. . . ." Instead of considering this to be a small contradiction, the reader of Philo should detect a signal here: the preceding hypotheses mark out a moral itinerary instead of proposing an exclusive and logically arranged theory. The first hypothesis denies that Noah had any special favor, but it is noted in order to give Philo a reason to return to the topic of the Universe, where "all natures, both the complex and the simple and elementary, all have been judged worthy of favor" (*Deus* 104). We will now stay with this anagogical consideration of the Universe in both the second and the third hypotheses. This third hypothesis, which is a bit difficult to understand at first, adds that there is no contradiction between special favor and universal favor. God has made all things, and it is the Universe which is a "favor," but a favor for whom? For God himself? God needs nothing. There remains only that this "favor" is said of parts of the Universe in relation to each other (*Deus* 107b). But this immanence of "favor" permits Noah to integrate himself into the Universe, to understand, we might say more abstractly, that Noah saves humanity as its new origin specifically *because he is willing to be* ***one single*** *being,* and because, although it might seem contradictory at first, the act of assimilating oneself into "banal" universality is the way to acquire the greatest individuality. If Philo had not brought up the idea of universal creation at the beginning, he could not thereafter explain how Noah saves *all* humanity. The negation heard in the first hypothesis (*Deus* 104) is therefore a "moment" of the dialectic, the time of self-rejection. The other hypotheses, which are also founded on a consideration of the Universe, correspond in reality to the moral journey of Abraham: Abraham who is led from Chaldean wisdom (pertaining to astronomy and cosmology) to the recognition of God as Cause of the World. Without naming Abraham, Philo keeps a constant eye on Abraham's journey. In this way, without Philo saying so directly, the story of Abraham replaces the long list of characters which led us in *Leg*. 3.65-106 from Noah to Moses, the same characters discussed here. In this passage of the *Quod Deus*, the same Moses here celebrates the sole cause of creation, the single Power of Goodness.[37] Such was the essential result of the dialectic of the *Leg*. 3.65-106.

---

[37]One will note that each time Philo intends to pronounce the formula on "God" recognized as the Cause of Creation, he makes use of a rhetorical safeguard (see *Opif*. 21; *Leg*. 3.78; *Deus* 108). Philo is conscious then of touching the "great mystery" — which does not mean, of course, that for Philo there is some mystery-bound Jewish

Let us add that Philo's literary procedure is similar from one Treatise to the next. *Deus* 109-110 asserts a parallel between Noah and Moses, as *Leg*. 3.100-103 asserts that of Bezalel and Moses. Note that the difference between Bezalel and Moses derives from the fact that Bezalel arrives at the image of God (in "shadow," as suggested by the etymology of his name) by a "reasoning" (*Leg*. 3.102a -- ἐξ ἐπιλογισμοῦ). What is this reasoning? It suffices to look back at *Leg*. 3.101 to see that Moses, in fact, asks God to go beyond reasoning, which is to say the consideration of the Universe, which is to say the contemplation of an Abraham starting from Chaldea — which is to say, also, the middle term which Noah uses to arrive, in *Deus* 104-108, at the recognition of the Cause.

The complex and immense "dialectic" of *Leg*. 3.65-106 is pre-contained in that of *Deus* 104-110. When I say "pre-contained," I am not suggesting a chronological priority of redaction, but, on the level of logical organization, a relationship of matrix to finished production. But there is some dialectic, by which I mean a proceeding by paradox and a mediation, in the two Treatises. There is no dialectic in the Questions, not even in the Questions where the expression "to find grace" appears (*QG* 1.82,85; 4.4). *It is therefore not a difference of dimensions, but of literary genre*. The Questions are never the first stages of a Treatise; the Treatises are never Questions that have been developed.

We have now arrived at *QG* 1.51, the point at which there is no longer concurrence with *Leg*. 1-3. After a "lacuna" in the Treatises, *QG* 1.57 brings us to the *De Cherubim*. We will now continue to *QG* 1.100, the last Question in Book 1, in the company of the Treatises which follow, up to and including the *Quod Deus*. More precisely, we should state that Question 100 has no parallel in the Treatises and therefore the comparison will end with Question 99. We will not attempt as detailed a comparison as before because the result would be a tedious discussion leading to an analogous conclusion. So we will move very quickly through the text to the end of *QG* 1.

---

system; this language is metaphorical. But this "mystery," if metaphysical, is also exegetical. Philo has placed the existence of Two Powers, Goodness and Lordship, behind the words "God" and "Lord"; but the uses made of these sacred terms in the biblical text imply a device, a dialectic, and other subtle things (see the beginning of the *De Mutatione Nominum*.)

D. QG *1.57-99 and the Parallel Treatises, Especially* De Gigantibus *and* Quod Deus Sit Immutabilis

(1) QG *1.57-58 and* De Cherubim

These two Questions speak to the two major themes of *De Cherubim*. In its details, *QG* 1.57 presents, but in reverse order, the first two hypotheses of *Cher.* 26-28 on the subject of the Cherubim and their fiery sword; and *QG* 1.58 is the equivalent of *Cher.* 125-130. These Questions are characterized by brevity and total lack of organization. It is therefore relatively unfruitful to make a comparison, even if two isolated "notions" are found to be similar — which is not always the case. There is nothing more to say, except perhaps that *De Cherubim* is not just a regrouping of Questions treated in a more exacting or more elaborate manner. As proof, let us recall that two series, one a little after the beginning of *De Cherubim*, and the other a little before the end, echo each other in a parallel way, as shown below:[38]

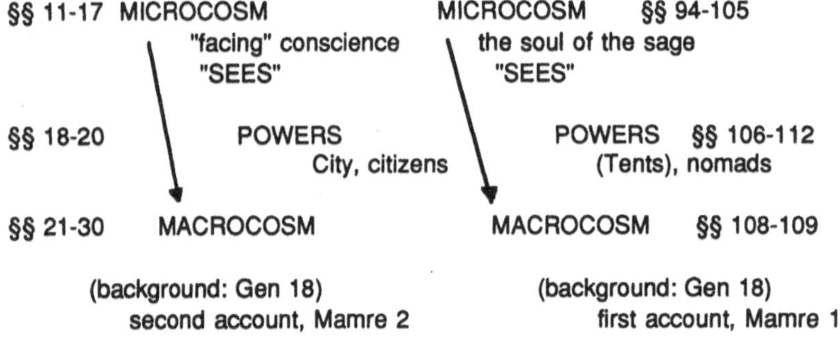

The rest of the Treatise offers a series of "chapters" that are organized and self-contained. Nothing in the hesitant lines of *QG* 1.57-58 leads us to expect the depth and the complexity of *De Cherubim* or the wealth of other biblical references found in that Treatise.

---

[38]See my discussion in Cazeaux 1983*b*, 12-84. Notice the inversion of the two accounts of Mamre: the second is located at the beginning; the first, at the end. There are other examples of these time rearrangements within some of the Treatises — see, for example, the *De Migratione*.

(2) QG *1.59-60 and* De Sacrificiis

In the same way, two other Questions suffice to cover the biblical text which is the basis of *De Sacrificiis.* The first sentence of *QG* 1.59 corresponds to *Sacr.* 11-45a; its second part, in a more precise way, makes a point corresponding to *Sacr.* 88. *QG* 1.60 deals with the same material as do *Sacr.* 52-71 and 72-139 (the conclusion of the Treatise). *QG* 1.61-63 has no attested parallel. Viewed as a whole, the *De Sacrificiis* presents an itinerary in three stages, connected by symmetries and a series of techniques of which I speak elsewhere.

(3) QG *1.64*

This Question sends us to *Agr.* 127-146. The "division" is allegorized there, but in a different way.

(4) QG *1.67-77 and* Quod Deterius

In this more extensive series of Questions, one finds a certain number of notions which are similar to those of *Quod Deterius* (thus, Question 73 can be studied with *Det.* 142, etc.). But the differences, even the difference in notions, are far more noticeable than the similarities. Note that the "groaning and trembling" of Cain receive only a few words in *QG* 1.72 but a long treatment in *Det.* 119-140, a passage marked by rigorous construction.[39] Farther on, in *QG* 1.87, we will find an echo of *Det.* 122-124a.

(5) QG *1.78-86 and* De Posteritate Caini

Questions 78-85 correspond in part to *De Posteritate* and in part to the beginning of *De Abrahamo,* which speaks about the very first Patriarchs, those before Abraham. But, once again, comparison of these texts teaches us very little. Thus, *QG* 1.82 on the words "Enoch was pleasing to God" has little resemblance to *Abr.* 17-26. Note that *QG* 1.86 evokes another biblical text, the story of Elijah being taken into heaven — but this is one of the standard "ascensions." *QG* 1.83 speaks about the symbolism of numbers, a major concern in *Quaestiones*.

---

[39]See Cazeaux 1984, 182-194.

(6) QG *1.89-99 and the Treatise Formed by* De Gigantibus + Quod Deus

QG 1.88 discusses the names of Shem, Ham, and Japheth as does *Sobr.* 31-44, 52 and 67-68 (in the Treatise, Japheth is closer to the good than he is in *QG).* The long *QG* 1.91 gives us the reflections we might expect on the number "120 years," the length of human life as restricted by the anger of God. But Philo patiently interprets this arithmological information in a *favorable* sense: it symbolizes various features of human nature in a positive way. Only at the end of the Answer are we reminded that God has punished perversity in that fashion, but the reason the idea is introduced is to allow the observation that penitence will eventually redeem this restriction, as is proved by the other, longer lives mentioned later in the Bible. Obviously, there is nothing like this interpretation in the pessimistic *De Gigantibus.* In that text, facing a discussion of the same number (120), Philo suddenly hesitates, as if faced with a dangerous, fathomless mystery capable of leading evil-minded persons or novices into error. *Gig.*56-57 refuses to examine[40] the problem of how it can be that Moses lived exactly 120 years, the same number assigned to the wicked men whom God punished by shortening the length of their lives to 120. Philo's attitude has changed altogether between *QG* 1.91 and *Gig.* 56-57: an extremely rich arithmological anthropology has replaced not only a "silence," but a "mystery" of the "initiated" (such is the expression used by *Gig.* 57). If the Treatise[41] *De Gigantibus* were a series of Questions, the refusal to interpret the Bible would be contrary to reason; if instead it forms a planned, organized whole, constructed with a movement in mind (with the *Quod Deus,* to which it is tied[42]), Philo's reserve is understandable: in a relatively subtle way, he thus announces that the remainder of his discourse will provide an answer — but only to those who read correctly, those who are the initiated. This

[40]See my reading in Cazeaux 1989. I consider this "crux" as the first example of the "ambiguities" or "medicinal lies" which Philo claims are found in the Bible — and that is the subject of quite a few pages of the *Quod Deus.*

[41]The word "Treatise" is commonly used, but it is evident that it does not really fit the majority of Philo's works, which are installments of a long commentary.

[42]Let us quickly sketch out some of the ties: the end of the *De Gigantibus* and the beginning of the *Quod Deus* share the character Abraham, the specific image of "military rank" (τάξις), and the condemnation of a "flesh" or of a "body" ἄψυχον. The beginning of the *Quod Deus* (§§1-4a) contains a summary of the *De Gigantibus*; and the end of the *De Gigantibus* (§64b) announces, through the theme of the "King's Highway," the ending of the *Quod Deus*, consecrated to the "Royal Road" (§§140-end). And these are merely correspondences in words.

answer, like all those in the Treatises, will be built upon a certain quantity of biblical texts, reflections, and dialectical digressions: Philo does not want interpretation to be based on an individual text or concept but instead to follow the course of a powerful presentation of the Words of the Logos, the contents of the Bible.

Next, *QG* 90, 93, 95, and 97-99 contain the same "notions" in their texts as the *Quod Deus,* in particular on the subject of the impossibility of discerning a change in God due, for example, to "repentance," or on the subject of the words "his way" which must be understood as "His Way" — a reference to God (*QG* 1.99 and *Deus* 142). The commentary of Question 99 on this last point ends with an enumeration of the cardinal virtues; and, in general, *QG* 1.99 is more explicit than the Treatise is on the same subject. We might say that *QG* knows that it must be comprehensive like a summary; while the Treatise *knows* that it will continue and develop the exegesis of the same biblical expressions in a different way using a *dialectical movement.* I repeat again: the presence of similar "notions" in no way permits us to assimilate two Treatises to one another, much less a Treatise and the corresponding material in *QG*. The only points in common are that the biblical texts under consideration are identical and that the conceptual "material" is the same. *QG* remains static; the Treatises move and live — and, like every living thing, each one lives for and in itself, even if the elements are found again and again in different places.

QG 1.89-99 juxtaposes allegories. In contrast, the two-volume commentary *De Gigantibus* + *Quod Deus* gives them an order. That this order was intended by Philo is proved in the three long developments which form the body of this grouping. *Deus* 20-50, 51-85, and 86-121, respectively, offer an exegesis of a phrase of Genesis 6. The first two sequences concern the eventual equivocalness of biblical language; and the third considers the words already cited above, "Noah found grace before the Lord God." Note that in all three, Philo proceeds in an analogous fashion: each time he gives *two series* of interpretations, with the first series preparing the second. *Deus* 20-32 prepares for 34-50; 51-69 prepares for 70-85; and, in a more subtle way, 86-103 prepares for 104-121, the first section of which (*Deus* 104-110) we have already discussed. The study of this device would force us beyond the scope of our present work on the *Quaestiones*. But this rapid glance reinforces our impression that the Treatises suggest a prescience and an organization which are totally absent in the *Quaestiones*. If we may use an image, there is the same difference between these two Philos as between the millions of cooks who have stirred a pot over a fire since both were invented and Denis Papin, who invented the dynamic principle of the "vapor machine" — inspired, it is said, by watching the agitations of a lid displaced by the vapor of his pot. Inertia in one case, movement in the other, with reference to the *same* biblical materials. It may be admitted that Philo invented nothing: neither allegory nor the techniques of allegory, nor the transformations of biblical proper names, nor even the conceptual transformations of situations or biblical phrases, nor their relation to the anthropological system or all that could be called "notions" in his work. But he *has* created *movement,* and this movement exists only in the allegorical Treatises, which includes almost all of them.

III. BOOKS 2-3 OF THE *QUAESTIONES IN GENESIM*[43]

A. *Book 2*

What we have said about *QG* 1 is substantially true of *QG* 2. The Questions have the same "insular" quality, despite a somewhat larger number of internal references (the general theme of the Ark as an image of the human body inspires this continuity, but it remains very textual in its basis — see, for example,*QG* 2.39, 46, and 47); occasionally, the same amount of attention is given to all the words of the biblical text (for example in *QG* 2.11), but with the same rigidity and without any internal movement. There is the same disproportion in both quantity and nature between the texts of the Questions and the corresponding Treatises: *QG* 2.66 covers the same material as the Treatise *De Agricultura*; *QG* 2.67, the *De Plantatione; QG* 2.68-72, the *De Ebrietate*; and *QG* 2.73-79, the *De Sobrietate*. We should of course note immediately that the building of the Ark and the Flood are not elaborated in the Treatises in a sustained fashion. The result is that *QG* 2.2, 3, 5-ll, 13-17, 19-52, 55-60, and 63-65 have no parallels in the Treatises. But it is unlikely that the style of a Treatise devoted to these chapters of Genesis would be similar to the style of the *Quaestiones* or much different than that of the Treatises mentioned above. One can, however, compare, for example, the description of the Flood as it is depicted in *QG* 2.18 and in the narrative of *Abr*. 41-46.[44] In *De Abrahamo*, the "purple passage" isn't one: Philo

---

[43]We should point out the presence of some Questions which are probably fragmentary: *QG* 2.30; 3.13, 14. *QG* 2.30 is continued by 2.33.

[44]In my opinion, the *De Abrahamo* is doubly an "allegorical" treatise, for Philo has introduced the mystery under the appearance of narration (cf. Cazeaux 1983*b*).

is emphasizing the image of the passions fighting against the mind, as he indicates in §§29-30. And Noah represents, in reality, the νοῦς, alone and majestically "at rest." *QG* 2.18, on the other hand, interprets the two inundations, one down from heaven and one up from earth, as the double perversion of the senses and of the human mind. We come to understand, then, that specifically in order to avoid having to say that the cataracts from on high symbolize the perversion of the νοῦς, which would ruin his allegory of the character of Noah, Philo has chosen to take a realistic (we might even say surrealistic) point of view when he tells the story of the Flood in the *De Abrahamo*. And we are better able to understand one detail of his narrative. *Abr.* 44 indicates that the air was also displaced, "with the exception of a small portion belonging to the Moon." Independent of any cosmological source and because of its completely material emphasis, this phrase "saves" the symbol of Noah, floating alone among the waves, for the title of 'mind' — for the Moon represents the boundary between the celestial world and the sublunary one. The *ekphrasis* of this realistic page of the *De Abrahamo* participates in an intention, a symbolical global movement, whereas *QG* 2.18 remains local and, in this sense, improvised, making reference to Philo's general anthropological system, but not to his dialectical transformation put in place to follow the sequence of the phrases in the Bible. In this example we can see once again that studying the correspondence between the Treatises and the *Quaestiones* of the elements of the "philosophical" system yields nothing more than some information about the raw material used by Philo; it shows nothing about the *form* he has created.

In the same way *QG* 2.69-72 deal with the episode of Noah's nudity, with the famous "report to the outside" made by Ham (Canaan), one of Noah's three sons. But it is hard to glimpse here any subtle analyses of "nudity" such as those found in *Leg.* 2.53-64 or in *Fug.* 188-193.[45] *QG* 2.73 interprets Noah's return to sobriety, but nothing is developed beyond the idea that sobriety allows one to "see" — especially, to see into the future (and in fact, Noah will pronounce oracles). The developments of *De Sobrietate* will go further. *QG* 2.74 briefly notes the paradoxical distinction of "new-old," but from a psychological and political angle, far removed from the usual metaphysical interpretation of this theme in the Treatises. *QG* 2.75 is based on the text of the benediction Noah gave to his other son, Shem: the word "God" is used twice in this text. *Sobr.* 51-58 does not give the same biblical text: "God" is not repeated.

[45]See Cazeaux 1983, 585-592.

(1) *A Meteorite?*

Let us stop for an moment to examine the text of *QG* 2.75. It is unlike anything else in Book 2, at least from our point of view. In it, Philo discusses the sequence of divine names, "the Lord God, God of Shem." Already, the juxtaposition of "God" and "Lord" recalls the idea that the One is accompanied by his two chief Powers, the Creative and the Kingly. But, says Philo, the repetition of "God" does indicate a difference between the meaning of each occurrence, an idea often found in his exegesis. Thus, the second "God" no longer stands for the Power θεός, but for that which is above the Powers — God as Being. The reader will recall the double dialectical progression in *Leg.* 3.67-104 and in *Deus* 104-110, which we contrasted with the static position of *QG* 1.48. Note that *QG* 2.75 anticipates the *dialectical movement* of the passages in the two Treatises. The argument used is that of "useful repetition," meaning observation elaborated from the biblical text according to its own syntax. Thus, considering both content and form, we suddenly discover one Question which emerges from the group and which, I believe, poses the problem of the uniformity of the literary genres in the *Quaestiones*. Here, for example, the argument of the double "favor" of which Noah is the beneficiary, the mediation of the "world"[46] discussed in the last line of *QG* 2.75, everything prepares for the discussion of the same subject in the two Treatises (using another biblical text). However, while acknowledging its "dialectical" merit, we should take note of the inchoate character of *QG* 2.75 and point out, in particular, the absence of either of the paired biblical characters, specifically Abraham and Moses. It is not impossible that the simple act of translating the Greek discourse into Armenian brought about the loss of a greater number of similarities between the *Quaestiones* and the Treatises, especially in the short Questions, in which it is harder to perceive possible echoes, if such echoes exist.

(2) *A Return to the Differences. . . .*

QG 2.76 (which should be read "that he extend Japheth so that he will live in the house of Shem") carefully ties "extension" to the return of Japheth to Shem. The allegory opposes an anarchic satisfaction of the

[46]See *QG* 2.2 for a discussion of the "grace" of the world.

senses. By contrast, in *Sobr*. 59-66 Philo hopes that the sage enjoys secondary goods. It is only at the end that he brings Japheth back to Shem (*Sobr*. 67-68). To be sure, this difference of emphasis would not be unheard of even between two passages of the Treatises. This, therefore, is the most important aspect: *QG* 2.76 is not only very much relativized by *Sobr*. 59-68; but the pages of the Treatise make up a strong and precise "dialectical" sequence, while *QG* 2.76 moralizes "on the spot," so to speak. *QG* 2.80 retains the same pessimistic view of the "extension."

Finally, *QG* 2.77 (the last question we can compare) discusses the relationship which Genesis establishes between Ham and Canaan. The translation of the name "Canaan" by "merchants" corresponds to biblical usage[47] but gives no hint of the possibility of translating "Canaan" by "agitation," as found in *Sobr*. 44. Again, this variation would not be of major importance if the idea of "agitation" referring to Canaan were not the main active device of an entire organized section of the *De Sobrietate* (§§31-49).

Thus the Questions of Book 2 evolve separately as far as content is concerned; and they also have little in common with the Treatises in their approach to form, movement, and "dialectic," by which I mean the capacity to shed light beyond themselves.

(3) *Soundings in* QG *2*

Comparing the Treatises to the *Quaestiones,* one finds many similar "concepts," Philo's habitual baggage, but only occasionally and with difficulty do we find in the Questions morsels of that which supplies movement in the Treatises. We are going to look quickly through Book 2, using the order in which the Questions are presented, and consider in as positive way as possible those questions which allow a Philo scholar who has had some practice to "foresee" such and such a passage in the Treatises. We cannot always find Treatise passages paralleling the Questions in content, and this non-parallelism is informative: one could, if one had the patience[48] to work painstakingly with detail, draw up an "archaeological" table of Philo's discourse.

[47]Thus, for example, Isa 23:8; Hos 12:8; Ezek 16:29 and the famous text of Zech 14:21.
[48]Such an undertaking is not to my taste, but it could illuminate the psychology of the literary creation, the "history of a text."

Let us note, in general, that Book 2, like Book 1, shows interest in arithmology (*QG* 2.5, 14, 17, 31-33, 45, 47). On this topic, let us make this commonsensical remark: Philo talks about numbers . . .when the Bible does. It is not surprising that *De Opificio* and the passages in *QG* which deal with the construction and measurements of the Ark contain many reflections on numbers. A statistical comparison would not, therefore, give good results. Let us say that, given their nature, the arithmological discussions are inevitably lengthy.[49]

Another general remark about the preparation of the "dialectics" should be made. Although it is true that, in general, there are few references to other biblical texts (*QG* 2.26, 29, 41, 43,45, 47, 54, 56, 59, 64, 66, if I am not mistaken), it does happen in several cases (*QG* 2.45, 56, 59, 64, and 66) that Philo finds one reference insufficient and instead gives two. This is the embryo of a combination. One could hypothesize that the reference used brings another to mind. In the Treatises, the system is organized perfectly, and the references do not follow each other as cumulative proofs, but instead are used as part of a deliberate, controlled, and dialectical linkage.

QG 2.43 presents not just two but three biblical texts to interpret the base text, "Noah knew that the water had diminished on the earth." This Question is elliptical and may have been more affected than the others by the translation from Greek to Armenian.[50] Let us add that even the most subtle of the Questions, those which are the most inchoately dialectical, if any exist, must certainly have suffered in the translation process. We can see obscurely that the reference to Creation ("the memory of good things bestowed at the origin") allowed Philo to speak in praise of "the Father for his great and kind goodness." The Father is the Creator, symbolized by the first Power, that Goodness which bestows good things. How then does Philo manage a transition to a quotation from Isa 1:9, where it is no longer "God" (Goodness) but the "Lord" (force and chastisement) who is named: "If the almighty Lord had not left us a seed . . ."? There is no doubt that Philo has intervened in the quotation of the Prophet. He continues, in fact, "we would have become like the blind and the barren." However, the text of Isaiah says, "We would have become like Sodom and Gomorrah." So Philo has "arranged" things by using his regular

[49]Thus, when he says that Enos is the "fourth" man, Philo feels the need to refer back to a longer treatment of the number four, which he seems to have written prior to *Abr.* 13, where this discussion of Enos is found. The brief notice is not considered sufficient, and the reader is invited to go back to a longer discussion of the idea.

[50]We have no Greek fragment for this Question.

code of name equivalences, according to which "Sodom and Gomorrah" stand for "sterility and blindness." This adaptation also represents an intended "brachylogy" and perhaps the "logos spermatikos" of a development analogous to that of a Treatise. In fact, in *QG* 2.43, Philo holds onto one single idea, that of the "seed" which flowers again: *QG* 2.42 had already so interpreted the olive leaf brought back by Noah's dove. We can see that there is, around these biblical phrases, the *beginning* of a more complex exegetical construction. The presence of several other biblical texts is at once the sign and the instrument of this approach, as is the explicit tie between Questions 42 and 43. Let us also mention a small detail found in Question 42: it follows the words of the biblical text, discussing the allegorical possibilities of each term in sequence; but the fifth part presents a small element of originality, since the symbol is presented before the quotation.[51] The Treatises often use this end-oriented procedure: a discussion precedes, sometimes by quite a distance, the biblical quotation on which it comments.

Question 34, which is a striking commentary on the "window" of the Ark, contains in brief the whole itinerary which Philo develops elsewhere when speaking of Abraham: the point of departure is in the contemplation of the world, through the eyes of the "Chaldean"; then "a more piercing look" allows him to go beyond the world of causalities to think about the Unique and transcendent Cause. This itinerary is certainly the one Abraham pursues: it is repeated, exactly, when Jacob becomes "Israel" — "the one who sees God." In *QG* 2.34 we can find a brief treatment akin to passages like *Praem*. 36-48, or (in even simpler form[52]) *Abr*. 72-84. But, we tirelessly repeat, the similarity of the "idea" should not make us forget that these two Treatises have a dialectic, fresh each time and each time tied to the whole of the commentary, whereas the Question is isolated and without overtones. The relation of Question 43 to Question 42, which we have already discussed, is really no more dynamic than that of Question 34 to the Treatises.

QG 2.54 prefigures certain developments in *Deus* 51-69, where Philo contrasts two biblical formulae on the subject of divinity: "God like

[51]*QG* 2.42 also has a special unity. Even the number of the symbols is symbolic: at the end is said: "And the sixth (symbol) is that the dry branch was in its mouth — since six is the first perfect number." We should also consider the possibility that Philo, interpreting the "mouth" as the location of "speech" — of the expressed logos — is alluding to the fact that this logos is the "sixth," added to the five senses (cf., e.g., *Abr*. 29, which discusses Noah, though from a different viewpoint).

[52]See Cazeaux 1979-80.

a man trains a son . . . ." — "God, not like a man." An important concept appears at the beginning of *QG* 2.54: the idea of a *distance*, within the biblical text itself, placed between truth and appearance, between unadorned reality and medicinal pedagogy. And in the remainder of the Question, one learns that this "idea" derives both from the opposition of the two contradictory elements and from the contents of the first formula, where the verb "to train" allows us to understand the entire phrase — another example of the technique of "redundancy" dear to Philo (both the words and the syntax of an inspired proposition function to indicate *one single* meaning, by a sort of regulated tautology). Farther on, also spoken of in *Deus* 21 and 33 ff., we are reintroduced to the difference between διανοεῖσθαι and ἐνθυμεῖσθαι. But even there, the problematic and isolated aspect of these notions differentiates the Question quite clearly from the Treatise. The *Quod Deus* is based almost entirely on the interplay of Reality and Appearance in the reading of the inspired text: already, the famous passage of *Gig*. 56-57, dealing with the subject of the exegetical difficulty created by the age of 120 years (the life span for bad men but also for Moses), refused to give an answer or offered it only to the "initiated." Then the alternating developments of *Deus* 21-50 and 51-69 completely rework these notions scattered in Question 54 and give them a more profound meaning. However, the mainspring idea of *Deus* 51-69, on the subject of the two opposite definitions of God, "not man" — "like a man who trains" (*Deus* 51-69), is already present in Question 54. In both the Question and *Deus* the "logical" reasoning given is the following: I find in the same Bible two contradictory definitions, "like a man" — "not like a man"; but the first is more developed, "like-a-man-He-trains." Thus "man" and "training" are brought into association. I must conclude that whatever is anthropomorphic in the expression concerning God is "pedagogical": moreover, the law of logical division then obliges me to say that the second definition, "not like a man," is connected with that which *complements* pedagogy. Since pedagogy is related to appearance, meaning untruth and medicine, I must conclude that the first definition is instead related to Reality, unadorned truth, and essence. In both Question 54 and the Treatise, the analysis of one of the two definitions permits the understanding of both, by ricochet and "division." But what *QG* 2.54 does not say and what the Treatise *Quod Deus* will later subtly show is that the difference between these two definitions is related to the difference between the two Powers, Goodness and Lordship. It is true that the end of Question 54 attributes the refusal to punish humanity with yet another Flood to a "Father who is good, kind, and a friend to mankind." But here we must pause to make a simple but important remark. *QG* 2.54 deals with the words of God *after the Flood*, whereas *Quod Deus* considers the words God uses *while deciding about sending the Flood*. *QG* 1.93 and 95 touch upon the problem of the "conversion," the change in God, and we also find slight suggestions of this topic in the *Quod Deus*. (Compare, for example, *Deus* 21 with *QG* 1.93 and *Deus* 52 with *QG* 2.95.) Thus the Treatise moves to the *beginning* of the Flood story that which *QG* keeps, in a tranquil and orderly way, for the end of the story. This means that the Treatise *Quod Deus* plays down the Power of chastisement, which is divine Lordship, and emphasizes instead the Power of Goodness, the Father as creator and savior. That means that Philo is going to make a *mental omission* of the Flood and, just as he does in our "chapter" (*Leg*. 3.64-106), save humankind and make Creation glisten when misfortune is over. These contrasting treatments in the *Quaestiones* and the Treatises are certainly more than just simple variations of the theme. What we see here is the invention of a powerful theology, one capable of wreaking havoc with the "note cards" of even the most elaborate of the *Quaestiones* — that whole "lexicon" of ideas and equivalencies, whether textual or even already symbolical ones. In fact, the *Quod Deus* avoids speaking of the Flood; as fast as sinister facts appear, this Treatise transforms them into effects of mercy. The most prominent proof of this sublimation is none other than the insistent presence of the Ἔλεγχος in this Treatise. It is precisely this "Witness of Conscience" which remains as the last image of the *Quod Deus* (§§180b-183). Perhaps this is why the Treatises have not given us any detailed analysis of the biblical Flood and also why Philo has taken refuge in the narrative whenever he is forced to talk about it (*Abr*. 41-46 and *Mos*. 2.54, 59-65, passages in which Philo surveys sacred history). In contrast, *Quaestiones* Book 2 fearlessly embarks upon a detailed, uniform, and instructive commentary — but one which lacks any movement whatsoever.

QG 2.56 interests me because of a similar observation. In the first third we read: "Observe carefully that scripture showed that the righteous man of the Flood (Noah) was equal in honor, not to him who was modeled and made of earth, but to him who was made according to the Image and the Form of the Being (the Logos)." Just as Philo "avoids" discussing the Flood in the Treatises, he also touches only briefly here on the story of Adam and Eve. In contrast, he certainly does not avoid it in the Treatises! Here in *QG* 2.56 Philo comments on yet another benevolent statement by the Creator, who gives Noah the order to populate the earth, as He had given it to the First Man (Philo emphasizes that this is the man of Genesis 1, not the man of Genesis 2 and 3). Now, let us consider the famous beginning of the *De Abrahamo*, the section in which Philo seems to set forth the classifying principle of his works. If one gives some thought to the choice he has made of the "first Triad" of Enos, Enoch and Noah, one sees that, in a parallel way, Philo avoids chapters 2 and 3 of Genesis, which contain the stories of Adam, Eve, Cain, and even Abel. The principle which guides Philo here is none other than the new γένεσις of Genesis 5. This word allows him to make several commentaries simultaneously. First of all, from Philo's point of view, it brings together and therefore connects chapters 1 and 5 of Genesis, thus authorizing the omission of the intervening chapters which are filled with the shame and misery of man — the project and "image of the Image of God." Secondly, it may be observed that the word γένεσις simultaneously introduces the Creation of the Universe and the story of the characters. For Philo, therefore, an identity or at least a parallelism exists between the macrocosm and the microcosm. It is this identity or parallelism that the term "Law" points to in both the Greek and Jewish traditions (Γένεσις is the first book of the Torah, and the ancient Greeks discussed νόμοι ἄγραφοι as a classical issue). This explains the commentary in *Abr*. 1-6 (or even *Abr*. 1-16, because the text on Enos is part of the Introduction[53]). Being the first book of the Jewish "Law," Γένεσις is set over against the second book, Exodus, where the written Laws are found, whereas the Patriarchs of Genesis are understood to be unwritten laws. We see that the beginning of the *De Abrahamo* is as exegetical as it is philosophical and, moreover, that each word of *Abr*. 1, for example, can be understood both philosophically and as an allusion to the specific contents of Genesis. But what catches our attention here is the direct transition from ideal Man, created on the Sixth Day, to Enos, the Man of chapter 5: *Abr*. 9 explains rapidly that "father and grandfathers had existed before, but (Scripture) interpreted them as founders of a mixed race, while Enos was the founder of a very pure race. . . ." There is no other reference to Adam, except one in which he is merely the "starting point" in the calculation of generations: "If we list the generations starting with the first (man), made of earth, we find that Enos . . . is the fourth" (*Abr*. 12).

[53]Which agrees fully with the idea that the Universe and Man imitate each other.

Question 56 gives Noah the role of Man in relation to the Image. The *De Abrahamo* introduces a "dialectic" starting with Noah, but in a specific manner. The γένεσις which introduces Enos by homonymy, meaning the total genealogical list of chapter 5, contains *three names that are emphasized by a theological "note" in the Bible itself:* Enos, who "hoped"; Enoch, "who was carried off"; and Noah, "calm and righteous." This similar treatment of these three characters lends them a common truth. In the *De Abrahamo*, Noah remains greater than Enos, just as he is the only one mentioned by *QG* 2.56. But Question 56 arrives at Noah without preparation; whereas the *De Abrahamo* comes to Noah slowly and only after considering the entire fabric of Genesis 5. *QG* 2.56 focuses simply on the idea of an Adam who is eclipsed and a Noah who is exalted. The *De Abrahamo* treats all of Genesis 5, but it also deals with the rest of Genesis. In fact, it must be noted that in *Abr*. 7-47 Philo is confronted with a delicate problem: he must exalt Enos, but he knows that Enos will be followed by greater men, Enoch and especially Noah. At first, the reader does not notice the devices Philo employs to give Enos a noble but still inferior stature. In the same way, Philo diminishes the character of Enoch, contrary to the tradition which ties Enoch to Elijah or even to Moses, a tie reinforced by the tradition that all three were carried off to heaven and no tomb is know for any of them. When he finally arrives at Noah, Philo confronts a similar problem: Noah is righteous, as righteous as anyone could wish, but what is his stature in relation to that of Abraham, who after all is the subject of Philo's book? So once again Philo calls on his dialectical expertise to manage this first Triad, already a noble group, yet less important and deficient by comparison with that of Abraham, Isaac and Jacob. All the allegories of *Abr*. 1-47 are dominated by the perception of the "structure" of Genesis in its totality. They do not evolve freely, inspired by chance or free association. Such is the difference between a Question and a Treatise.

It is a common error of perspective to think of Philo as an "allegorist" indefinitely producing "allegories" one after another, like a silkworm spinning its cocoon. The "ideas" and the "allegories" are only the raw material: Philo's work begins afterward, with an "economy" which imitates that of the Bible; and this movement is given us in the Treatises.

Question 65 speaks of Canaan in his relationship to his brother Ham. At the end of this text one can find elements which prefigure the allegories of *Sobr*. 30-50, despite the textual differences of proper noun interpretations: "Canaan—agitation" rather than "Canaan—intermediary, merchant." But the complexity of the *De Sobrietate* owes nothing to these equivalencies. Let us simply recall a technique used by Philo in the Treatises: the interpretation of the names of the two who are accomplices in evil, Canaan and Ham, is revealed only in *Sobr.* 44, during a subtle exegesis extending from §30 to §50. Thus, what preceded this interpretation of names was secretly prepared by it, attracted by it; and that is one of the principles of Philonic movement: a biblical text will appear at the end of a commentary to give it finality and authority. It is the opposite of the *vis a tergo* which the *Quaestiones* often exemplify — a model too often adopted by people who speak of Philo.

Question 79 contains a curious polemical statement criticizing "literalists." Philo illustrates and emphasizes this idea with the striking allegorization of the names of Shem, Ham, and Japheth. Once again we have an isolated but interesting "idea." In the middle is Ham himself, who of course incarnates evil. Noah, because he is a prophet, is able to foresee that Canaan, the son of Ham, will accomplish the evil which remains in the state of intention in Ham (see Question 65). Shem, though the last in the genealogical sequence, is the oldest in merit — as was to be expected. Japheth, the eldest, becomes youngest in the order of good; we know, moreover (*QG* 2.80 and *Sobr.* 59-69), that Japheth is a combination of bad and good and a friend of external manifestations of goodness such as virtue, which explains the end of Question 79. In brief, then, the two friends of goodness, Shem and Japheth, distance themselves from Ham (evil). This moral movement is modeled on an alternation within the Bible: the order of the names of Noah's sons varies according to whether their names are listed alone (Shem, Ham, Japheth — Gen 10:1) or along with their descendants (in which case the order is Japheth, Ham, Shem — Gen 10:2, 6, 22). Ham is always in the middle.

Perhaps the allegory built on these specific texts reflects something profound and active in the composition of the exegetical series which form the Treatises and their movement. It often happens that a series of examples, tied together by Philo's choice, are arranged so that the middle is occupied by a biblical figure who incarnates evil, the many, or dispersion. Thus, in the series of the five meanings of the term "source," the third evokes the menstrual flow, while on either side are two quotations which designate completely positive meanings and which progress, moreover, from the least to the most elevated meaning (*Fug.* 177-201). Likewise *Migr.* 94-104 explains the grandeur of a mode of life in which reality is matched with appearance. Five biblical examples are provided, of which the third is of evil women capable of setting the camp on fire (§§99-100). Evil flourishes in the middle of the dialectic formed by biblical references. Other examples may be found. Philo seems to have transferred his idea of "evil as circumscribed by good" (as *QG* 2.79 puts it, referring to Ham set between Shem and Japheth or Japheth and Shem) into an active literary technique, a process involving form, not just content, in allegorical exposition, giving it movement and the drama of a sort of Descent into Hell in the middle of the moral itinerary proposed by every Philonic "chapter." Such is the profound transformation of what I call the immobile "idea" (notions, proper name transformations, even the allegories in Philo) into a movement — from the genre of a Question to that of a Treatise.

B. *Book 3*

QG 3 deals with texts found in Gen 15:7-17:27, the same material treated in the Treatises *Quis Heres* (*QG* 3.2-16), *De Congressu* (*QG* 3.18-35), *De Fuga et Inventione* (*QG* 3.26-35), and *De Mutatione Nominum* (*QG* 3.39-60). The questions of *QG* 3 share a great number of "ideas" with these corresponding Treatises. Since we have just studied Books 1 and 2 in some detail, I will not linger over a similar comparison of Book 3 and the Treatises. In *La trame et la chaîne* [54] I have tried to demonstrate the complexity, erudite art, and dynamic which prevail in this series of Treatises devoted to Abraham's character. In these Treatises we see the moral importance of the patriarch, the father of the Jews, and the continuing role he has in the development of the spiritual itinerary which dictates the broad outlines of Philo's allegorical universe. These aspects, as well as the beauty and subtlety of *De Abrahamo,* which like the other Abraham Treatises appears deceptively simple, invite us to investigate the interconnections of the two series, the Treatises and the Questions. But the result would be discouraging. *QG* 3.26, containing only a few words, is the only text corresponding to the long passage *Fug.* 1-118. *QG* 3.30 speaks of the return of Hagar to Sarah's control, but fails to hint at the established theory of relationships between the encyclical studies and Wisdom, although *QG* 3.32 does mention the relationship. At the beginning of 3.39, three lines give us a sense of the double appellation "Lord-God," whereas *Mut.* 1-51 establishes the movement from one Power to the other in a slow and refined manner. *QG* 3.43 is very eloquent and would be worthy of a Treatise — if a

[54]Cazeaux 1983 *a*.

Treatise were the equivalent of a group of Questions. The justification of circumcision in *QG* 3.48-52 would readily recall the frontispiece of *De Specialibus Legibus* 1 except for the fact that the Treatise gives the subject a prominent place: at the beginning of all the Jewish laws. The apologetic motive (*Spec.* 1.1: "I shall begin with [the law] which is held in derision by the crowd") should not make us forget the deeper reason for this choice: the fact that circumcision was required of Abraham. That requirement precedes as one fundamental practical rule all the determinations of the Law. *QG* 3.49 connects circumcision with the order of the world, and this development is made very impressively. But it does not enter into a dynamic relationship with the context, as it should have were it in accord with the mysterious analysis of the rite between *De Decalogo* and *De Specialibus*. Choosing another Question almost at random, we note that in *QG* 3.55, where there is a discussion of the text about Abraham falling and laughing, Philo speculates in a rather abstract way on the opposition of these two actions and insists on a particular interpretation of the expression "to fall on one's face." In the corresponding discussion in *Mut.* 154-175, Joy is the aspect most stressed: Philo connects the laughter of Abraham with that of Sarah (§166), and he opposes the essential laughter of Isaac (§§157-165) to the false joys of Egypt (§§167-174). The whole forms a harmonious "chapter" in the Treatise, which is in equilibrium and filled with other biblical quotations and careful analyses of them. *QG* 3.56 discusses the ages of Abraham (100) and Sarah (90). Here the importance of arithmological values is heavily stressed. The parallel passage in *De Mutatione* keeps only the biblical examples (*Mut.* 189-192, like the last part of *QG* 3.56), but they are more elaborate. Also there is a difference of style. *QG* 3.56 explains that the advanced age of the parents makes God's power more evident, while *Mut.* 188 presents Abraham praying that Joy (Isaac) "will be conceived by the numbers 100 and 90,"[55] and these numbers have a symbolic meaning.

Among the "ideas" contained in the Questions of Book 3 we should emphasize the theoretical passage in *QG* 3.3, in which Philo attacks the literalists who imagine that Abraham, seated before the animals he has sacrificed, interprets their entrails conjecturally like an augur. Philo instead views this passage as the deployment of a whole world of thoughts and multiplied correspondences between the universe and the

[55]In passing we note that *Mut.* 192 is illuminated by *QG* 3.56, making plausible Wendland's correction, reading δευτέρας instead of δεκάτης.

Bible, a text which reflects this unity and is a guide to the true reader. Despite the immediate application to the cosmological and moral relations which Philo proposes in order to explain the sacrificial animals and the prolonged contemplation of Abraham, who does the sacrificing, one must consider this profession of faith in totality as the awareness which Philo has of the unity of the Bible: it is the unified mirror of the cosmos and of God's designs. This principle is decisive for the commentaries found in the Treatises. They always stress totality in the precise sense that they assume and show the interconnecting of the largest possible number of passages distant from one another in the Bible as well as the connection of scripture with philosophy. Thus the "chapters" of the Treatises obey an interior law of equilibrium, composition and movement which one might call "gravitation": "Divine law exists, and one must contemplate it as a whole, in its totality. One must take it all in with eyes wide open, embracing scripture with a circular view and with exactitude and great clarity, without breaking its harmony or dismantling its unity . . ." (*QG* 3.3). The *Quaestiones* are still very timid in their application of this principle. The Treatises, however, do it complete justice.

QG 3.5 discusses the allegory of the "division" of all things. For the reader, the long "chapter" of *Her*. 130-229 immediately comes to mind. *QG* 3.5 simply establishes the bipartite composition of humans, who have bodies and souls. At the end, the name of Heraclitus allows the observation to be extended, not to an application to the entire Cosmos but to the sublunary world of meteorology and geography. One notices that *QG* 3.3 had already discussed the elements and the heavenly bodies in a more elaborate way, but in the context of a tripartite division rather than a bipartite one — the text of reference (Gen 15:9) had spoken of the three animals of Abraham's sacrifice, "the heifer, the goat, and the ram — each one three years old." The number "three" required its own allegory.[56] Here is the probable reason why *QG* 3.5 treats only examples which can be divided by "two." However, there is an additional major difference between the scholarly development of *QG* 3.5 and the treatment in *Heres*. Absent from *QG* 3.5 are all the examples borrowed from the Bible itself, and especially those from the Jewish cultus. Also missing is the movement found in all the individual interpretations in *Heres*, those techniques which transform what could

[56]In *QG* 3.3 the allegory of the three animals is cosmological; in *Heres* it is related to education, which allows cosmology to be held in reserve.

have been a tedious, static, and cumulative list into an increasingly dramatic treatment. A single example: at the beginning of the "chapter" on division, Philo anticipates what will follow, alluding in *Her.* 132b to the case of "the birds left undivided." This simple detail announces a sort of "superior division" between what can be divided and what cannot be. The purely mechanical concept of a world systematically divided in two is relativized even before it is discussed. And, in fact, a detailed analysis[57] shows how Philo softens this dichotomy, despite the fact that it is so easy to assert and to prove. One can say, without exaggerating, that the care Philo takes to speak of these indivisible birds, well before the citation of the biblical text which discusses them, is a discreet but firm hint to his reader. The well-known idea of universal "division" will be carefully treated in a nuanced way: interconnections will be proposed, types of division will be specified, some distortion will be present — all those aspects are necessary for the development of a dialectical and a mental itinerary. And of course, there is no hint of any of that in *QG* 3.5. We have already said that *QG* 3.3 already contains another division, into "three," which of course limited the applications of the division by "two," the subject of *QG* 3.5. Reciprocally, we see that *Her.* 125-126 considerably limits the allegorical exegesis of the "three" animals, "the ram, the goat and the heifer" and their "three" years. A few words suffice, and Philo undertakes no discussion which could be compared to the list found in *QG* 3.3. Thus Philo avoids contradiction in the cases of *QG* 3.3, 5 and *Her.* 122-229, and he is well aware of what he is doing in both cases. Here the difference between the two approaches is quite visible, a difference not really of "allegory" but rather of the "genre" chosen, one static and the other dynamic.[58]

IV. BOOK 4 OF THE *QUAESTIONES IN GENESIM*[59]

We cannot begin to study *QG* 4 without first making clear just how long we understand it to be. The Armenian translation is divided into four books, and the fourth book in this grouping contains as many

[57]See Cazeaux 1983*a*, 260-309.

[58]As in Books 1-2, there are Questions in which the *incipit*, the initial question, is already complicated. Such is the case in *QG* 3.23, 47, and 56. There is also one series of Questions which share an allegory: the questions of *QG* 3.3-10 share several notions, including that of "prophecy."

[59]This section dealing with *QG* 4 is by A. Méasson.

questions (245) as do the first three books put together. On the other hand, the florilegia which have preserved the Greek fragments for us refer to a division into six books.[60] The French edition (PAPM) has adopted the latter; however, it keeps the unbroken numbering used in Book 4 of the Aucher translation and applies it to Books 5 and 6. We also will adopt this division. Book 4, then, contains 70 questions.

These Questions, numbered from 1 to 70, are commentaries on Genesis 18-20. Since Book 3 ends with a commentary on the last verse of Genesis 17, there is continuity between Books 3 and 4. On the other hand, Book 5 does not follow Book 4 directly because it skips to Gen 23:1. As it has come down to us, therefore, the text of *QG* contains no commentary on Genesis 21-22.

Book 4, moreover, ignores certain verses of Gen 18-20: 18:18, 25-26; 19:6,15,25,33-36; 20:5,8,9,13-15. It is interesting to note that these verses are neglected not only in *QG* but also, with a single exception (Gen 19:33-36), in all the Treatises of Philo. It is possible to find plausible reasons for these omissions, at least in certain cases. Gen 18:18 repeats, in abridged form, Gen 12:2-3 which is discussed in *Migr.* 53-126 (Gen 12:2 is also cited in *Her.* 277); v. 25 repeats v. 23; and v. 26 is God's acceptance of the proposition made by Abraham in v. 24. In Gen 19, one can consider that v. 25 is included in the discussion of v. 24, as is the case of *Abr.* 137-142. As for vv. 33-36, all they do is tell how the two daughters of Lot brought about what the elder had proposed to the younger in vv. 31-32.[61] With regard to Genesis 20, v.5 (which is not cited in the biblical lemma) is alluded to in Question 64. Verse 9 is repeated, in a certain way, by v. 10, which is cited in the lemma of Question 67. The justification of Abraham contained in v. 13 might be viewed as superfluous after v. 12; and a similar view might hold for v. 14 since v. 16 is discussed.

Book 4 of *QG* has no real parallel in the Treatises, except for the fact that its first 58 questions correspond to *Abr.* 107-166, a commentary on Gen 18-19. Elsewhere only commentaries on isolated verses exist, as the following table shows:

---

[60]Cf. Mercier 1979, 25-26.

[61]Verses 33-36 are treated in *Post.* 176-177 and in *Ebr.* 164-166 (v. 33 being cited in §166), and in *Ebr.* 203-205 (vv. 33 and 35 being cited in §203).

A. *The Treatises and QG 4*

Genesis	*QG* 4	Treatises
18:1-2	1	*Abr* . 107, 119
18:2	2-3	*Abr* . 107 and 119-131!
18:3	4	*Abr* . 131
18:4	5	—
18:5	6-7	—
18:6-7	8	*Abr*. 108-109; *Sacr*. 59-60
18:8	9-10	*Abr* .110, 117-118
18:9	11	*Det*. 59-61
18:10	12	*Abr* 110-111, 132; *Cher*. 106; *Migr*. 126
18:10b	13	—
18:11	14-15	*Abr*. 111; *Leg* 3.218; *Cher*. 50;*Det*. 28;*Ebr*. 6;*Fug*. 128, 167; *Post*. 134; *Somn*. 2.185; *Spec*. 2.54
18:12	16	*Leg*. 3.218; *Ebr*. 62; *Mut*. 166-7; *Abr*. 206; *Spec*. 2.54
18:13-14	17	—
18:14	18	—
18:15	19	*Abr*. 112-113, 205-207
18:16	20	*Migr*. 173-175
18:17	21	*Leg*. 3.27; *Sobr*. 56-57
18:18**[62]	—	—
18:19	22	—
18:20	23	*Ebr*. 222; *Abr*. 133
18:21	24	—
18:22	25	*Leg*. 3.9; Cher. 18-19; *Post*. 27-28; *Somn*. 2.226-228
18:23	26	*Leg*. 3.9-10; *Cher*. 18-19; *Deus* 161; *Migr*. 132; *Her*. 30; *Prov*. 1.55

[62] The double asterisk indicates a passage in Genesis that is totally ignored in the extant commentaries of Philo.

18:24, 28-32	27	*Sacr.* 122-125; *Migr.* 122-123; *Congr.* 109-110; *Mut.* 228-229
18:25-26**	—	—
18:27	28	*Deus* 161; *Her.* 29-30; *Somn.* 1.214
18:33	29	*Somn.* 1.70-71
19:1	30-32	*Abr.* 142-146
19:2	33	—
19:3	34-35	—
19:4	36	*Conf.* 27-28
19:5	37	—
19:6**	—	—
19:7-8	38	*Ebr.* 164
19:9	39	*Mos.* 2.58
19:10-11	40-41	*Fug.* 144
19:12-13	42	—
19:14	43	—
19:15**	—	—
19:16	44	—
19:17	45-46	—
19:18-20	47	*Abr.* 165-166
19:21	48	—
19:22	49-50	—
19:23-24	51	*Deus* 60; *Ebr.* 222-224; *Somn.* 1.85-86; *Abr.* 138-141; *Mos.* 2.53-58; *Prov.*1.55
19:25**	—	—
19:26	52	*Leg.* 3.213; *Ebr.* 164; *Fug.* 121-123; *Somn.* 1.246-248
19:27-28	53	—
19:29	54	—
19:30	55	—
19:31-32	56	*Post.* 175; *Ebr.* 165
19:33-36**	—	—
19:37-38	57-58	*Leg.* 3.81; *Post.* 177
20:1	59	—
20:2	60-61	—
20:3	62	—

20:4	63-64	—
20:5**	—	—
20:6	65	—
20:7	66	*Her.* 258-262
20:8-9**	—	—
20:10-11	67	—
20:12	68	*Ebr.* 61-62; *Her.* 62
20:16	69	—
20:17-18	70	—

Studied as a separate unit, *QG* 4 offers a particularly interesting illustration of the literary genre of the *Quaestiones*. We will first discuss the 70 Questions of which it is composed in a general way and then look more carefully at the first 29 of them, with special emphasis on Questions 1, 2, and 8, which are noteworthy because of the length of their development.

B. *The Independence of the Questions and the Lines of Force that Traverse Them in* QG *4*

Two characters dominate Genesis 18-20: Abraham and Lot. If it is possible to group the Questions of Book 4, it is around episodes in which they are the heroes.

On Genesis 18: Questions 1-29 deal with God's appearance to Abraham and the hospitality the patriarch offered the three strangers.

On Genesis 19: Questions 30-41 concern the hospitality Lot showed to the angels who had come to punish Sodom and Gomorrah;

——————— Questions 42-54 treat the destruction of the two cities and the saving of Lot and his daughters;

——————— Questions 55-58 comment on the scabrous story of Lot's daughters.

On Genesis 20: Questions 59-70 discuss the attitude of King Abimelech toward Sarah, whom Abraham had introduced as his sister.

This grouping of the Questions of Book 4, built upon the story told in Genesis, obviously does not infringe upon their independence.[63] In the course of a careful sequential reading of the 70 commentaries it contains, however, one particular aspect becomes visible. A theme runs through this book from one end to the other, even if it is explicit only where it is directly discussed: the parallel between "the perfect one" and what Philo calls " the one who progresses."

The Bible itself invites us to compare the two characters whose stories are told in Genesis 18-20; for the Bible shows each in succession fulfilling the duty of hospitality. Philo's only addition was to give each character an allegorical interpretation: Abraham embodies "the perfect"; and Lot, "the progressive." Question 30, which links the two episodes, sheds much light on this subject. Philo asks himself why "when three had appeared," the Bible says: "The two angels came to Sodom at evening"? (Gen 19:1). The entire commentary is a comparison between Abraham, the "perfect one" who saw the triad, and Lot, the "progressive man" who saw only the dyad, which Philo interprets as "the servant-Powers without the Father." In addition, the triad appeared to the former in the bright sunlight of noon; but the dyad appeared to the latter during the "intermediary period" of twilight. This "intermediary" situation, which is precisely that of one who is "progressing," is evoked in *QG* 4.31-32. This parallel returns in *QG* 4.33: the strangers who appear to Abraham immediately accept his invitation because they know he is perfect; in contrast, the Powers refuse Lot's invitation at first and, according to the Bible, when they do accept it, it is only a detour (Gen 19:3). *QG* 4.34 insists on the fact that their acceptance was not perfect because Lot had to "force" them. In a curious twist in the development, Lot is portrayed as the one being forced, rather than the one who does the forcing. In effect, the "perfect" man desires "wisdom willingly," whereas the one who is "progressing" receives "an education despite himself." Escaping the stereotypical forms found elsewhere, the question of *QG* 4:30 foreshadows the commentary, and the same is true of the question of *QG* 4:35 : "Why did he (Lot) prepare drink and unleavened bread for them; but Abraham (prepared) bread under ashes, without drink?" (Gen 19:3).

These two forms of hospitality do not receive the same reward. Abraham receives the birth of Isaac, laughter, and perfect joy; as for Lot, it is probable that his reward is to be saved.[64] On the evidence of

[63]J. Cazeaux would call it their "insularity."

[64]The theme of Lot, the "progressive one," is found again in *QG* 4.38, 46, 47, 49-52.

Gen 19:27, the character Abraham reappears in Question 53 as an example of saintliness and love for mankind. *QG* 4.54 is a commentary on Gen 19.29: ". . .God remembered Abraham, and sent Lot far from the midst of destruction." The literal sense is clear: Lot was saved above all because of Abraham. The allegorical sense is the following: "When the Father remembers the perfect race, he also saves its kinsmen and the progressive man." There ends the parallel between Abraham and Lot.[65] But the "perfect man" and the "progressing man" are once again shown in parallel in *QG* 4.66. Abraham has told Abimelech that Sarah is his sister. Although this tie is not mentioned by Gen 20:7, which is treated here, Philo writes that Sarah, who is Virtue, is "related to those who progress as to a brother, but she cannot be a wife to one who is not a perfect man." In this case, Abraham at the same time embodies the one who "progresses" which he was so long as he was not yet worthy to act as a true spouse to Sarah, and also the "perfect one," which he became later.[66]

In the Treatises Abraham is often the allegorical figure of the "perfect one" (*Leg.* 3.203, 244; *Deus* 4; *Her.* 275, *Mut.* 270.) In contrast, Lot is never the symbol of "one who progresses." *Mos.* 2.58 notes only that he was not at the summit of wisdom and was not saved because of his perfection. The Treatises are not, however, ignorant of the theme which brings together "the perfected" and "the progressive." The most significant development is found in *Leg.* 3.125-159, but in that case it is Moses who is designated as "the perfect one" and Aaron who is "the one who progresses."

Once the exegete has allegorized Abraham and Lot, it becomes quite natural to present the theme of "the perfect one" and "the progressing one" in a large number of the questions of *QG* 4. Genesis suggests this connection; Philo makes it systematic. But the most interesting aspect lies elsewhere: in the persistent appearance of the theme even when one of the characters has disappeared and another has been brought forward to take on its meaning. Philo thereby avoids the rigidity of an allegorical system based on simple repetition, which does not always enrich the theme, and develops a device with a variety of approaches. If such is

[65]The theme of "the progressing one" is found in *QG* 4.55, and the theme of "the perfect man" reappears with Abraham in *QG* 4.59-60.

[66]Cf. *QG* 3.18. *QG* 4.60 interprets the opposition sister/spouse differently. For more on the concept of Abraham being at first unworthy of being the husband of Sarah, see *De Congressu.*

indeed the case, *QG* 4 contains examples of the flexibility and the extension of the Philonic allegorical system.

C. QG *4.1-29*

The first 29 questions of Book 4 are of especially great importance. Not only is Abraham represented as the allegorical symbol of "the perfect man," but it is also indicated that he has this rank because of divine favor and because of the welcome Abraham gave this show of favor. An additional proof of this importance is the place which these 29 questions would have occupied in the architectural ensemble of the *QG* if, as an Armenian translator claims,[67] it is true that Philo had already written a first book which went from the creation of all the creatures to the birth of Abraham's first-born child (Gen 1: 1-17:27), and then a second book which went from God's appearance to Abraham at the Mamre oak up to Moses (Gen 18: 1-50:26).

Philo also provides a commentary on Gen 18 in *Abr.* 107-132, discussing there each part of the passage in sequence. In addition, there are passages in various Treatises where, dealt with separately, certain verses of this same chapter are discussed.[68] Finally, there are a few pages which have come down to us only in Armenian making up the little Treatise called *De Deo*; and, once again, these are devoted to the appearance of the three "men" to Abraham in vv. 1 and 2.[69]

It is hardly necessary to repeat that the only reason these 29 Questions of Book 4 form a grouping is because of the text of Genesis. *QG* 4.1 is a commentary on v. 1 and the beginning of v. 2: "And the Lord God appeared to Abraham at the oak of Mamre. . . ." Question 29 deals with v. 33, which marks the end of the appearance: "The Lord went away, when he had finished talking with Abraham. . . ." The development of each Question concerns only the text under discussion, as is true in the rest of the work. Thus the commentary is not continuous. Moreover, these developments vary greatly in length (from 7 to 110 lines)[70] and approach the texts from quite different points of view. *QG* 4.7, for example, is no more than a moralizing statement. However, when Philo discusses Gen 19:1, "Two angels came to Sodom in the

---

[67]Cf Mercier 1979, 25.
[68]See table above.
[69]See Harl 1967, 189-203.
[70]In the Marcus edition.

evening," Philo opposes Lot and Abraham, as we have seen; and this opposition can be interpreted as a sort of point of separation from what has come before.

All the questions of this grouping are not equally interesting. We have therefore chosen to analyze only three of them: Questions 1, 2, and 8. These are the ones which are the most developed. Marcus's translation contains 110 lines for the first of them, 81 lines for the second, and 104 lines for the eighth. Developed interpretations of this length have great value for the study of Philo's exegetical techniques and the investigation of how they are used in the *Quaestiones*.[71]

(1) *God appears to Abraham* — QG *4.1*

The biblical lemma introduced by the first question corresponds to Gen 18:1-2a: "And the Lord God appeared to Abraham at the oak of Mamre, when he was seated at the door of his tent in the heat of the day, and he lifted up his eyes."[72]

The long discussion which follows is a linear exegesis of the text. Philo comments on each part of the sentence in sequence: "And the Lord God appeared to Abraham at the oak of Mamre," "when he was seated at the door of his tent," and "in the heat of the day." Only the last words of the text are not the object of an explicit interpretation, but it soon becomes apparent that they are inseparable from what has gone before. These words place face to face the one who appears ("the Lord God") and Abraham, not only the one for whom the appearance is destined but the one who in fact receives its direct impact: "And the Lord God appeared to Abraham . . . and he lifted up his eyes."

(a) At the beginning Philo writes, "The literal meaning seems quite clear to me," but he is not speaking of the entire text but only of its first part. Already, the expression "the oak of Mamre" seems to him to be allegorical. His commentary is therefore devoted to a discussion of that part. He cites Heraclitus' statement "Nature likes to hide itself" to confirm the need for an explication.[73] That explication is then divided

---

[71]We deplore the fact that we must rely on translations of the Armenian text (which is itself a translation): Aucher, Marcus, Mercier. We have based our own work on the French translation of Mercier.

[72]For the order in which the complements of place and time are cited, see Mercier 1979, 44: "Les lemmes du livre IV."

[73]For this quotation in the Armenian text, see Marcus 1953 1.265, nn. *i* and *j*.

into two parts. The first part deals with the meaning of the Hebrew word "Mamre," and the second is concerned with the oak itself.

The interpretation of *"Mamre"* is based on etymology. For Philo, the Hebrew word means "that which derives from sight" — in other words, "the act of seeing." In *Migr.* 164-165, he gives the same etymology of this word and concludes "there is a close connection between seeing and contemplation."[74] In the *QG* "the act of seeing" becomes the appanage of "a virtuous intellect endowed with good sight." This is the way the character Abraham is allegorized. Note that the sight that he possesses allows him to see "this created world," "the forms" of this world whose contemplation is "related to philosophy" and "the Father and Creator" of this world, "God uncreated and unbegotten."[75] We recognize the three kinds of sight which are presented more distinctly in *Abr.* 57-58: that of the eyes in the body, which perceive "those most beautiful of created things . . . the ensemble of the heavens and the universe"; that of "the dominant element of the soul" which is wisdom, "the sight of the intellect" whose object is to comprehend through the understanding everything encompassed by nature, and the sight of the eye of the soul which is capable of seeing "the Father and Creator of all." Despite appearances, only two different organs correspond to these three forms of sight, for the intellect is nothing more than the sight of the soul, as *Deus* 45-46 says. The text of *QG* does not even oppose the eyes of the body to the intellect: speaking of the latter, Philo seems to indicate that it is capable of apprehending both the sensible world and the intelligible world and God. Finally, if we understand the translations of this passage correctly, "the act of seeing," signified by "Mamre," makes the sight of the intellect sharp and the intellect itself so vigilant that it cannot sleep.

Afterwards Philo suggests an objection, but at the same time he refutes it. His ideas unfold more or less in this way: how can one talk of seeing God, since God is incomprehensible not only "to the human race, but also to all the purest parts of heaven"? However, how could it be that God would come if it were not in order to be seen? He must therefore make himself visible, and in order to do that he must give off light,[76] which he does. He shines with a certain radiance which "we most

[74]See Cazeaux 1965, 200, n. 1.

[75]However, it seems that Aucher's translation avoids dealing with "the forms," the sight of which is related to philosophy. Marcus 1953, 1.266, n. *g*, proposes τὰ εἴδη or τὰς μορφάς as a Greek equivalent for what he translates as "the forms."

[76]Here we are using the Aucher and Marcus translations.

properly call forms," and envelops the whole soul with this radiance and "fills it with a light which is incorporeal and supercelestial." This light will conduct the intellect from the form to the archetype.

Even in the absence of the Greek text, the vocabulary in this passage suggests a Platonic inspiration. What is this incorporeal and supercelestial light if it is not the αὐγή which in the great myth of the *Phaedrus* does not confound itself with the forms but instead inundates them, thereby offering them to the contemplation of souls whose charioteers have raised their heads high enough? Sensible world, intelligible world — Philo borrows his representation of the universe from the Platonic myth, and he crowns it with the addition of God. In his Treatises, the word "archetype" is usually applied to the Ideas, but rather often also to the Logos of God and, occasionally, to God himself. We read in *Cher.* 86 "For the things in the world which are beautiful would never have been what they are, if they had not been modeled on the archetype, the true beauty, the Uncreated, the Blessed, the Imperishable." In general, therefore, God is placed in direct opposition to the created world, and the world of Ideas is not invoked. However, in *Somn.* 1.75, Philo writes: " . . .God is light . . . and . . . he is not only light, but the archetype of every other light, or rather prior to and high above every archetype. . . . "[77] A little farther on, in *Somn.* 1.115, we read lines which have some resemblance to our text from *QG:* "In the time of fruitfulness and uplifting, from all sides there shine upon it (the intelligence of the spiritual athlete, which is to say Jacob) the incorporeal rays of the Archetypes, which come from the spring of the Logos, meaning God through whom all is accomplished."

The etymological sense of the Hebrew word "Mamre" thus leads Philo to introduce the theme of spiritual sight and to make Abraham the symbol of an intellect endowed with the clearest sight possible. In addition, since there is no sight without light,[78] the image of light is introduced in its turn. Around and within the virtuous intellect God himself sheds a light which is different from that of the sensible world.

---

[77]A comment on Ps 26:1. Cf. Mercier and Petit 1984, 149 (4.1).

[78]Cf. Plato, *Rep.*6.507 D-E, 508 E -509 A.

The interpretation of *the oak* makes us regret all the more that the Greek text has disappeared.[79] Since it is unavailable, we will depend on the translation and examine it section by section.

First, Philo expresses his admiration for "the extremes," by which he means, on the one hand, the One who appears (God) and, on the other, the one to whom God appears and who sees. That is why, he suggests, the Bible places between them an oak -- a tree which to Philo seems "very symbolic." The problem is to discern the exact meaning of this symbol, and Philo proceeds to address this issue.

He remarks that the oak is "the most powerful and the greatest in authority, since it is one of the most familiar undomesticated (trees)." In Philo's Treatises, the oak has two symbolic meanings, one positive and one negative: it represents either unswerving effort (*Migr*. 223) or stupid bullheadedness (*Congr*. 61, *Fug*. 39). In both cases the proverbial hardness of the oak inspires the interpretation. There is no allusion to this hardness in the passage under discussion. Moreover, this oak is both wild and domesticated, which Philo explains a few lines later by saying that its trunk is wild but its fruit is "a domesticated nut." Several times the Treatises set those trees which are essentially wild over against those which are cultivated (*Opif*. 40, *Leg*. 1.49), the former being sterile and the latter bearing fruit. The oak, whose acorns traditionally made up the food of the first men, would therefore be a noteworthy exception. But, in his extant writings Philo says nothing about that.[80]

If Marcus is right to think that the Greek verb translated by the Armenian here should be αἰνίττεται,[81] such an oak should signify "the sage who has become altogether an eye." If that is so, the entire sentence seems to teeter on the edge of absurdity. That the sage should become "altogether an eye" is not surprising, for the same affirmation will reappear in the second answer which clarifies that what is meant is the eye or the eyes of the soul;[82] but how can this oak be the allegorical designation of the sage when it is placed, according to what we have seen above, between the sage and God? Philo will also say on this subject that, since the oak has nourished primitive men with its fruits, it has been

[79]See Marcus 1953, 1.267, nn. g and h; the latter is repeated by Mercier and Petit 1984, 147, n. 5.

[80]For a discussion of the oak as a wild tree, cf. *Aet*. 64.

[81]Marcus 1953, 1 267, n. *d*.

[82]Cf. Mercier and Petit 1984, 153-154. Cf. also Marcus 1953, 1.267, n. *e*, where he suggests that the original Greek must have read ὀφθαλμιζόμενον, translated by "grafted."

given "preeminence" by life.[83] Would it then be completely impossible to see in this oak an allusion to the tree of life and to remember a passage from *Plant*. 44: "For the man formed by the breath of God in his image differs not at all, it seems to me, from the tree whose fruit is immortal life: both are considered imperishable and masters of the most central and important part for it is said that the tree of life is in the middle of the garden" (Gen 2:9). Note that in this text the man formed in the image of God is opposed to the moulded man as defined afterwards, in the same way that the soul, or even more correctly its master part, meaning the intellect, is presented in opposition to the body. If this is correct, the oak is the image of the intellect of the sage, whose perfection makes possible the vision of God.

The contemplation of the intellect seems to pass through different stages, but the phrase which suggests them is as difficult as the preceding one; it is obscure from one end to the other. Certain pages of the Treatises seem however to throw a little light on this passage. In *Praem*. 37-39[84] we see Jacob painfully open the eye of the soul and realize, although he is blinded by the brightness of the vision, that the intelligible world has a charioteer. He perseveres in his contemplation and receives the aid of God who reinforces "the penetration of his eyesight." Returning to the oak, it seems that before discussing the special divine attention that was shown, Philo first wishes to evoke the difficulties of contemplation when he speaks of the "rays which struggle until they accommodate themselves to the sight" of the intellect.

But perhaps one should ask oneself if this phrase is in its proper location. The following phrase, which opposes the wild trunk and the domesticated fruit, would be more logically connected with the earlier description of the oak as both wild and domesticated. The part that deals with the sight of the intellect would seem to be a sort of parenthesis. By contrast, the mention of the acorn, a domesticated nut which served as food for men, is closely tied to that which follows: "For this reason," Philo writes in effect, "life attributed preeminence to it, considering the

---

[83]Mercier and Petit 1984, 147, n. 6, asks if the Greek text here read ἡγεμονία or ἀρχή, thinking of a possible allusion to the longevity of the oak. But isn't it enough to remember the service rendered to primitive men and which allowed them to survive? Cf. the proverb cited by Dicéarque: ἄλις δρυός = "Let us be finished with the oak." Cf. Vidal-Naquet 1975, 374-390. Cf. Hesiod *Op*. 230-233; Lucretius 939-940, 965; Virgil *Georg*. l. 5-9, 147-149, 159.

[84]Cf. *Abr*. 70 and 79.

oak as the temple and altar of the only God," an important linking phrase, since one here finds the oak assigned two new attributes.

The declaration that the oak is the temple and altar of God makes one wonder if these two images are compatible with the meaning previously assigned to it, "the sage who has become altogether an eye." The solution is found in Philo's Treatises, several passages of which represent the soul (and more precisely the intellect) as either the dwelling or the temple of God (or both at the same time). We read in *Somn.* 1.149, "Work therefore with all your strength, O my soul, to become the lodging of God, his holy temple, his shining dwelling!" and, a little farther on in the same Treatise, "For there exist . . . two sanctuaries of God: one is the visible universe . . . the other is the rational soul (§215)." And Philo writes in *Cher.* 100: "One house alone is worthy of him (God): the soul which conforms to his wishes."[85] As for the altar, it is erected in honor of God and upon it are offered sacrificial victims; the most appropriate victim is "a soul intact in all its parts." [86] According to Philo, every sacrifice accomplished according to the rites of the Law is the symbol of an invisible offering of the soul. *Ebr.* 85-87 depicts Moses erecting two altars, "one, on the outside, for the sacrificial ritual; the other, on the inside, for burning incense." The first symbolizes the exterior life, the second, the interior life; and the incense and perfumes on it represent that which is produced by the intellect and which with its sweet fragrance fills "the whole region of the soul."

It is therefore not impossible that the oak stands for two things at the same time: the sage become eye and rewarded by the vision of God, and the sage become temple and altar of God. This oak is situated between the sage and God because, on one hand, the sage has had to strip himself of all that is not intellect and, on the other hand, God sends his light to manifest his presence. Everything occurs as if each one had taken a step in the direction of the other and as if the oak marks the place where they meet.

That would explain why the discussion of the oak has two parts: the first considers the oak as the allegory of the sage's intellect blessed with good sight; the second shows the oak as the temple and altar of God. It is to this latter aspect that life has attributed preeminence. Hence the second part exalts the oak as the tree par excellence. It is at first

---

[85]See Colson's translation: " . . the soul that is fitted to receive Him." Cf. *Sobr.* 62-64 and *Somn.* 2. 246-248.

[86]Cf. *Sacr.* 139 in Méasson 1966 and 209-210, n. 23. Cf. also *Somn.* 1.243; 2.183.

assimilated to the laurel and the olive and then designated as the greatest of trees.

Oak, laurel, and olive — Philo here brings together three trees the Greeks had consecrated to a divinity: the oak of Dodone, sacred to Zeus; the laurel, sacred to Apollo; and the olive, sacred to Athena.[87] Moreover, these associations with particular gods do not prevent the olive from crowning the statue of Zeus at Olympia;[88] and it was an olive branch heavy with fruit and wrapped with wool (ἡ εἰρεσιώνη) which was carried to the temple of Apollo during the Pyanepsies and the Thargelies.

In our text, the assimilation of the oak to the laurel and the olive could suggest a return to the image of light. But we dare not affirm it without some qualifications. When Philo speaks of the "laurel of the sun," it is probably a reference to the laurel of Apollo who is god of the sun. It is likely that Philo uses this turn of phrase to avoid naming a pagan deity. However, the sun is mentioned not because it gives light[89] but because of the supremacy it exercises in the world. The theme goes back to Plato; Cleanthes considers the sun the *hegemonikon* of the world because it determines the day, the year, and the other divisions of time.[90] We find the idea in *QG* 1.57. That is why Philo can interpret the sun allegorically as the Logos and God himself.[91] If it is hard to dissociate the sun from the idea of light, that is not the primary association here. By contrast, the olive tree is linked to the oak through its relationship to light. "The olive tree," writes Philo, "(is) of an ever-virginal essence and the most pure found in the sphere of the fixed,[92] for olive oil is the material of light. . . ." This strange and beautiful affirmation evokes other Philonic texts.[93] In *Somn.* 2.58, we find olive oil cited for its benefits to the body: "It makes the skin smooth, soothes away fatigue, gives an excellent physical form. . ."; and in *Mos.* 2.152 olive oil is the purifying oil used by priests. But it can take on yet another meaning. In

[87]In the oracular oak, the Greeks worshipped the presence of the god whose voice they believed they heard in the rustle of the leaves. Cf. Frazer 1963*a*, 349-375 ("The Worship of the Oak"), esp. p. 358, and Plutarch *Table Talk* 7.4 (703 C). For the laurel, see Frazer 1963*b*, 81-82. It is thought that the crown of laurel replaced a crown of oak.

[88]Frazer 1963*b*, 91. This crown was given to the winners of the Olympic games. Cf. Pausanias 5. ll.1.

[89]The translation of Mercier, "he works in the service of health," would seem instead to refer to Apollo as physician.

[90]Cf. *Rep.* 6.509 B 2-4; *SVF* 1.499, p. 111-112; see also Méasson 1986, 38-39.

[91]See *Somn.* 1.85-87.

[92]Mercier translates: "le globe fixe."

[93]Cf. also Plutarch *Table Talk* 6.9.2 and "On the Cause of Cold" 13.

Det. 115-118, Philo speaks of the virtues as the nourishment of a soul which is able to suck "honey from the rock and oil from the hard stone" (Deut 32:13). This stone represents the wisdom of God, and the source of wisdom does not always flow with equal force: "when its flow is calm, it sweetens like honey; when the flow is quite rapid, it is a thick liquid like olive oil, which becomes the light of the soul." Philo thus establishes a close tie between olive oil and light. This tie is confirmed in the following paragraph when honey and oil represent two aspects of learning: "first of all, it gives birth to a sweetness in the mind upon contact with the objects of knowledge, and then it makes a blinding light shine on those who do not easily tire of the objects they love. . . ."[94] Last of all, olive oil is what feeds fire and, in that way also it is a source of light. According to *Fug.* 176, the contemplative life provides "a joy which is unmixed" and "an intelligible light, like that given off by a flame which is oil-fed."

The preeminence accorded the oak appears also in the vocabulary used. The fact that the name "oak" is used as a sort of generic noun[95] shows clearly that it is the "leader" of trees. This fact can be verified more particularly by examining compound nouns: δρυηκόποι,[96] which etymologically means "cutters of oaks," is applied to woodcutters who cut down all kinds of trees; δρύφακτοι[97] means "a barrier of wood" and not just a "barrier of oak"; fruits of trees which are both domesticated and wild are referred to as "fruits of the oak and olives" and fruits which mature on the tree are called δρυπεπεῖς,[98] "tree-ripened."

Thus ends the allegorical exegesis of the "oak of Mamre," an exegesis which still has its obscure parts. No Philonic parallel exists to illuminate it. No reference to the oak of Mamre is present in *De Abrahamo*, which tells the story without citing the biblical text, nor is there any help in the *De Deo*, a text specifically devoted to the first two

[94]Cf. *Fug.* 110 in Starobinski-Safran 1970 (PAPM) and p. 184, n. 1: "Olive oil here stands for intelligible light. . . . In rabbinical literature, olive oil symbolizes the light of the Torah, of the mind, and of the human soul itself."

[95]Cf. Hesychius: δρῦς· πᾶν ξύλον καὶ δένδρον. Cf. also Homer *Il.* 11.86, scholium: δρῦν ἐκάλουν οἱ παλαιοὶ πᾶν δένδρον, in relationship to the word δρύτομος = δρυοτόμος, carpenter, woodcutter. Cf. Soph. *Tr.* 766 where δρῦς means "the pine" and Eur. *Cycl.* 615 where it means "the olive tree."

[96]Marcus's hypothesis. Mercier thinks it is δρυοκόποι.

[97]Marcus.

[98]Ibid.

verses of Gen 18, for the biblical lemma given does not even include this expression.

(b) Philo then turns to the second part of the phrasing in his text. In the order that the words are presented, but without quoting that section again, he discusses "when he was seated" and "at the door of his tent." Although the two explications are complementary, each deserves to be studied separately.

After *the seated position* has been discussed on the literal level, it becomes the object of an allegorical exegesis. At the allegorical level, such a posture should no longer be attributed to a man, even one as great as Abraham, but rather to "the intellect of the virtuous man." This position clearly represents the absence of change, a stability in the image of the immutability of God himself, even though it can only be an obscure image "in comparison with the archetype." What is required of this intellect is the knowledge of "intelligible life," for which we should read "the life which is fitting to an intelligible nature." No human can have lasting access to it, because for a human it is an "unliveable life," ἀβίωτος βίος. The contrast of stability, which makes us more like God, to change, which is characteristic of creatures, is a theme particularly dear to Philo; and in his work we often see Abraham embody an attitude which raises him momentarily above human nature.[99]

The *tent* at whose door the intellect is seated represents the body. Philo himself alludes to the "tunics of skin" with which, according to Gen 3:21, God clothes Adam and Eve when they are forced to leave Paradise. Since the body makes paths available to the sensations which they can use to penetrate to the soul, it is fitting that the virtuous intellect take on the role of guardian of the senses, which are the doors to the body.

Philo's Treatises contain a theme which is close to this idea, that of the intellect submerged by the flood of sensible objects which penetrate to the interior by the orifices of the senses.[100] Here Philo is no longer speaking of "doors" but, in the strict sense, of "mouths" (στόμια). Therefore the image of a doorkeeper is no longer appropriate. That image is replaced by one of a chain, δεσμός, which represents self-control (*Det.* 103). For the same reason, in *Post.* 182, Phinehas is not

---

[99]Cf. *Cher.* 18-19, an allusion to Gen 18:22; *Somn.* 2.226-227 where Abraham (Gen 18:22) and Moses (Deut 5:31) are discussed; and the same in *Post.* 27-28. Also cf. *Deus* which cites Deut 5:31 and where Moses is discussed.

[100]Cf. *Det.* 100 and *Mut.* 107. Cf.Méasson 1986, 184-185, "l'âme submergée par les flots."

the doorkeeper, but the "controller (ὁ δίοπος) of the orifices and openings of the body," and his name is explained as "muzzle of the mouth."

In the answer of this Question we are examining, we are presented with a sort of double role for the intellect, since it has two aspects: it is that which, in the body-clothed soul, must be carefully protected from the assaults of the sensible world; and it is also that which provides protection against whatever might intrude from this sensible world.[101]

The words "he was seated at the door of his tent" mean, therefore, that the intellect was not only in a state of stability (an image of divine immutability) but also that it was on guard, protecting against any aggression from the exterior. Without such vigilance, its stability would be lost.[102]

(c) To this indication of place, Genesis adds an indication of time: *"in the heat of the day."* Philo substitutes the expression "at noon," which in fact is found in the Septuagint. This specific indication is a perfectly appropriate one to use for an appearance, for this hour is "the most luminous hour in the entire day."[103] The image of light inseparable from vision is thus reintroduced by the biblical text itself and is the last image discussed in *QG* 4.1. Allegorically, the noon sun is "the intelligible sun" — "it sends out incorporeal rays which are very luminous and brilliant and shine on pure souls." Here we recognize what Philo had written previously in his commentary on "Mamre." These are the same rays, the same incorporeal light, the same αὐγή. It surrounds and illuminates the intellect, giving it "a clearer and more certain perception of things that really exist." Probably Marcus is right to think that the Greek text read τῶν ὄντως ὄντων, the Platonic formula which designated the Ideas. The pure souls are virtuous intellects which turn their gaze toward the light, "drawn forward by feelings of piety and becoming familiar with heaven." But the eyes of the soul cannot look for long at this brilliant light which dazzles and blinds them. Every act of contemplation involves this experience, which evokes the Platonic myth of the cave. Philo's Treatises offer several examples: that of Jacob, who,

---

[101]Cf. *Det.* 53.

[102]Cf. *Cher.* 12-13; *Leg.* 2.53-64; *Fug.* 188-193, but, in these two latter passages the error of the soul, or, better stated, of the sensations, is to go toward the exterior, whereas in *QG* 4.1, its error is to allow what is outside to penetrate within. At any rate, the result is the same. Cf. Cazeaux 1983*a*, 451-455, 585-592.

[103]As Marcus translates it.

however, received the gift of the vision from God (*Praem*. 38-39); that of philosophers who study heavenly bodies and who should serve as models for those who search for the essence of God (*Spec*. 1.37); finally, that of the intellect which has raised itself up to the summit of the arch of intelligible things (*Opif*. 71). Speaking of the noonday sun in *QG*, Philo quite naturally insists on the intensity and the purity of shadowless light. The same biblical text is discussed in *Abr*. 119. Filled with the light of intelligible nature, the soul itself becomes shadowless and "apprehends a triadic vision of one single object." This "triadic vision" refers to Gen 18:2, which Philo discusses here with Gen 18:1.

(d) *Remarks*. Thus *QG* 4.1, which began without an introduction, ends without a conclusion. As we have seen, only one method is used: the exegesis is linear, with the biblical text divided into three parts which are discussed in sequence. Each comment first touches on the literal sense, if only to point out explicitly where the meaning is perfectly clear. Such is the case of the first phrase discussed. For the second, Philo begins with a rapid definition of "the seated position"; for the third, with a reminder of what characterizes that moment of the day called "noon." After these introductions on the literal level, the exegesis is allegorical from one end to the other. That is why Abraham's name never appears and why "the virtuous intellect endowed with excellent sight" has its role in the entire presentation.[104] For the same reason, after affirming that the literal sense of the first section of the quotation is plain, Philo detaches an expression in the text — "the oak of Mamre" — which he thinks is exclusively allegorical and suggests that this one expression would suffice for the commentary. But then Philo breaks it down to consider first the meaning of "Mamre" and then the meaning of "oak." In the second part of the scriptural sentence, this time explained as a whole, he distinguishes two elements which he interprets separately, "as he sat" and "at the door of his tent." This fragmentation of the text does no harm, however, to the unity of the exegesis. Everything contributes to our understanding of God's appearance to Abraham, with the result that the first two words of v. 2 cited in the biblical lemma require no commentary: the appearance of God and the sight of the intellect cannot be viewed separately.

The exegetical techniques used here are the same as those found in the Treatises: the interpretation of "Mamre" is based on etymology,

---

[104]Abraham is cited in *QG* 4.8.

while the exegesis of "oak" is based, at least in part, on a vocabulary study. Elsewhere, the biblical text itself furnishes images which allegory transposes; and in order to interpret them, Philo refers to another verse of Genesis (3:21). Finally, his explicit reference to Heraclitus and implicit references to the cosmology of the *Phaedrus*, to the idea of the vision offered by the *Republic,* or to the bedazzlement of the prisoner in the cave show that Philo reads the Bible in the light of his Greek culture.

A single theme: the appearance of God to the patriarch; but, in order to discuss it, Philo uses two images which dominate this long stretch of exegesis: that of sight, of the gaze, of the eye(s) of the intellect, and that of light, without which eyes cannot function. We find these images in the comments on both "Mamre" and "at noon." The latter exegesis no longer emphasizes the characters in the scene, but rather the light itself, whose blinding brilliance and pureness is exalted. Between these two commentaries, the exegesis of the words "when he was seated at the door of his tent" introduces the image of the stability of the intellect. Although this differs from the images of sight and light, it is not completely unrelated to them because it expresses a state without which the intellect is incapable of contemplating God.

Because all of the Questions in *QG* 4.1-29 deal with the same biblical episode, it is not surprising that the same images reappear in several of them. In his commentary on v. 3, "Lord, if I have found grace before you, do not pass over your servant," Philo writes: "because of eyes which are more open and because of a more enlightened sight, the intellect has a clearer vision (*QG* 4.4)." In the same Question, God is shown filling the soul with "his incorporeal light." The image is tied here to the theme of the presence of God, who is himself associated with the theme of the happiness which his presence brings. In contrast, the image of shadows is associated with the theme of God's absence and thus, with unhappiness.[105] *QG* 4.8, to which we will return, is a commentary on vv. 6 and 7 (Abraham's order to Sarah and the servant to prepare quickly what was fitting to offer the three visitors): it explains that God appeared as a triad in order to show consideration for "the weakness of those who looked" — "For the eye of the soul, which is very luminous and very brilliant, will become dimmed before falling upon and gazing on Him who is in his oneness. . . ." *QG* 4.21, which discusses v. 17 ("I shall not conceal from my servant Abraham what I do") considers "blind" " those who do not philosophize properly with the eyes of the

[105]Cf. *QG* 4.18-19.

soul," meaning persons who do not develop a healthful theology from the study of nature. Question 22, which discusses v. 19, returns to the same subject: "the eyes of the intellect with their piercing gaze" slowly become capable of perceiving "the incorporeal light" which leads the intellect to discover the true Cause. As for Sodom, the cursed city, its name means "Blindness" or "Sterility"(*QG* 4.23).[106]

We also rediscover the image of the stability of the intellect. In *QG* 4.25, which is a commentary on v. 22 ("And Abraham was still standing before the Lord"), stability is interpreted as "constancy in truth," a firmness which remains "immovable and enduring." *QG* 4.29, which discusses the words "The Lord went away when he had finished talking to Abraham, and Abraham returned to his place," is of particular interest to us. Philo here explains that God chooses to be the first to depart out of consideration, once again, for the weakness of human nature. Note that, starting with *QG* 4.1, the stability of the intellect which contemplates God is clearly shown to be a pale imitation of divine immutability. Therefore human contemplation of God can only be temporary.

QG 4.1 offers an exceptionally long discussion. We think it also presents some rather unique aspects when compared to the rest of the work. It is true that it contains dense and confusingly obscure passages which make parts of it incomprehensible, and the thread which ties ideas and images together sometimes seems to break. Moreover, while at first glance allusions appear to be present, a closer examination makes that seem much less sure. But all of these flaws are not necessarily the fault of Philo. On the other hand, this commentary does not neglect anything in the biblical text, and it has a genuine unity to which each of its parts contributes. The exegetical method is very close to that found in the Treatises. Even the same themes and images are found. Finally, these pages contain an exegesis which is of interest not only in relation to Gen 18:1 but also, viewed as a sort of beginning piece, in relation to the entire text of chapter 18.

---

[106]The image of light is also found in *QG* 4.14, applied to virtue. Question 26 speaks of those who have not lost the capacity "to rekindle the brightness of the ray, the glow of the fire of justice" and who will thus recover "good spiritual health." Cf. in *Migr*. 122-123 the images of "the live coal" and "the spark."

(2) *The Three Visitors or The Ambiguous Vision* — QG *4.2*

The biblical lemma of *QG* 4.2 closely follows the text subsequent to the one dealt with in the first Question: "He saw, and behold, three men were standing over him" (Gen 18:2a). The commentary begins with an introductory phrase which announces the subject in a completely abstract way: "In the deepest sense, he (Moses) presents the idea that, for those who are able to see, it was possible for the One to be three, and for the Three to be one, because they are one according to a higher principle."

The translators seem to agree that the Greek text probably began with the adverb φυσικώτατα, which etymologically means "in the way which is most in harmony with the nature of things," often interpreted by Philo to mean "in the most profound sense," meaning "in an allegorical sense."[107] Therefore we are not surprised that Abraham is not named and that "those who are able to see" is substituted instead.

Whereas *QG* 4.1 shows the Lord God, who takes the initiative to appear, standing opposite the virtuous intellect which receives the vision, *QG* 4.2 is devoted to the contents of the vision itself. The first Question emphasizes the impossibility of seeing God unless God sends his light, but the second Question responds to the implied query, "Exactly what does the intellect see when it is said to see God?" The introduction gives a first answer, which — if the biblical text were not present in the background — would present all the abstraction and enigma of Philo's speculations on numbers found elsewhere in his works. Verse 1 spoke of the appearance of the Lord God; and it is still the Lord God to which the expression "One" refers. For Philo, in effect, "one" can have several meanings: in addition to being the first number, it can stand for the Parmenidian notion of Being, which is pure of all which is not itself, and consequently for God as One. *Virt.* 215 describes Abraham walking "with unfaltering zeal in quest of the One (ἐπὶ τὴν τοῦ ἑνὸς . . . ζήτησιν)."[108]

It therefore becomes the task of allegory to reveal who the two other visitors are and to explain the reciprocity of the two formulae: "(it was possible) for the One to be three, and for the Three to be one."

---

[107]According to Leisegang 1941, cols. 37-39, Philo's use of φυσικώκατα often means the same thing as συμβολικώτατα.

[108]Cf. *Leg*. 3.48 and 126. Elsewhere, in order to safeguard transcendence more clearly, Philo says of God that He is more pure than the one; cf. *Praem*. 40 and *Contempl*. 2.

Initially the development appears to be a linear exegesis. Everything is organized as if Philo, having divided the biblical lemma into two parts, were interpreting them one after the other. The words to which the first commentary refers are not quoted, but it immediately becomes clear that the exegete is reading the text in the following manner: "He saw three (persons)." Philo then discusses the end of the text, which he quotes in this way: "they were standing over him." But the commentary does not stop there.

(a) The first half of the first exegetical discussion is devoted to the meaning of the number three, and the second to the meaning of "he saw."

Philo tells us three times what we must understand by the triadic appearance of which v. 2 speaks, in contrast to v. 1, which spoke only of the Lord God. The first explanation immediately reveals the identity of the three characters: "the first Powers, the Creative and the Royal" to which the One adds itself, that one being God. God chooses to present himself as a triad out of consideration for human weakness, which renders the human intellect incapable of apprehending him as "distinct from all others."[109] The second explanation follows the gaze of the intellect which directs itself toward God and discovers simultaneously the Powers which are in his service. For, once again, instead of appearing alone, God makes a triad appear. The third explanation once again follows the gaze of the intellect, a gaze which has become more penetrating, one must think, since Philo writes "when the intellect begins to have an apprehension of the Existent One" and since, despite its obscurity, the text of the Question seems to mean that one cannot speak of God except as unique and playing the role of principal. However, the following phrases designate the Existent as Him whom the intellect was unable to see without the Powers: "the Creative which is called God" and "the Royal which is called Lord." The exegesis is therefore not satisfied with proposing an interpretation of the three characters which gets richer through repetition, but suggests that there is a sort of alternation between the One and the triad, as if each time the One were "aimed at" but the triad was where the gaze "landed."

---

[109]Cf. *QG* 4.1, the last part, the commentary of "at noon."

When Philo begins to discuss the words "he saw," he substitutes "he lifted up his eyes,"[110] the beginning of v. 2, already cited in the biblical lemma of Question 1. The exegesis, however, emphasizes only the image of sight, leaving aside the question of the direction of the gaze, the meaning of which should be evident to anyone who thinks of the world in the image of the mythical universe of Plato.[111] Question 1 had already discussed it in length; Question 2 returns, in part, to the discussion devoted to the sight of the virtuous intellect.[112] What is new is the explicit opposition set up between the eyes of the body and the eyes of the soul, as well as the importance assigned to the images of sleep and wakefulness as a way to contrast those whose spiritual eyes are always closed and the virtuous intellect, whose eyes are in such a state of wakefulness that the intellect cannot sleep. Philo insists upon the necessity of speaking in the plural of the "eyes" of the soul, for "the virtuous man" (we are to understand his intellect) "has become an eye altogether." The expression has already appeared in Question 1. And these variations on the theme of the sight of the soul finish in the same way as did the exegesis of the triadic appearance: of the virtuous man "become eyes" it is said that "he begins to see the divine and holy vision of the Lord,"[113] as was said above "when the intellect begins to apprehend the Existent One." In both cases, however, the result is the same: "the single appearance appeared to him as a triad, and the triad, as a unity." What is presented is thus not a gaze which would progress from the triad to unity: it initially aims at unity and reaches the triad, but, through the triad, it becomes capable of apprehending unity.

---

[110]According to Mercier, Philo here is taking up the text in an alternate form; Aucher and Marcus quote the text as it appears in Question 1.

[111]In *QG* 4.4 (Mercier and Petit 1984, 161), Philo writes that only "the souls which have been seized by celestial desire" can present themselves before God. Cf. *QG* 4.20 (Mercier and Petit 1984, 187).

[112]Cf. Mercier and Petit 1984, 145 and 147. For the image of the sight of the soul in Plato's works, cf. *Rep*. 519 B, *Symp* 219 A; for the eye of the soul, cf. *Rep*. 533 D, and in its plural form, *Soph*. 254 A. Philo often uses the image of the eye or the eyes of the soul in his works. Cf. for the singular use *Sacr*. 78, *Post*. 8, *Ebr*. 44, *Sobr*. 3, *Migr*. 39, 191, *Congr*. 135 (see Alexandre 1967, 199, n. 4); for its plural use see *Sacr*. 69, *Post*. 18, 118, 167, *Plant*. 22.

[113]The Armenian text contains 3 adjectives. Marcus 1953, 1.271, n.*g*, proposes the expressions κυρίαν καὶ ἁγίαν καὶ θείαν as Greek equivalents and wonders if Philo were not therefore suggesting: God (ἅγιος), flanked by the two Powers, the Creative (θεῖος), the Royal (κύριος). However attractive this hypothesis, it seems confirmed neither by the end of the phrase nor by the phrase to which it is parallel.

Philo then goes on to the second part of the biblical lemma, "they were standing over him." The commentary is brief and banal: if it is true that the appearance is made up of God and his two first Powers, how could such a triad not be above any created being?

(b) Suddenly, right when the exegetical analysis seems to have arrived at its conclusion, Philo sets off to explore a new path. At the end of this second part, we discover that it is an explanation of a small bit of biblical text neglected up to this point. It is written, in effect, "and behold, three men. . . ." Note that, although Philo's commentary certainly discussed the triadic appearance, he has nowhere yet spoken of the fact that the appearance took the form of three human figures. That is why Philo here introduces the idea of two appearances which are probably two interpretations of a single and same appearance.[114] But it is important to note that there is no intent here to oppose a literal to an allegorical meaning. We have not left allegory. Abraham still has not been named and the intellect continues to be substituted for him. In addition, the exegete is no longer Philo, properly speaking, but rather the intellect which hesitates between the two interpretations and decides finally to accept both of them. In the preceding section, the commentary spoke continuously of the first interpretation. It is taken up again here and the function of the two Powers said to be "superior" is clarified further: "the Creative, through which he (God) created the world and operates it, and the Royal, through which he has authority over what he has created." The second interpretation limits itself to the appearance of three strangers — not just any strangers, however, but "the most perfect according to human nature both in body and in the honors due to their merit."[115] Pulled first toward one appearance and then toward the other, the intellect adapts its conduct to each one in turn: in its attention to God it manifests its piety, in its attention to the noble strangers its love for mankind — meaning in this specific case its hospitality.

Note that, according to Philo, both the uncertainty of the intellect and its care to practice these two fundamental virtues are revealed in the play of singulars and plurals which the biblical text itself offers: ". . .everything which is said concerning one or to one or by one bears

[114]The phrase which introduces the theme of the two appearances is obscure, but the theme itself becomes clear in what follows.

[115]We are following the translation of Aucher, which is the most satisfying for the meaning. According to Marcus 1953, 1.272, who is probably thinking of *Abr.* 113, these are three angels. We depart from him on this point.

witness to an appearance as God, but whatever is said concerning several or to several (bears witness to an appearance) as human strangers." The range of the exegesis is then enlarged to vv. 1-16, where the words considered most important are lifted out to be regrouped according to whether the reference is singular or plural. According to Philo, seven phrases, with references in the singular, concern the appearance of God. Two of them, however, contain surprising elements. The approbation given to Abraham in v. 5, "Do as you have said," does not allow us to judge if one or many are speaking. In the Septuagint the phrase is introduced by a plural, εἶπαν, but an alternate reading suggests εἶπεν.[116] In the same way, quoted as "and it was said to him: Where is Sarah. . .?", v. 9 in no way implies that there is only one speaker. Perhaps the Armenian translator is responsible for these difficulties. Above and beyond the anomalies presented by the text, what is really important to note here is that Philo is no longer establishing a parallel between the divine triad and the three strangers, but that he is opposing the three men to God considered in his oneness.

Since scripture has literally confirmed the two appearances, Philo returns once again to the importance of the two virtues of piety and love of mankind. If we judge by the translations, however, the text is far from clear. We seem to be very close to the literal sense: although Abraham still has not been named, it is not hard to recognize him in the phrase "the leader and founder of a line." He is probably still the symbol of the virtuous intellect which appears, in these lines, to guide "every man who is enrolled, toward life in the city."[117] What city? Perhaps it is the world, in which, according to *Spec.* 2.45, "the companions of wisdom are the citizens, counted as such by virtue (ἀρετῆς ἐγγραφούσης), which has the charge of presiding over the universal commonwealth." Or perhaps it is above the world, "the commonwealth of imperishable and incorporeal Ideas" where live, after having been registered (ἐγγραφέντες) as freemen, the priests and the prophets "who do not wish to be involved as citizens in the commonwealth of the world" as we read in *Gig.* 61. The contexts are different, but it is not impossible that in Philo's thought the city of Stoic inspiration has joined Plato's Republic of Ideas. There is a new theme in this discussion: that of the virtuous

[116]See the edition of Rahlfs, who gives εἶπαν in the text and sends the reader to A (Codex Alexandrinus) for εἶπεν.

[117]Mercier translates: "(l'esprit) dirigera tout homme. . . ?" For Marcus, the subject of the verb here is scripture.

intellect put forward as an example and as a leader of men. If such really were the sense of the text, the shadow of Moses, whose φιλανθρωπία Philo has praised, might be seen in the background, profiled behind Abraham.[118]

The lines with which *QG* 4.2 ends do not really constitute a conclusion as such. They are instead a warning against an erroneous interpretation. "Having used that as a pretext," Philo writes, "certain people, when they attribute (to God) measures and weights of proportion and structure, have gone astray in their way of thinking." But how could they have gone astray in thinking thus, when *QG* 4.8 says that "the measure of all things, intelligible and sensible, is God alone" and that that which preceded shows the Powers also taking on, according to their rank, the role of measure? Unless those of whom Philo speaks (since they attribute not only to God but also to the Powers "the measures and weights of proportion and structure") have considered the Powers divinities, thus falling into the error of polytheism? As the translators have rendered this phrase, the meaning remains obscure. A few lines later on, those who "think that it (the divinity) has often appeared in beautiful human forms"[119] are accused of polytheism. Thus formulated, the accusation is addressed to those who are tempted to see three gods in the three men Abraham sees, and thus the error of polytheism would be made even worse by that of anthropomorphism.

The originality of the passage is found in a reference to Homer which is not limited to three verses of the *Odyssey*. Philo mentions "austere Homer, full of knowledge" because he set forth "the way of conducting oneself, meaning that it is not fitting to be overly proud, which is to one's own detriment." Now, this banal lesson of wisdom would have nothing to do with the exegesis we are studying if it did not send us back to the context in which appear the verses of the *Odyssey* which are then cited. In Book 17 Ulysses, who has disguised himself as a beggar, is insulted and struck by Antinous, one of the suitors, who refuses to give him a little food. In Book 22, when the hour of vengeance has arrived, Antinous is the first to pay. This character is guilty of arrogance toward others rather than pride. Nevertheless, it is likely that Philo was thinking here of Antinous' tragic adventure when he reminds us of the words by which another suitor had tried to warn him:

---

[118]Cf. *Virt.* 51-79: περὶ φιλανθρωπίας.

[119]According to Marcus, this opinion is held by Homer; according to Aucher and Mercier, it is attributed by Homer to others.

"And yet the gods, in the likeness of strangers from other lands, in all kinds of forms go about unknown, seeing and beholding the many enmities of men and their lawlessness and also their good laws." Placed at the end of the Question, these verses seem in a sense to present a Greek version of the appearance to Abraham of the three strangers.[120]

(c) *The Following Questions*

The next Questions return to the theme of the appearance made to Abraham and treat it in various ways. Sometimes we are reminded of the virtuous man's hesitation between two appearances: he sees either three strangers or God accompanied by his Powers.[121] Sometimes only the appearance of God is considered, without mention of those Powers.

QG 4.10 recalls the two interpretations and the virtues exhibited by the virtuous man in either instance: ". . . if he believed them to be men, it is the sign that he practices hospitality, and . . . if he believed them to be divine Powers appearing with the Father, it is the sign of a worthy moral disposition and his love for God. . . ." *QG* 4.5-6 again point out certain grammatical features in the biblical text which tend to prove the alternation of the two appearances. According to Question 6, these constitute the literal sense of the text. In *QG* 4.20, on the other hand, Philo considers that the interpretation in which strangers appear corresponds to the literal sense, while the interpretation which shows "the soul of the virtuous man . . .granted a very clear appearance of God and his Powers" is related to the allegorical meaning.

QG 4.4, a commentary on v. 3, seems at first to be a continuation of the commentary on v. 2, "When he saw (them), he ran to meet them and worshipped (them). . . . " But Philo speaks only of "he ran," making no comment on the plural in "to meet them"; and he also forgets what he had written in preceding Questions on the impossibility of seeing God without his Powers: " . . . he runs toward the One and the One shows Himself without the Powers which are under him . . . ." As for *QG* 4.3, it no longer even mentions the presence of the Powers and speaks against the "strangers" interpretation: ". . . if by chance they had been men, he would not have worshipped these mortals, but God." In *QG* 4.12 also

[120]Cf. *Somn.* 1.233, but the quotation is not literal. Philo is speaking of an old proverb and uses the singular.

[121]It is hard to tell when Abraham is actually named in the text.

there is only one appearance, but it is composed of "the Father of all things with his Powers."[122]

Elsewhere the triad has disappeared and only God is named. Finally, in *QG* 4.29 (concerning v. 33, "The Lord went away . . . ") we no longer see the virtuous man manifest his piety toward God and his love for mankind toward the strangers. The strangers have disappeared. The alternation of the two appearances is replaced by an alternation of privileged moments of divine possession and ordinary moments of ordinary life: the former are manifestations of piety, the latter permit the expression of love for humanity.

(d) *Abr.* 107-132 offers an exegesis of Gen 18:1-15, although the biblical text is not quoted word for word. *QG* 4.2 offers us a rare opportunity to compare the rather elaborate treatment within this Question to the treatment of the same material in a Treatise. One might object that the Question deals only with v. 2. But the Treatise attaches such importance to the appearance of God to Abraham that the exegesis of the entire episode hinges on its interpretation.

As the Question interprets it, v. 2 is completely allegorical. The commentary of *De Abrahamo* presents a literal interpretation followed by an allegorical one. The study of the literal meaning is itself composed of two parts, of which the first is devoted to the φιλανθρωπία of the hero (§107); the second, to his θεοσεβεία (§114). If we look more closely, we find that things may perhaps not be quite so clear-cut. Already, according to J. Cazeaux, only the first part of this passage is a literal interpretation while the second is half-allegory, so that "the movement from literal to allegorical . . . becomes progressive here."[123] It seems to us that this "movement toward the allegorical" is visible even in this first part where certain sure indications can be found.

First of all, nowhere in the entire passage is either Abraham or Sarah named,[124] although certain translators do reinsert their names. Who, then, is the one whose love of men will be praised? "He who had to undergo" the inhospitality of the Egyptians (*Abr.* 107). Why the haste of the hero and his wife? Because "in a wise man's house, no one is slow to show love for humanity"(§109). As for the guests, they are less touched by the quality of the food than by "the quality of the soul of their

[122]Cf. Question 25.

[123]Cf. Cazeaux 1983*b*, 126. Cf. also Cazeaux 1984*b* , 25.

[124]Apart from a biblical quotation in *Abr.*132.

host" (§110). Even more significant is the absence of a subject before προσεῖχον in §111. After the promise of a son, we of course expect the names Abraham and Sarah. Further, when Philo moves from the virtue of hospitality to piety (§114), he restricts himself to speaking of "the hospitality of our hero" (τοῦ ἀνδρός).[125] Meanwhile, the mysterious visitors have only consented to enter because they regard the master of the house "as a kinsman and fellow servant who had sought refuge with their master (§116)." In §118 Philo says that he who received their visit is "the man of worth" (ὁ ἀστεῖος) and that the purpose of this special favor was "to cause the wise man to perceive through his sight, rendered clearer, that the Father did not fail to recognize his wisdom." All that is needed, then, for the exegesis to become completely allegorical is for the sage to be replaced by his soul which is inundated with divine light.[126]

We arrive at the same conclusion if we stay with the appearance itself. In the first part of the commentary, the part considered literal (§107), Philo, who does not quote the Bible but stays very close to the text, says of the hero that "he saw three beings, in the form of men, who were traveling. . . ." A few lines later, the enigmatic nature of the characters is evoked again, when the text shows them able to read the thoughts of their host and then promise him a son (§110). His "wife" finally wonders if they might not be prophets or angels (§113). The second part of the commentary confirms her intuition: the visitors are angels (§115). We are on the verge of allegory, but allegory will commence when the appearance is moved from the sensible world to the spiritual world.

The literal exegesis of *Abr.* 107-118 is concerned with the identity of the three travelers and what happened during the meal they were offered. The allegorical exegesis (§§119-132), on the other hand, deals only with the appearance of God; it thus has the same subject as the response found in *QG*. It also presents, with only one exception, the same general plan.

Everything begins with the interpretation of the divine triad. Three separate times the Question lists the members of the triad, but the interpretation remains strictly theological. *Abr.* 119-122, on the other hand, tries to express the inexpressible by associating sight with the theme of divine light developed by Question 1. This evocation will also return three times, but it is done so that, using successive

---

[125]We are using J. Cazeaux's translation for this entire text.

[126]Cf.Mercier and Petit 1984, pp. 147 and 151.

approximations, a symmetrically composed tableau will appear. The two Powers seem first to be two shadows shining out from the Existent, then two characters who stand on either side of him, and finally they become his bodyguards.[127]

After having interpreted the appearance, both the Question and the commentary in *De Abrahamo* focus on those persons who are able to receive it. According to the Question, some souls keep their eyes shut while the eyes of others are wide open. *De Abrahamo* does not mention the first group and rearranges the grouping of the second according to the level of their vision. In keeping with its degree of purification, the soul sees either a single or a triadic appearance. In an even more nuanced way, Philo distinguishes between souls capable of apprehending the Existent, those whose gaze reaches up to grasp the Creative Power, and those who perceive only the Royal Power.

This long development in *De Abrahamo* takes the place of the exegesis of the "three men" in *QG* 4.2. In the Treatise, the "three men" are the subject of a literal interpretation.

Finally, the Question justifies the differentiation of the two appearances, that of God and that of the three strangers, by pointing out that the biblical text alternates between singular and plural expressions. At the end of the allegorical exegesis, *De Abrahamo* also concentrates on the letter of this text, which, however, does not in our opinion mean that it returns to the literal level of meaning. The expressions Philo picks out here and which have a similar tendency are also found in the Question; but in the Treatise they are present only to demonstrate the oneness of the appearance, thus undermining the literal sense. Already, the first exegesis suggested a movement toward unity by the unanimity manifested by the three visitors. At the end of the allegorical exegesis, it is no longer a question of unanimity; now we are given the impression that only one visitor is present: " . . . εἷς ὑπισχνεῖται ὡς μόνος αὐτὸς παρών. . . . " (§132).

These two commentaries are interesting because of the difficulty of explaining a biblical text which is ambiguous at the literal level. *QG* 4.2 concentrates on the passage from the appearance of the Lord God, announced in v. 1, to that of the three men in v. 2. This explanation sets forth two appearances between which Abraham, as their interpreter, oscillates. But subsequently the eyes of the body and those of the soul

---

[127]Cf. *Sacr*. 59.

seem to be differentiated no longer and, in consequence, the sensible and spiritual worlds also are no longer distinguished. All this confusion has disappeared from the Treatise, and Philo has returned to his role of interpreter, thanks to a double exegesis. However, the ambiguity of the biblical text shows up again in a literal exegesis which, as we have pointed out, is, partially because it cannot be helped, already on the road to allegory.

(3) *Abraham's Hospitality or the Mystical Exchange:* — QG *4.8*

QG 4.8 treats Gen 18:6-7: "Abraham hurried to the tent to Sarah and said to her, 'Hurry and mix three measures of wheat-flour and make bread under ashes.' And he ran to the cattle and took a tender calf and gave it to the servant, and he hurried to prepare it." Given the biblical text's emphasis on the eagerness of the three characters, it is not surprising that Philo has decided against the banal interrogative expressions which he uses almost systematically in *QG* and substitutes the most appropriate question, "Why do they all hurry?" However, the commentary devotes only a few lines to this question; and its principal subject is totally different — or so it would seem. Moreover, Philo interprets these two verses in the light of the biblical context within which they are placed, so that, in a sense, this Question addresses all of Gen 18.

The introduction presents the two appearances which cause the virtuous man to hesitate. If he saw strangers, "his love of humanity and his hospitality" would be admirable. We therefore expect that, if he saw God and his first Powers, the virtuous man would be praised for his piety. Note, however, that Philo does not state that he is pious, but rather that he is "happy." It is only at the end of the Question that we understand the importance of this adjective, which denotes the joy Abraham intends to give to his guests through his attentions and the joy he receives in return.

The presentation has three parts: the first offers an interpretation of each character named in the two verses; the second, which is the most important (not only because it is four times as long as each of the other parts[128] but also because of its interesting topic) is the allegorical exegesis of the three measures of flour and of the bread cooked under ashes; the

[128]In the Marcus edition, it occupies 65 lines. Both the first and the third parts are 16 lines long. Could this be accidental?

third part evokes, again allegorically, the feast which will follow these preparations, although the verses cited make no reference to it.

(a) At the beginning of the first part, the theme of the two appearances is stated again, but we observe that Abraham is no longer the only one involved: if the visitors appear as strangers, Sarah and the servant are depicted sharing in the offer of hospitality; and, if those who are welcomed are God and his Powers, the welcomers themselves are no longer human "but incorporeal beings." Without saying so explicitly, Philo thereby moves from the literal sense to the allegorical sense: the welcomers are understood to be the most pure intellect (which bears the name "Abraham"),[129] the perfection of virtue (named "Sarah"), and "the utterance of thought"[130] (which is called "the servant"). "And without delay or hesitation, intellect and virtue hurry to please God and serve him and his Powers." This is the only answer given to the question, "Why do they hurry?" The end of the first part is only a sort of paraphrase of the two verses. It continues to emphasize the haste with which intellect and virtue do the task proper to them. All that is said of "utterance" is that it offers the designated victim. Note that a paraphrase such as this one is allegorical to the extent that it uses the equivalences established above, but it mixes the literal meaning with the allegorical when it speaks of the three measures and of the ash-cakes. These measures and cakes are the subject of the lengthy discussion which follows.

(b) Philo himself calls attention to the importance of this second part: "The passage concerning the three measures has a very profound meaning."[131] The exegesis is introduced by some considerations of the meaning and the properties of the number three: "in reality all things are measured by three, for they possess a beginning, a middle, and an end." Homer said so when he wrote τριχθὰ δὲ πάντα δέδασται, "all things are divided into three," a hemistich found in *Il.* 15.189 in which πάντα refers to the entire world which Zeus, Poseidon and Hades divided among themselves. The authority of the Pythagoreans is invoked in its turn, because they "give, as the foundation of the birth of all things, the triad in numbers and the right triangle in figures." It will soon be

[129]According to Marcus 1953, 1.279, n. *e*: ὁ καθαρώτατος νοῦς. See, e.g., *Her.* 64.
[130]ὁ προφορικὸς λόγος. Cf. e.g. *Mut.* 69.
[131]Marcus and Mercier give φυσικώτατος as the Greek equivalent.

apparent that these speculations are closely linked to the interpretation which follows. Thus they can be compared to the cosmological developments with which Philo begins certain interpretations in his Treatises, as if he wanted to set forth some concepts at first so he could use them later to support his argument.[132]

The exegesis of the three measures here is both cosmogonic and theological. At the beginning, Philo points out that they correspond to a tripartite division of the universe: one measure has served to make up "the incorporeal and intelligible world"; a second, the perceptible heaven, which has as its share "a fifth and divine substance"; the third is the measure of the sublunary world. Then these measures which, as we have just seen, play the role of causes, are identified: the measure of the incorporeal world is "the most important of the causes"[133] — in other words, the supreme cause (which is God); the cause of the fifth element that "heaven received as its share" is the Creative Power of the Existent; and, finally, the cause of the sublunary beings is the Royal Power.

The lines which immediately follow are particularly obscure in their location.[134] It may well be that a lacuna is responsible for the unintelligibility of the text. Why, right after the interpretation of the measures, does the text apparently move to a reference to the "utterance of thought" bringing its aid "to direct that which should be done"? Should we explicate this phrase with the aid of *Mut.* 69, which interprets the name of Abraham etymologically as "elect father of sound," interpreting "elect father" as the intellect of the sage and "of sound" as the utterance of thought? How should we interpret the distinction apparently made afterwards between sinners, whose punishments put them back on the right path, and others who are lost forever? Even more important, how can we establish a connection between these two groups and what, according to the translations, follows: " . . . so that . . . the measure of all beings, the intelligible and the sensible, is God alone, who, in his unity, makes himself appear as a triad, because of the weakness of those who look."[135]

---

[132]Cf. *Cher.* 21b-22; *Gig.* 7-11; *Somn.* 1.134-135.

[133]The translations allow us to recognize the Greek expression: τὸ πρεσβύτατον τῶν αἰτίων, familiar to Philo. Cf. *Conf.* 124. See Méasson 1986, 56 and notes.

[134]Cf. Marcus 1953, 1.281, n. *g*.

[135]Mercier uses only a comma to separate this consequence from what precedes it. Aucher and Marcus use a period and start a new paragraph, but it is clear that we are to understand that a consequence is being stated.

There are many reasons why we should stop to look at this phrase or end of phrase. First of all, it expresses a Philonic theme present in the Treatises: that of "the true and just measure" of God (*Congr.* 101)[136] and perhaps, at the same time, the polemical theme related to it, that God is the measure of all things, a repudiation of the famous affirmation of Protagoras (*Post.* 35-36; *Her.* 246, *Somn.* 2.192-194). Moreover, this phrase is not just a simple conclusion to the exegesis; it assimilates the three measures to the triadic appearance received by Abraham by bringing us back to the theme of contemplation, the prerogative of the eye of the soul.

The weakness of Abraham's gaze, his inability to apprehend the One, and the goodness of God who presents Himself as a triad, all are echoes of Question 2. What is new, however, is the reference to another biblical text, Exod 33:13. Genesis shows Abraham favored by the appearance of God who manifests himself as a triad; Exodus presents Moses addressing this prayer to God: "Show Thyself to me, so I can see Thee distinctly." Is not Moses therefore asking to see the One alone, without his Powers, a grace reserved only for "a God-loving soul"?[137]

After the exegesis of the three measures of flour comes that of the bread cooked under ashes. The Greek word is ἐγκρυφίας, from ἐγκρύπτω. That is why this bread, made from flour worked and kneaded by Sarah, means, first, that "the knowledge of the Father and of his two superior Powers (is) hidden," and, secondly, that such a subject of study *should be* kept hidden. In this way Philo connects the image of mysteries which must not be revealed to the uninitiated with the theological doctrine under discussion.[138]

Thus ends the important exegetical discussion which occupies the central part of the Question. We should keep in mind that Sarah, representing the virtue of the intellect, has prepared for these guests a meal which symbolizes the guests themselves.

(c) Although we can only judge from the translations, the last part of *QG* 4.8 seems to have a literary quality which is quite rare in *QG*. We should first note the lyrical outpouring at the beginning, even if the rhetorical treatment is banal: "O thrice happy the soul in which God has

---

[136]Cf. *QG* 4.23: "The true and just measure is the divine Word, by which everything has been and is measured."

[137]The same verse is cited in *Leg.* 3.101; *Mut.* 8; *Post.* 13,16.

[138]For the image of the mysteries and the law of silence, cf. *Cher.* 48-49.

not disdained to dwell . . . !"[139] The abundance of images is also noteworthy: the soul which God makes "his palace and his home," "the springs of good which pour forth forever" into which truly pure people "may dip," and also "the food of the voluntary law of incorruptible and pure wisdom." And especially, in a progression whose rhythm seems to accelerate, the text at first shows us an astonishing reciprocity between the very pure intellect which offers the feast and his guest, God; at the end of QG 4.8, we encounter a true inversion of roles since we there see that God himself is giving the feast.[140] This text is essentially a veritable hymn to joy. Under different forms, one idea is repeated over and over: if God agrees to dwell within a soul, it is "so that the giver of joy may have joy." "Those who receive men offer rejoicing and festivities." "As for the very pure intellect, which is wholly filled with the appearance of God, seeming to be joyful and to rejoice (?), it becomes joyful." And the beverages offered are "beverages of joy." Behind this term, which is repeated with fervor and liveliness, we can divine not only the promise of a son's birth but already Isaac's actual presence.

(d) We have seen the importance given the interpretation of the three measures by the length of the discussion and the place it occupies in Question 8. We shall now return to it once more, this time to study its sources. Philo himself refers in a vague way to the Pythagoreans for the arithmology; but he makes no reference to any philosophical authority for the cosmology which he then connects with his theology.

The symbolism of the triad is discussed by Aristotle at the beginning of the *De Caelo* 1.268a 10-13, in terms not far from those Philo uses in this Question: "In truth, as the Pythagoreans also say, the All and the totality of things are determined by the number three; end, middle and beginning form the number characteristic of the All, and their number is the triad."[141] In the *Timaeus* 53 C, Plato places the right triangle at the origin of surfaces and thus of elements: "And every surface in a rectilinear shape is composed of triangles. Note that all triangles are based on two types of triangles, both of which contain one right angle and two acute angles."[142] Speusippus attributed this doctrine to the Pythagorean Philolaos. In his Treatises, Philo often speaks of the

---

[139]Cf. *QG* 4.21.

[140]Cf. *Abr*. 167 and *QG* 5.124.

[141]See the translation of P. Moraux 1965. Cf. *QG* 2.5.

[142]See the translation of A. Rivaud 1970. Cf. Taylor 1928, 370-371.

marvelous properties of the right triangle whose sides are 3,4,5. He writes in *Opif.* 97 that "the right triangle is the principle of figures and qualities."[143]

Two characteristics of cosmology which underpin the exegesis orient us toward Aristotle or, at least, an Aristotelian tradition: the distinction between heaven and the sublunary world on one hand and the nature of the elements, which constitute them, on the other hand (since "a fifth and divine substance" served for the construction of the perceptible heaven, while the sublunary world is made of four elements). Note that in *De Caelo* 1.2-4 Aristotle intends to demonstrate the existence of what he calls "the first body," which the doxographers, and Philo also, call "the fifth substance" (*Her.* 283b) or "the fifth body" (*Somn.* 1.21). This body is moved with a circular movement which indicates that it is the substance of heaven and the stars and makes it superior to the four elements which form the sublunary world — so superior that it is worthy of the epithet "divine." That is why "the first body" of the *De Caelo* escapes the processes of generation and corruption, just as it neither grows nor diminishes (*De Caelo* 1.270a 33-35).

It seems clear that the fifth substance described in *QG* 4.8, which we are studying here, is also endowed with a circular movement. Is it not what Aucher understood when he spoke of "periodica essentia"? Marcus, however, translates "circular essence" and Mercier "the circular substance," equivalent expressions in which the adjective indicates the form rather than the movement.[144] On the other hand, it is certain that, as a Greek fragment of this Question attests,[145] a substance such as this one is described as "divine": πέμπτην λαχὼν (ὁ αἰσθητὸς οὐρανὸς) καὶ θειοτέραν οὐσίαν. According to the same fragment, this substance is, moreover, ἄτρεπτος καὶ ἀμετάβολος ("exempt from change and immutable"), two epithets which are more or less synonymous. Aristotle uses the adjective ἀμετάβλητος (*De Caelo* 2.288b 1) which for him is in no way incompatible with κινούμενος.[146] There is therefore reason to believe that the same might be true for Philo.[147]

We should next consider whether Aristotle admitted the existence of an intelligible world above and beyond heaven in any of his Treatises. In

143Cf. *Contempl.* 65; *Spec.* 2.177; *Mos.* 2.80.

144Cf. *Her.* 283: Πέμπτη . . . ἔστω τις οὐσία κυκλοφορητική.

145Petit 1978, 148 = Marcus 1953, 2.214.

146Cf. Pépin 1964, 161-162.

147Marcus is certainly correct to translate "unaltered and unchanged" in the passage where Mercier translates: "immuable et immobile."

the *De Caelo* 1.279a 18, "things of over-there," τἀκεῖ, are untouched by place and time. That is why, among so many other interpretations, one might think that they designate the "forms."[148] It is certain, on the other hand, that the doxographies attribute a tripartite conception of the universe to Aristotle.[149] Everything takes place as if on Aristotle's sublunary world with the perceptible heaven above it there had been superimposed the intelligible world of Plato's *Phaedrus* . Such a division, either explicit or implicit, is often found in Philo's work.[150]

(e) Two Treatises, *De Abrahamo* and *De Sacrificiis,* offer parallels to *QG* 4.8. The former speaks only of the haste of Abraham, and the latter adds an interpretation of the three measures which does not correspond exactly to that of the Question.

Gen 18:6-7 is interpreted rapidly in the literal-level exegesis which *De Abrahamo* devotes to Abraham's hospitality (*Abr.* 108-109). The only section of the biblical text which is quoted is a part of the patriarch's exhortation to Sarah. Stress is placed on the haste with which Abraham himself acts and on the haste he demands of Sarah and the servant. The meaning is that "No one is slow to love men in the home of a sage." However, from the very first words, Abraham's haste is be explained by the joy which fills his soul; and this joy announces what will be said later about the happiness of the house which angels have deigned to visit.

The allegorical exegesis in *Sacr.* 59-60 is restricted to v. 6. Once again, the biblical text is not quoted word for word; and Philo's free rendering of it permits him (somewhat as he did at the end of the first part of our *QG* 4.8) to express Abraham's haste with not one term but three: he invites Sarah to hurry in turn with eagerness (σπουδή), rapidity (τάχος), and ardor (προθυμία). Note that Abraham showed this zeal "when God, escorted by the two highest Powers (Sovereignty and Goodness, and between the two, he who is One), offered three images to the patriarch's contemplative soul." The assimilation of the triadic appearance to the three measures of wheat reveals itself slowly. None of the three images received a measure, for neither God nor his Powers have any limits; instead, each one of them gave a measure to all that exists. At this point, the exegesis seems quite close to that of the three

148Cf. Elders 1966, 144-145 and Méasson 1986, 73-74.
149Cf. Pépin 1964, 164-170.
150Cf. *QE* 2.83. See Harl 1966, 92-94 and 94, n. 2.

measures in *QG* 4.8. In *De Sacrificiis,* however, the creative action of God and of his two highest Powers is not exercised over a tripartite universe. By a sort of tautology, it is said that the goodness of God, the first of the Powers, is the measure of that which is good, and that his sovereignty, which is the second, is the measure of all that is under his authority, while "he who directs all himself is the measure of all corporeal and incorporeal beings." To this last statement corresponds the affirmation of the Question, "the measure of all beings, intelligible and the sensible, is God alone."

Though the triadic appearances of *De Sacrificiis* and *QG* 4.8 are similar so far as the figures' identity is concerned, they differ in grouping the figures. In the Treatise, God appears between his Powers; in *QG* 4.8, in harmony with the tripartite cosmology which underlies the exegesis, the three figures are arranged vertically: the Royal Power below, above it, the Creative Power, and God at the top. *QG* 4.2 gives no indication of the position each figure occupies. On the other hand, *Abr.* 119-122 insists that God's position is between the two Powers even more than does *De Sacrificiis* . In both these Treatises the Powers are designated as God's bodyguards: ὁ θεὸς δορυφορούμενος ὑπὸ δυεῖν τῶν ἀνωτάτω δυνάμεων (*Sacr.* 59)[151]. One would therefore be tempted to think that the importance accorded to "the middle position" appears only in the Treatises. Thus a passage in *Spec.* 4.168 reads: ". . . within the triad, the middle occupies the place which directs, coordinates, and, with indissoluble bonds, ties to itself its two neighbors who escort it[152] as they might a king." However, this image is not restricted to the Treatises since *QG* 4.30 speaks of "the Father who is in the middle and is served by the two chief Powers."

In *De Sacrificiis,* on the other hand, Philo does not limit himself to an interpretation of the three measures of flour; he also explains the meaning of "to knead": the soul must come to be "convinced of the existence of the most high God, who is master of his own Powers, since he can at the same time be seen without them and manifest himself with them." This revelation is what he calls the initiation into the mysteries and even, in *De Sacrificiis,* "into the greatest mysteries," an image which leads to the evocation of the law of silence, whose symbol is found in the ash-cakes. The image of the mysteries and the law they impose is also present in *QG* 4.8, which, however, lacks an interpretation of kneading.

---

[151]Cf., e.g., *Spec.* 1.45.

[152]Literally: "by which it is escorted" (δορυφορεῖται).

The exegetical parallelism between *De Sacrificiis* and the Question is plain. To be sure, there is no cosmology in the Treatise. Its interpretation of the action of "kneading," however, sheds light on the abrupt transition in *QG* 4.8 from the explication of the three measures to the image of the mysteries.

D. *Conclusion:* QG *4 and the Treatises*

The *Quaestiones* and the Treatises of Philo belong to two different literary genres. It is no more possible to compare *QG* 4 as a whole to a Treatise than it is to consider each of the Questions which compose it as a section of a Treatise.

(1) *A Predominant Theme in* QG *4*

(a) We have called attention to the recurrence of an exegetical theme in the 70 Questions of *QG* 4. It is certainly not by chance that the first Questions of *QG* 4 deal with the appearance at the oak of Mamre, a text which allows Abraham to represent the virtuous intellect. With the biblical verses devoted to the story of Lot we find the motif of comparing "progressive" and "perfect"; that continues until, with the disappearance of Lot, the two allegorical figures merge into one: progress and perfection express two successive moments of the same spiritual itinerary (*QG* 4.66). *QG* 4 ends on the theme of the righteous savior (*QG* 4.70).[153] If we think of Abraham less as a biblical character[154] and more as allegorical symbol of the intellect which has attained perfection, he is the hero of this book, even if he is not present in all the Questions.

(b) Even though this allegory returns with particular insistence in *QG* 4, this repetition is not enough to make a grouping of questions and answers comparable to a Treatise. The carrying over of the same themes and images from one Question to another does not produce that effect; nor do Philo's allusions to what came before: *QG* 4.12, for example,

[153]Cf. *QG* 4.54.

[154]*QG* 3 is devoted to the story of Abraham before Mamre (Genesis 15-17).

begins in this way: "Why the singular? That has already been said. . .," a clear reference to *QG* 4.2.[155]

The independence of the Questions is so great that the interpretations they propose can be quite different. In *QG* 4.60, a commentary on Gen 20:2, we read that "the intellect, friend of virtue, calls virtue 'sister' but not 'wife' in order . . . to show that his zeal and desire are common to all those who have an authentic and true desire for perfect probity" — meaning that Abraham calls Sarah "sister" so that all wise people can claim this kinship with her. But, when *QG* 4.66 alludes to Sarah's statement about Abraham: "He is my brother" (Gen 20:5), the interpretation offered is that virtue "can be related to the one who progresses as to a brother,[156] but she can only be a wife to the 'perfect man'." This is no longer the same intellect which can claim a simultaneous double bond with virtue as is the case in *QG* 4.60.

A succession of independent commentaries do not make up a Treatise. But the predominance of the allegorical symbol of "the perfect man," a predominance no doubt suggested to Philo by the biblical verses, is a characteristic aspect of *QG* 4.

(2) *The Questions and Answers of* QG *4 and the Treatises of Philo*

(a) There are many similarities between the Questions of *QG* 4 and the Treatises. Like the Treatises, and even more systematically, the Questions distinguish between literal exegesis and allegorical exegesis. One good example is *QG* 4.1.

The exegetical techniques used in the Questions are the same as those used in the Treatises: etymology, at least in the case of proper nouns (Questions 1, 17, 23, 50, 58, 59), and grammatical study (Questions 2, 5, 11, 12).

In the Questions, as in the Treatises, Philo calls on the knowledge of philosophy and literature he has accumulated in his secular studies:

In the background, behind Question 1, we glimpse the mythical universe of the *Phaedrus*. The cosmology of Question 5, which reminds us of the cosmology underpinning the discussions in *Gig*. 7-11 and *Somn*. 1.134-137, goes back to the *Timaeus*.[157] In Question 8, we find a

[155]Cf. *QG* 4.24 which refers to *QG* 4.22.

[156]Mercier's translation uses a plural here, which does not seem to fit the text; Aucher and Marcus use the singular.

[157]Cf. especially *Gig*. 11 and *Somn*. 1.136. See Méasson 1986, 269-281.

cosmology influenced by scholarly Aristotelianism along with speculations on the triad explicitly attributed to the Pythagoreans. In Question 1, a quotation from Heraclitus is included and the name of its author given; Homer is also named, once when four verses of the *Odyssey* are quoted (*QG* 4.2) and again in connection with a hemistich from the *Iliad*[158] (*QG* 4.8).

We also find the following quotations from the Bible:

> **Genesis**: 1:2 in *QG* 4.5; 3:21 in *QG* 4.1; 4:13 in *QG* 4.4; 28:12 in *QG* 4.29;
> **Exodus:** 19:22 in *QG* 4.4; 19:24 in *QG* 4.29; 33:13 in *QG* 4.8;
> **Isaiah:** 60:5 and 66:14(?) in *QG* 4.16.

It would take too long to list all the Philonic themes and the images connected with them which are shared between *QG* 4 and the Treatises. Some of them have been discussed in the preceding pages.

(b) Despite these similarities, an essential difference exists between the Questions and the Treatises: the Questions are static, as we have said; but the Treatises are dialectical.[159] A rapid overview of the Questions of *QG* 4 shows that they use affirmations, confident declarations, and allegorical equivalences. One finds such expressions as these: "It must therefore be known that . . ."(*QG* 4.1), "(the Bible) manifestly and very clearly shows that . . . ." (*QG* 4.18), and also "Setting aside the opinion of certain scholars . . . we say that here it is a question of. . . ." (*QG* 4.61). Affirmations are often defended: "because . . . ." or "that is why. . . ." In general, the movement of the thought does not go beyond two successive phrases.

This absence of true argumentation is noticeable even in the most developed of the Questions, where space is available for more ample presentations. As we have seen, the exegesis of Gen 18:1 found in *QG* 4.1 is perfectly linear from one end to the other. The etymological meaning for "Mamre" is "that which (is derived) from sight" — the sight of the virtuous intellect which sees not only the created world, but also "its Father and Creator." The proof is clear: "After all, what would be

158Cf. *QG* 4.20 where *Od* .15.74 is quoted. Homer is here designated as "the poet," as was customary in antiquity.
159See the Preface above.

the use of his (the Father) coming without being seen?" Farther on, the symbolism of the oak will also be explained and justified. The same method is used for the rest of the Question.

In relation to what we are discussing, *QG* 4.2 is much more interesting because it allows us to see, so to speak, how the schema of an argument begins to take shape. The question is stated in a banal way: "What is meant by . . . ?," followed by the words of Gen 18:2. Yet this does not seem to correspond to the difficulty Philo notes, a problem which might be formulated thus, "How can a verse in which it is said that God (the unique God) appeared to Abraham be followed by another verse which speaks of a triadic appearance?" Philo furnishes a satisfactory explanation for this contradiction with his hypothesis of the two visions seen by Abraham, but then scriptural justification for the hypothesis must be found. Found it is in the alternating singulars and plurals of the biblical text. Thus we have here the skeleton of a demonstration.[160]

QG 4.8, whose circular composition we have analyzed, also contains an implicit argument. We have noted the substitution of a "happy" Abraham for the "pious" Abraham we expected. It is clear that Abraham's happiness is the cause of the haste he shows and that his happiness is caused by his certainty that he is being visited by God and his Powers — in other words, his happiness is caused by his piety.[161]

As for Abraham's certainty, how is it acquired? It would seem that it is acquired as a result of the kneading of the three measures of wheat. We should note that the meaning of these three measures becomes clear only when they are seen in the light of Philo's doctrine that nothing can be offered to God which has not previously been given by Him. The Question, however, does not refer to this doctrine; it does not even interpret the verb "to knead." Obviously many shortcuts have been taken in the Questions.

Finally, one might think that the use of biblical references would introduce movement into the discourse. However, once again, a closer study turns up little of interest. *QG* 4.1 speaks of "the tunics of skin" mentioned in Gen 3:21, but the only sense assigned to the expression is metaphorical. In *QG* 4.4 a contrast is developed: on the one hand we

[160]*QG* 4.51 is a commentary on Gen 19:23-24, but it also deals with v. 25. When he comes to this verse, Philo writes: "It is appropriate to wonder: Why. . . ?" But no true discussion is offered. Philo continues: "To that, it must be said . . . ," and then comes the justification: "because. . . ."

[161]Cf. *Abr.* 108.

find Abraham, who addresses this prayer to God, "Do not pass over your servant" (Gen 18:3), and on the other hand Cain, who is abandoned by Him (Gen 4:13) and the Hebrew people from whom Moses fears the Lord may be removed (Exod 19:22). There is no movement, properly speaking, here, but only a contrast between the presence or absence of God for the soul and the distinction between two forms of absence. *QG* 4.8 cites Exod 33:13. According to Genesis, God appeared to Abraham as a triad; according to Exodus, Moses prayed to God "Show Thyself to me, (so) I may see Thee distinctly" -- a petition in which Philo sees the expression of a desire to contemplate God alone, without his Powers. Here we perceive the beginnings of a movement of thought which immediately comes to a halt.

(c) Lack of movement is characteristic of the Questions. We must add that the literary genre to which they belong makes it impossible for them to undertake the vast compositions which the Treatises present. We have already examined side by side two interpretations of the three measures of flour kneaded by Sarah at Abraham's request (Gen 18:6): one occupies most of *QG* 4.8; the other is from the *De Sacrificiis*. Note that, unlike the commentary in the Question, the commentary in the Treatise is a section of an important development in five parts. Without giving a detailed analysis,[162] we will try to point out how they fit together.

The text under discussion is Gen 4:3, and Philo declares that Cain was guilty of having been slow to give thanks to God (*Sacr*. 52). Philo contrasts this verse with Deut 23:21: "If you make a vow, do not be slow to fulfill it" (*Sacr*. 53). "To be slow" or "not to be slow" doing what one owes to God — these are the two antithetical poles of the exegesis.

> In a first section (*Sacr*. 54-58) Philo enumerates the reasons for being slow: forgetfulness, presumption, conviction of one's own merits. Three passages from Deuteronomy present antidotes for each of these attitudes.
>
> The second and third sections (*Sacr*. 59-63) extol haste: Abraham's haste, and then that of the Hebrews. Thus we have moved from "to be slow" to "not to be slow" and finally to "to make haste": when the causes of slowness are removed, nothing hinders the haste of the soul. Abraham's haste cannot be dissociated from the task he gives Sarah. When she kneads the three measures, it is Abraham who is initiated into the greater mysteries which must be kept secret in accord with the law symbolized by the loaves cooked under ashes. From the secrecy required by the great mysteries, we pass to the secrecy required by the

[162]See J. Cazeaux, "Etude littéraire du Traité 'De sacrificiis'" (forthcoming).

lesser mysteries. Exod 12:39 tells that the Hebrews "had the dough which they had carried from Egypt cooked in flat cakes without leaven." This act of cooking is another example of an initiation which is in this case manifested by their victory over passion. Passover has precisely this meaning of passing over from passion to virtue, and it is at this point that Exod 12:11 recommends that the meal be eaten "with haste." Abraham, the "perfect man," and the Hebrews, who here are "progressing," have thus given examples of haste in the service of God.

The following section (*Sacr.* 64-68) shows human swiftness transcended by the instantaneity of divine gifts (Gen 27:20). For God "arrives first," before everything, even before time. The haste required of man is thus to be placed in the context of a larger precept which invites him to imitate God.

The final section (*Sacr.* 69-71) returns to the theme of tardiness. Pharaoh, who prefers to postpone having Moses pray for him and his servants, is presented as a symmetrical and caricatural analogue to Cain.

We thus are led from the slowness of Cain, which seems to affect God because it is the result of a man's forgetfulness or sense of self-sufficiency, to the slowness of Pharaoh, which turns against a man and brings about the evil that comes to him. The passage itself is based on a double exegetical reflection: on the haste which is joy or deliverance because it involves a quest for God and revelation, and on the unimaginable speed of God which humans can only try to imitate.

Earlier in this article, Jacques Cazeaux has shown the radical difference which exists between the *Quaestiones* and the Treatises. His analysis was based on two important discussions, one found in *Leg.* 3.65-106, the other in *Deus* 104-110. The same dialectical movement underpins them: the passage from the Royal Power to the Creative Power, the first absorbed by the second so completely that Moses, the just man par excellence, sees only the Goodness of God. In each discussion, this passage is accomplished through a mediation: an exegetical one in *Legum Allegoriae* (as in our text from *De Sacrificiis*) and a philosophical one in *Quod Deus*. Cazeaux's twofold analysis arises from a study of *QG* 1, but his conclusions reach beyond the limits of that Book and also apply to *QG* 4.

QG 4, though interesting and distinctive, contains not one commentary in which a dialectical movement is clearly visible. It is true that in some Questions the biblical references provide the potential for movement, but these opportunities are not exploited. *QG* 4.2 seems to imply a genuine line of argument, but the argumentation is "left out" of the exegesis and only implied by the train of thought.

V. *QUAESTIONES IN GENESIM* 5 AND 6[163]

The fact that the commentary skips from Gen 20 to Gen 23 is the most convincing reason to divide "Book 5" from the text that precedes it. "Book 6" is separated from the preceding material by a smaller lacuna consisting of Gen 25:9-19.

Nothing really new is to be found in these texts at the end of *QG*. It is hard to make any systematic comparison between these texts and the Treatises because no Treatise offers a detailed commentary of the biblical text beyond Genesis 17.

As in the other books, we find rather elaborate questions, for example *QG* 5.82, 88, 95, 108, 110, 122, 140, 145; and 6.167,175. In the answers, Philo continues to alternate the literal interpretation and the interpretation closest to "the nature of things," but a clear system is lacking. From time to time he expresses admiration or gives way to a diatribe against the enemies of the Bible.

I want to point out a phenomenon which might be thought of as "tangential" when comparisons are drawn between the interpretations in the *Quaestiones* and those in the Treatises with regard to the characters Isaac, Jacob, and Esau. On the subject of Esau, we can compare *Congr.* 61-62 with *QG* 6.172 and 225, in which Esau is described as a "theater buffoon" or as a "drunken buffoon." Why? The Questions do not say. But *Congr.* 61-62 builds an argument on the basis of the interpretations that can be given to Esau's name and character. We here see that "buffoon" (end of *Congr.* 61) is an interpretation of the word σκηνή (end of *Congr.* 62), which in Greek means both "theater" and "tent"; and since Jacob, Esau's rival, himself lives in "a house," it is clear that Esau lives somewhere else — in a "tent." His tent becomes, for this evil man, the symbol of hypocrisy and playacting and buffoonery, through a sliding of meaning from "tent" to "stage of a theater." Hence Esau is the nomad — uncertain, changeable, unstable. Let us note that *QG* 6.165, which comments on the fact that Jacob lives in a house, says nothing corresponding about Esau's tent: the opposition set up has nothing to do with the theater, and the contrast between two ways of living is handled by depicting Esau as a savage, opposed to the civilized Jacob.

However, the existence of this "theater buffoon" image seems to imply that the same subterranean device of the allegorical contrast "house-tent" is operating in the Questions. Philo is in possession of the

[163]This section on *QG* 5-6 is by J. Cazeaux.

complete allegory in both the Questions and the Treatise; but, in the Questions, he keeps it simple. The end of *QG* 6.172 suggests a commonplace psychological explanation for Esau's hypocrisy: bad people never admit they are bad. . . . Furnished with this detail,[164] we might ask if Philo, in the Questions and in the Treatises, might not be *deliberately* choosing one genre or the other. If so, we may be dealing with something other than a progression of thought or dialectical discovery in the case of the Treatises; what we may rather discern here is a choice, conditioned, for example, either by the public or the usage of Philo's various texts. The Questions provide the minimum needed for an orthodox reading of the Bible; the Treatises, on the other hand, propose a reading to the limit, a sort of maximum or intellectual luxury. I will return to this idea in the Conclusion.

In an even more curious way, *QG* 5.88-89 seem to suggest a general interpretation of Isaac rather different from the usual presentation of him in the Treatises, in which he embodies the immobile perfection of the End, Joy, and Nature. Here, Isaac continues to represent Joy and Nature, but Abraham seems to fear that the Sophists might still be able to corrupt what Isaac represents. In the same way, *QG* 5.89 seems to extend the hypothesis of an Isaac who is compromised and eventually tempted. But the modern translators tell us that the Armenian is unclear at this point. And one must add that the biblical context here forces Philo to speak of Abraham being worried. In my opinion we cannot learn much from these passages.[165] Let us add, while we are talking of curiosities, that *QG* 5.87, which comes before the two Questions about Isaac, seems also to give some weight to a theory of the Powers which is less clear: the term "Lord" here seems to assume one of the two roles ordinarily assigned to "God," meaning Providence. But we should not exclude the hypothesis that the "care" of the world which is referred to is the care of governing it with authority and punishment.

A good example:

A group of Questions, *QG* 5.99-107, can be compared with the presentation found in *Post.* 130-157. Many specific and almost identical

---

[164]Like the print of a single step in the middle of a desert, one detail can reveal a whole reality.

[165]*QG* 5.146 already implies a perfectible Isaac! Correspondingly, §198 imagines an Esau who is capable of conversion . . . ; this same idea is found in §200 where, in addition, Isaac is represented as a good and voracious giant.

allegories are found in both texts. The idea of the good master and true sage, as opposed to the sophists, is a thread running through both *QG* 5.99-107 and the parallel passage in *De Posteritate*. A study of this textual parallelism is instructive because it brings to light a major difference between these two texts: although many of the elements are present in the Questions, the guiding principle of movement which animates *Post.* 130-157 (and which continues present to the very end of the Treatise!) is totally absent. This guiding principle is the larger comparison Philo establishes between Rebecca (the subject of both these Questions and *Post.* 99-157) and Hagar. Note that Hagar, the Egyptian woman, is the mother of Ishmael, the model of the sophists. This difference is enough. That which is isolated, apparently limited to the text at hand in the Questions, becomes architectonic in the Treatise. This is the reason the Treatise continues by posing the new question: what is the difference between the "Spring" which, thanks to Rebecca, quenches the thirst of the servant of Abraham on the one hand, and, on the other, the "well" from which she draws water for his camels (*Post.* 153-164)? We note that Hagar, the Egyptian, mother of the sophist Ishmael, also gives her son water from a "well." We then discover that there is a whole organized larger grouping in *De Posteritate*: §124 speaks of "Seth," interpreted as "Quenching"; and this dialectic using the themes of water, truth and sophistry continues up to §169. *Post.* 170 once again speaks of Seth, but this time it is to move the commentary in a new direction. But is it really a new direction? No, because the theme of §§170-185 is the theme of self-sufficiency, the first theme proposed in this Treatise. (Moreover, we can see that Seth appears as early as §10 — a warning to readers who may entertain doubts about the inner coherence of a Treatise, in contrast to the *Quaestiones*.) All these interweavings make a Treatise a true tapestry. They are wholly lacking in Book 5 and the other Books of *QG*. The Treatise and the *Quaestiones* share in common certain particular "allegories" (the camel represents memory, etc.), certain identical "ideas" (e.g., the sage portrayed in contrast to the sophist), and even the technique of referring to other biblical texts (*QG* 5.102 reminds us of Manna and a sacrificial law to explain why Abraham's servant asks Rebecca for only "a little" water). The one crucial feature that is clearly unique to *De Posteritate* is the premeditated and carefully interlocked organization which makes it a Treatise. A Treatise can never be just a collection of Questions because, once again, the essence of a Treatise's literary genre is neither "allegory" nor "ideas" nor biblical concordance, but rather dialectical movement — a unifying vision which is original, premeditated, dynamic, and often difficult to perceive. Philo seeks to produce a discourse that parallels the discourse of the Logos in scripture so that the wonderful unity of the Bible gives birth to a second unity in human discourse and understanding — a mysterious unity which demands the reader's active involvement, as does the one in the Bible.

VI. CONCLUSION: "CATECHISM" AND "THEOLOGY"

Here, at the end of these investigations, which have varied greatly in depth, our conclusions remain those we have proposed as we studied the sequence of the *Quaestiones in Genesim.* They may be summarized in one sentence: one cannot compare two different "literary genres" — we cannot speak of "Questions" in the text of the Treatises, nor of a Philonic method in the Questions. Philo has produced two unequal series, distinct one from another and different in kind, in the sense that the *Quaestiones* does not claim to be a "a definitive work" or "discourse," whereas the Treatises are both things because the discourse technique raises them to the higher level.

Nevertheless, the *Quaestiones* are not merely some notes or scratch copies prepared as preliminary materials for a Treatise. We can find an intention in them, one which is very simple and general: whoever writes in the *Quaestiones* format should offer the reader of Genesis a simple work which is elevating and orthodox in thought. It would seem that the "doctor" tried to preclude a subjective, materialistic, and too-literal reading of the Bible which would impoverish its meaning. Perhaps the Questions reflect the meditative reading of the Therapeutae described in *De Vita Contemplativa.* By offering a *minimum* of transposition, the Questions save and preserve the Meaning. In contrast, the Treatises — as we have suggested — demand the highest intellectual effort. There are greater risks, because the Treatises ask a *maximum*, first of the biblical text, and then of the reader's mind. Viewed in this way, the Questions constitute a kind of *catechism*, and the Treatises a *theology*. We might say that the catechism is more solid, more elementary and yet indispensable, while the theology is more ambitious, more attractive, and better suited for infusing the Truth into the human mind — but, for all that, a sort of luxury. Faith and Reason form the two poles of these two "literary genres." Faith is guarded by the *Questions*, and Reason in turn is enlightened by the *Treatises*. Of course the boundaries are not clearly fixed, except in the context of the inborn "insularity" of the *Quaestiones:*

the "catechism" of the Questions implies a preliminary "theology," and the "theology" of the Treatises has some connection with the simplicity of the "catechism." Whoever speaks of "literary genre" restricts himself to the codes of writing and composition, and that is how we envision the coexistence of the *Quaestiones* and the Treatises. But "Philo" is himself only in the Treatises.

BIBLIOGRAPHY OF WORKS CITED

Adler, Maximilian. 1929. *Studien zu Philon von Alexandreia*. Breslau: M. & H. Marcus.

Alexandre, Monique. 1967. *De Congressu Eruditionis Gratia*. PAPM 16. Paris: Editions du Cerf.

Allenbach, J. et al. 1982. *Biblia Patristica Supplément Philon d'Alexandrie* Paris: Centre d'analyse et de documentation patristiques: équipe de recherche associée au Centre National de la Recherche Scientifique.

Amir, Yehoshua. 1983. *Die hellenistische Gestalt des Judentums bei Philon von Alexandrien*. Neukirchen: Neukirchener Verlag.

______. 1984. "The Transference of Greek Allegories to Biblical Motifs in Philo." In *Nourished with Peace: Studies in Hellenistic Judaism in Memory of Samuel Sandmel*, ed. Frederick E. Greenspahn, Earle Hilgert, and Burton L. Mack, pp. 15-25. Chico: Scholars Press.

Arnaldez, R. 1961. *De Opificio Mundi*. PAPM 1. Paris: Editions du Cerf.

Aucher, Johannes Baptista. 1826. *Philonis Iudaei paralipomena Armena. . . nunc primum in Latinum fideliter translata*. Venice: St. Lazarus.

Awetik'ean, G., X. Siwrmelean, and M. Awgerean (J. B. Aucher). 1836-37. *Nor bargirk' haykazean lezowi*. 2 vols. Venice: St. Lazarus.

Belkin, Samuel. 1960. "The Midrash *Quaestiones et Solutiones in Genesim et in Exodum* of Philo Alexandrinus and Its Relation to the Palestinian Midrashim" (Hebrew). *Horeb* 14: 1-74 .

______. 1964. "*Questions and Answers to Genesis and Exodus* by Philo Judaeus: The Earliest Source for the Midrash" (Hebrew). In *The Abraham Weiss Jubilee Volume*, pp. 579-633. New York: Shulsinger Brothers.

Blass, F., Debrunner, A., and Funk, R. W. 1961. *A Greek Grammar of the New Testament and Other Early Christian Literature*. Chicago: University of Chicago Press.

Bolognesi, Giancarlo. 1970. "Postille sulla traduzione armena delle *Quaestiones et Solutiones in Genesin* di Filone." *Archivio Glottologico Italiano* 55: 52-57.

Borgen, Peder. 1984*a*. "Philo of Alexandria. A Critical and Synthetical Survey of Research since World War II." In *ANRW* II.21.1: 98-154.

______. 1984*b*. "Philo of Alexandria." In *Jewish Writings of the Second Temple Period: Apocrypha, Pseudepigrapha, Qumran Sectarian Writings, Philo, Josephus*, ed. Michael Stone, pp. 233-52. Compendia Rerum Iudaicarum ad Novum Testamentum. Philadelphia: Fortress.

Borgen, Peder and R. Skarsten. 1976-77. "*Quaestiones et Solutiones*: Some Observations on the Form of Philo's Exegesis." *SPh* 4: 1-16.

Borgen, Peder and Roald Skarsten. 1971. "Bibelvitenskap, gresk och EDB." *Forskningsnytt fra Norges almenvitanskapelige forskningsråd.* 16,3: 37-39, 50.

Bréhier, Emile. 1950. *Les idées philosophiques et religieuses de Philon d'Alexandrie*. 3rd edition. Paris: Vrin.

Cazeaux, J. 1965. *De migratione Abrahami*. PAPM 14. Paris: Editions du Cerf.

______. 1979-80. "Système implicite dans l'exégèse de Philon. Un exemple: le De praemiis." *SPh* 6: 3-36

______. 1983*a*. *La trame et la chaîne, ou les Structures littéraires et l'Exégèse dans cinq des Traités de Philon d'Alexandrie* . Vol. 1 ALGHJ 15. Leiden: Brill.

______. 1983*b*. *L'épée du Logos et le Soleil de Midi*. Collection de la Maison de l'Orient méditerranéen 13, Serie littéraire et philosophique 2. Lyon: Maison de l'Orient.

______. 1984. "Philon d'Alexandrie, exégète." In *ANRW* II.21.1: 156-226.

______. 1987*a*. "Mystique et sagesse: le repas des trois anges et d'Abraham à Mambré vu par Philon d'Alexandrie." In *Prière, Mystique et Judaïsme* (Coll. Strasbourg, 1984). Paris: Presse universitaires de France.

______. 1987*b*."Le voyage inutile, ou la création chez Philon." In *La création dans l'Orient ancien, Coll. Lectio Divina*, ed. Louis Derousseaux, pp. 345-408. Paris: Cerf.

______. 1989. *La trame et la chaîne*. Vol. 2. Leiden: Brill.

______. "Etude littéraire du Traité 'De sacrificiis'" (forthcoming).

Christiansen, Irmgard. 1969. *Die Technik der allegorischen Auslegungswissenschaft bei Philon von Alexandrien*. Beiträge zur Geschichte der biblischen Hermeneutik 7. Tübingen: J. C. B. Mohr (Siebeck).

Cohn,.Leopold. 1899. *Einteilung und Chronologie der Schriften Philos.* Philologus. Suppbd. 7.3: 387-435.

Cohn, Leopold and Heinemann, I. 1909-1929. *Die Werke Philos von Alexandria in deutscher Übersetzung*. 5 vols. Breslau: Marcus.

Cohn, Leopold and Wendland, Paul (eds.) 1896-1930. *Philonis Alexandrini opera quae supersunt*. 7 vols. Berlin: G. Reimer.

Colpe, Carsten. 1961. "Philo." *RGG* . 3rd ed. 5:341-46.

Conybeare, Frederick C. 1895. *Philo about the Contemplative Life, or the Fourth Book of the Treatise Concerning Virtue*. Oxford: Clarendon Press.

Conybeare, Frederick C. and Stock, St. George. 1980. *A Grammar of Septuagint Greek.* Grand Rapids, Michigan: Zondervan.

Courcelle, Pierre. 1971. "Philon d'Alexandrie et le précepte delphique." In *Philomathes: Studies and Essays in the Humanities in Memory of Philip Merlan*, ed. Robert B. Palmer and Robert Hamerton-Kelly, pp. 245-250. The Hague: Martinus Nijhoff,

Dähne, August Ferdinand. 1833. "Einige Bermerkungen über die Schriften des Juden Philo, angeknüpt an eine Untersuchung über deren ursprüngliche Anordnung." *TSK* 6:984-1040.

Daniel, S. 1975. *Philo: De specialibus legibus I et II*. PAPM 24.

Dillon, John. 1979-80. "Ganymede as the Logos: Traces of a Forgotten Allegorization in Philo." *SPh* 6: 37-40.

______. 1983. "The Formal Structure of Philo's Allegorical Exegesis." In *Two Treatises of Philo of Alexandria: A Commentary on "De Gigantibus" and "Quod Deus Sit Immutabilis,"* ed. John Dillon and David Winston, pp. 77-87. Brown Judaic Studies 25. Chico: Scholars Press.

Elders, Leo. 1966. *Aristotle's Cosmology*. Assen: Van Gorcum.

Erbse, Hartmut. 1974. *Scholia Graeca in Homeri Iliadem.* 3 vols. Scholia vetera. Berlin: de Gruyter, 1974.

Ewald, H. 1858. *Geschichte des Volkes Israel*. 2. Aufl. Göttingen: Dieterich.

Frazer, James G. 1963*a* . *The Golden Bough 1.2:The Magic Art and the Evolution of Kings*. Vol. 2. New York: Macmillan.

______. 1963*b The Golden Bough 3 :The Dying God.* London: Macmillan.

Früchtel, Ludwig. 1937. "Griechische Fragmente zu Philons *Quaestiones in Genesin et in Exodum*.." *ZAW* N.F. 14: 108-115.

Gessner (Gesner), Conrad. 1546. *Sententiarum sive capitum, theologicorum praecipue, ex sacris & profanis libris, Tomi tres, per*

Antonium & Maximum monachos olim collecti. . . . Zurich: Christopher Froschover. Reprinted in PG 136, cols. 765-1244.

Goodenough, Erwin R. 1932. "A Neo-Pythagorean Source in Philo Judaeus." *Yale Classical Studies* 3:115-64.

______. 1935. *By Light, Light: The Mystic Gospel of Hellenistic Judaism.* New Haven: Yale University Press.

______. 1962. *An Introduction to Philo Judaeus.* 2nd ed. New York: Barnes & Noble, Inc.

Goodhart, H. L. and Goodenough, E. R. 1938. *A General Bibliography of Philo Judaeus.* New Haven: Yale University Press..

Gorez, J. 1962. *Philo: De sobrietate.* PAPM 12.

Greenspahn, F. E., Hilgert, E, and Mack, B. L. (eds.) 1984. *Nourished with Peace: Studies in Hellenistic Judaism in memory of Samuel Sandmel.* Chico, California: Scholars Press.

Grossmann, Christian. 1841-42. *De Philonis Judaei operum continua serie et ordine chronologico commentatio.* Leipzig.

Harl, M. 1966. *Philo: Quis rerum divinarum herese sit.* PAPM 15.

______. 1967. "Cosmologie grecque et représentations juives dans l'œuvre de Philon d'Alexandrie." In *PAL*, pp. 189-203. Paris: Centre national de la Recherche scientifique.

Harris, J. Rendel. 1886. *Fragments of Philo Judaeus.* Cambridge: Cambridge University Press.

Hay, David M. 1979-80. "Philo's References to Other Allegorists." *SPh* 6: 41-75.

______. 1980. "Literalists and Literal Interpretation in Philo's World." Unpublished paper presented at the 1980 Annual Meeting of the Society of Biblical Literature.

______. 1987. "The Psychology of Faith in Hellenistic Judaism." In *ANRW* II.20.2: 881-925.

Hecht, Richard. 1979-80. "Patterns of Exegesis in Philo's Interpretation of Leviticus." *SPh* 6:77-156.

Hilgert, Earle. 1984. "Bibliographia Philoniana 1935-1981." In *ANRW* II.21.1: 47-97.

Holladay, Carl R. 1983. *Fragments from Hellenistic Jewish Authors. Vol. 1: Historians.* Texts and Translations 20/Pseudepigrapha Series 10. Chico: Scholars Press.

Jensen, Hans. 1959. *Altarmenische Grammatik.* Heidelberg: Carl Winter.

Karsten, Simon. 1838. "De effatis Delphicis μηδὲν ἄγαν et γνῶθι σεαυτόν." *Symbolae literariae* 2: 78.

Katz, Peter. 1950. *Philo's Bible: The Aberrant Text of Bible Quotations in Some Philonic Writings and Its Place in the Textual History of the Greek Bible*. Cambridge: Cambridge University Press.

Leisegang, H. 1941. "Philon." *RE* 20.1: 1-50.

Lewy, Hans. 1932. "Neue Philontexte in der Überarbeitung des Ambrosius. Mit einem Anhang: Neu gefundene griechische Philonfragmente." In: *Sitzungsberichte der preussischen Akademie der Wissenschaften*, Phil.-hist. Kl., 23-84.

______. 1936. *The Pseudo-Philonic De Jona*, Part I. London: Christophers.

Lieberman, Saul. 1950. *Hellenism in Jewish Palestine: Studies in the Literary Transmission, Beliefs and Manners of Palestine in the I Century B.C.E. - IV Century C.E.* Texts and Studies of the Jewish Theological Seminary of America 18. New York: Jewish Theological Seminary of America.

Lucchesi, E. 1976. "La Division en six livres des *Quaestiones in Genesim* de Philon d'Alexandrie." *Muséon* 89: 383-95.

______. 1977. *L'usage de Philon dans l'œuvre exégétique de saint Ambroise*. Leiden: Brill.

Mack, Burton L. 1984*a*. "Decoding the Scripture: Philo and the Rules of Rhetoric." In *Nourished with Peace: Studies in Hellenistic Judaism in Memory of Samuel Sandmel*, ed. Frederick E. Greenspahn, Earle Hilgert, and Burton L. Mack, pp. 81-115. Chico: Scholars Press.

______. 1984*b*. "Philo Judaeus and Exegetical Traditions in Alexandria." In *ANRW* II.21.1: 227-71.

Mai, Angelo 1831. *Classicorum auctorum e vaticanis codicibus editorum*. Rome: Vatican.

______. 1833. "Λεοντίου πρεσβυτέρου καὶ 'Ιωάννου τῶν ἱερῶν βιβλίον δεύτερον." In Mai, *Scriptorum veterum nova collectio*. 7.83-109. Rome: Vatican. Reprinted in PG 86A.

______. 1834. "Προκοπίου χριστιανοῦ σοφιστοῦ εἰs τήν Γένεσιν τῶν ἐκλογῶν ἐπιτομή." In Mai, *Classicorum auctorum e vaticanis codicibus editorum* 6.1-347. Rome: Vatican.

______. 1837. "Συναγωγὴ ἐξηγήσεων εἰs κατὰ Λουκὰν ἅγιον εὐαγγέλιον." In Mai, *Scriptorum veterum nova collectio e vaticanis codicibus edita*. 9.626-74. Rome: Vatican.

Mangey, Thomas. 1742. Φίλωνος τοῦ 'Ιουδαίου τὰ εὑρισκομένα ἅπαντα. *Philonis Judaei opera quae reperiri potuerunt omnia. Textum cum MSS. contulit, quamplurima etiam è Codd. Vaticano, Mediceo, & Bodleinao, scriptoribus item vetustis, necnon catenis graecis ineditis, adjecit, interpretationemque emendavit, universa notis & observationibus illustravit Thomas Mangey.* 2 vols. London: William Bowyer.

Mann, Jacob. 1940 (rep. 1971). *The Bible as Read and Preached in the Old Synagogue.* New York: KTAV.

Marcus, R. 1930. "The Armenian Translation of Philo's *Quaestiones in Genesim et Exodum.*" *JBL* 49: 61-64.

______. 1933. "An Armenian-Greek Index to Philo's *Quaestiones* and *De Vita Contemplativa.*" *JOAS* 53: 251-282.

______. 1953. *Philo, Supplement, Vol. 1: Questions and Answers on Genesis, Vol 2: Questions and Answers on Exodus.* Loeb Classical Library. Cambridge and London: Harvard and Heinemann.

Massebieau, L. 1889. "Le classement des œuvres de Philon." *Bibliothèque de l'Ecole des Hautes Etudes, Sciences Religieuses* 1: 1-91.

Massebieau, L. and Bréhier, E. 1906. "Essai sur la Chronologie de la vie et des œuvres de Philon," *RHR* 53 : 25-64, 164-85, 267-89.

Mercier, Charles. 1979. *Quaestiones et Solutiones in Genesim I et II e versione armeniaca.* PAPM 34A. Paris: Editions du Cerf.

Mercier, Charles and Petit, Françoise. 1984. *Philo, Quaestiones et solutiones in Genesim III-IV-V-VI e versione Armeniaca. Complément de l'ancienne version latine.* PAPM 34B. Paris: Editions du Cerf.

Méasson, Anita. 1966. *De sacrificiis Abelis et Caini.* PAPM 4. Paris: Editions du Cerf.

______. 1986. *Du char ailé de Zeus à l'Arche d'Alliance — Images et mythes platoniciens chez Philon d'Alexandrie.* Paris: Etudes Augustiniennes.

Moehring, Horst R. 1978. "Arithmology as an Exegetical Tool in the Writings of Philo of Alexandria." SBLSP 1.191-227. Missoula: Scholars Press.

Mondésert, Cl. 1962. *Legum Allegoriae I-III* PAPM 2. Paris: Editions du Cerf.

Moraux, Paul. 1965. *Du ciel (De caelo).* Collection des universités de France. Paris: Société d'Edition "Les Belles Lettres."

Nikiprowetzky, Valentin. 1967. "La spiritualisation des sacrifices et le culte sacrificial au temple de Jérusalem chez Philon d'Alexandrie." *Sem* 17: 97-116.

______. 1973. "L'exégèse de Philon d'Alexandrie." *RHPR* 53: 309-29.

______. 1977. *Le commentaire de l'Ecriture chez Philon d'Alexandrie.* ALGHJ 11. Leiden: Brill.

______. 1983*a*. "L'exégèse de Philon d'Alexandrie dans le De Gigantibus et le Quod Deus." In *Two Treatises of Philo of Alexandria: A Commentary on "De Gigantibus" and "Quod Deus Sit Immutabilis,"* ed. John Dillon and David Winston, pp. 5-75. Brown Judaic Studies 25. Chico: Scholars Press.

______. 1983*b*. "Le Bible de Philon dans le De Gigantibus et le Quod Deus sit Immutabilis." In *Two Treatises of Philo of Alexandria: A Commentary on "De Gigantibus" and "Quod Deus Sit Immutabilis,"* ed. John Dillon and David Winston, pp. 91-118. Brown Judaic Studies 25. Chico: Scholars Press.

Paramelle, J. 1984. *Philon d'Alexandrie, Questions sur la Genèse II 1-7. Texte grec, version arménienne, parallèles latins. Interprétation arithmologique* by Jacques Sesiano. Cahiers d'Orientalisme 3. Geneva: Patrick Cramer.

Pearson, Birger A. 1984. "Philo and Gnosticism." In *ANRW* II.21.1: 295-342.

Pépin, J. 1964. *Théologie cosmique et théologie chrétienne.* Paris: Presses universitaires de France.

Perrot, Charles. 1973. *La lecture de la Bible dans la synagogue.* Publications de l'Institut de Recherche et d'Histoire des Textes. Hildesheim: Gerstenberg.

Petit, Françoise. 1973. *L'Ancienne version latine des Questions sur la Genèse de Philon d'Alexandrie.* 2 vols: I: Edition critique. II: Commentaire. TU 113-114. Berlin: Akademie Verlag.

______. 1977. *Catenae graecae in Genesim et in Exodum, T. I: Catena sinaitica.* Corpus Christianorum, ser. gr. II. Turnhout/Leuven: Brepols.

______. 1978. *Philo, Quaestiones in Genesim et in Exodum: Fragmenta Graeca.* PAPM 33. Paris: Editions du Cerf.

______. 1979. "Les fragments grecs du livre VI des Questions sur la Genèse de Philon d'Alexandrie." *Muséon* 89: 93-123.

Pitra, Johannes Baptista. 1884. *Analecta sacra spicilegio solesmense parata.* Florence.

Praechter, Karl. 1896. "Unbeachtete Philonfragmente." In: *Archiv für Geschichte der Philosophie* N.F. 9:415-26.

Radice R. 1984. "Introduzione." In R. Radice and C. Mozzarelli, *Filone di Alessandria: le origini del male.* Milan: Rusconi.

Rahlfs, Alfred. n.d. *Septuaginta*. 6. Aufl. 2 vols. Stuttgart: Württembergische Bibelanstalt.

Rhodes, Erroll F. 1972. "Limitations of Armenian in Representing Greek." In *The Early Versions of the New Testament: Their Origin, Transmission and Limitations*, ed. Bruce M. Metzger, pp. 171-181. Oxford: Clarendon Press.

Richard, Marcel. 1964. "Florilèges spirituels, III. Florilèges grecs." In *Dictionnaire de Spiritualité*, vol. 5, cols. 475-512. Paris: Beauchesne.

Richter, C. E. 1828-30. *Philonis Iudaei opera omnia*. Leipzig: E. B. Schwickert. 8 vols. Reprinted 1851-53, Leipzig: Tauchnitz; reprinted again 1880-93, Leipzig: Otto Holtze.

Rivaud, Albert. 1925. *Platon Oeuvres Complètes: Tome X Timée-Critias*. Collection des universités de France. Paris: Société d'Edition "Les Belles Lettres."

Robertson, A. T. 1934. *A Grammar of the Greek New Testament in the Light of Historical Research*. 4th ed. Nashville: Broadman Press.

Royse, James R. 1976-77. "The Original Structure of Philo's *Quaestiones*." *SPh* 4:41-78

______. 1984. "Further Greek Fragments of Philo's *Quaestiones*." In *Nourished with Peace: Studies in Hellenistic Judaism in Memory of Samuel Sandmel*, ed. Frederick E. Greenspahn, Earle Hilgert, and Burton L. Mack, pp. 143-153. Chico: Scholars Press.

Runia, David T. 1984. "The structure of Philo's allegorical treatises: a review of two recent studies and some additional comments." *VC* 38 (1984) 209-56.

______. 1986*a*. *Philo of Alexandria and the* Timaeus *of Plato*. Philosophia Antiqua 44; Leiden: Brill.

______. 1986*b*. "How to read Philo." *NedTTs* 40:195-98.

______. 1987. "Further observations on the structure of Philo's allegorical treatises." *VC* 41: 105-38.

Sandmel, Samuel. 1954. "Philo's Environment and Philo's Exegesis." *JBR* 22: 248-53.

______. 1979. *Philo of Alexandria: An Introduction*. New York and Oxford: Clarendon Press.

Schürer, Emil. 1909. *Geschichte des Jüdischen Volkes im Zeitalter Jesu Christi*. 4. Aufl. Leipzig: J. C. Hinrichs.

______. 1987. *The History of the Jewish People in the Age of Jesus Christ*, rev. and ed. by G. Vermes *et al.* Vol. 3:2. Edinburgh: T. & T. Clark.

Shroyer, Montgomery J. 1936. "Alexandrian Jewish Literalists." *JBL* 55: 261-84.

Sichard, J. 1527. *Philonis Iudaei Alexandrini, libri antiquitatum. Quaestionum et solutionum in Genesin. De essaeis. De nominibus Hebraicis. De mundo*, Gvlielmo Bvdaeo interprete. Basel: Adamus Petrus. Reprinted in 1538 as *Philonis Judaei quaestionum et solutionum in Genesim liber*. Basel: Henricus Petrus; reprinted again in 1550 as "Philonis Judaei antiquitatum biblicarum liber, quaestionum et solutionum in Genesin liber, liber de statu Essaeorum i.e. Monachorum, qui temporibus Agrippae regis monasteria sibi fecerunt; de nominibus hebraicis N. et V. Testamenti liber, latine" in Μικροπρεσβυτικον *Mikropresbutikon, Veterum quorundam breuium Theologorum, sive Episcoporum, sive Presbyterorum*. Basel: H. Petri.

Smyth, Herbert W. 1956. *Greek Grammar*, rev. by G. M. Messing. Cambridge, Massachusetts: Harvard University Press.

Staehle, Karl. 1931. *Die Zahlenmystik bei Philon von Alexandreia* Leipzig-Berlin:Teubner.

Starobinski-Safran, Esther. 1970. *De fuga et inventione*. PAPM 17. Paris: Editions du Cerf.

Stein, Edmund. 1929. *Die allegorische Exegese des Philo aus Alexandreia*. BZAW 51. Giessen: Alfred Töpelmann.

______. 1931. *Philo und der Midrasch: Philos Schilderung der Gestalten des Pentateuch verglichen mit der des Midrasch*. BZAW 57. Giessen: Alfred Töpelmann.

Taylor, A. E. 1928. *A Commentary on Plato's 'Timaeus.'* Oxford: Clarendon Press.

Terian, Abraham. 1980. "Syntactical Peculiarities in the Translations of the Hellenizing School." In *First International Conference on Armenian Linguistics: Proceedings*, ed. John A. C. Greppin, pp. 197-207. Delmar, New York: Caravan Books.

______. 1981. *Philonis Alexandrini De Animalibus: The Armenian Text with an Introduction, Translation, and Commentary*. Studies in Hellenistic Judaism, 1. Chico: Scholars Press.

______. 1984. "A Critical Introduction to Philo's Dialogues." In *ANRW* II.21.1: 272-94.

______. 1985-86. Review of Mercier 1979. *Journal of the Society for Armenian Studies* 2:187-189.

Tobin, Thomas H. 1983. *The Creation of Man: Philo and the History of Interpretation*. CBQMS 14. Washington, D. C.: Catholic Biblical Association of America.

van der Valk, Marchinus (ed.) 1979. *Commentarii ad Homeri Iliadem pertinentes*. Leiden: Brill.

Vidal-Naquet, P. 1975. "Le mythe platonicien du Politique, les ambiguités de l'âge d'or et de l'histoire." In *Langue, Discours, Société. Pour Emile Benvéniste*, ed. Julia Kristere, Jean-Claude Milner, Nicholas Ruwet, pp. 374-390. Paris: Editions du Seuil.

von. Arnim, Johann 1903-1905. 3 vols. *Stoicorum veterum fragmenta*. Leipzig: Teubner.

von Tischendorf, Constantinus. 1868. *Philonea, inedita altera, altera nunc demum recte ex vetere scriptura eruta* . Leipzig: Giesecke et Devrient.

Wendland, Paul. 1891. *Neu entdeckte Fragmente Philos*. Berlin: Reimer.

Wilkins, Eliza G. 1926. "Μηδὲν ἄγαν in Greek and Latin Literature." *Classical Philology* 21: 141-142.

Winston, David. 1981. *Philo of Alexandria: The Contemplative Life, the Giants, and Selections*. The Classics of Western Spirituality. New York: Paulist Press.

______. 1985. Review: T. Tobin, *The Creation of Man*. In: *JBL* 104: 558-560.

Winston, David and Dillon, John. 1983. *Two Treatises of Philo of Alexandria: A Commentary on* De Gigantibus *and* Quod Deus Sit Immutabilis. Brown Judaic Studies 25. Chico: Scholars Press.

Wolfson, Harry A. 1947. *Philo: Foundations of Religious Philosophy in Judaism, Christianity, and Islam*. 2 vols. Cambridge: Harvard University Press.

CONTRIBUTORS

JACQUES CAZEAUX is Director of Research at the Centre National de la Recherche Scientifique at the University of Lyon. His Philonic publications include *La trame et la chaîne* (2 vols; Brill, 1983, 1989) and numerous articles. He edited volume 14 of the Lyon edition (*De migratione Abrahami*).

DAVID M. HAY is Professor of Religion at Coe College (Cedar Rapids, Iowa). He is the author of several articles on Philo, including "Philo's References to Other Allegorists" (*Studia Philonica* 6 [1979-80] 41-76) and is preparing a monograph on all of Philo's references to other exegetes. He is also Co-Chair of the Seminar on "Hellenistic Judaism and the New Testament" of the Studiorum Novi Testamenti Societas.

EARLE HILGERT is Professor Emeritus of New Testament at McCormick Theological Seminary (Chicago). He was co-editor of the journal *Studia Philonica* and Secretary of the Editorial Board of the Studia Philonica series in the Brown Judaic Studies. Among his publications is "Bibliographia Philoniana 1935-1981" in *Aufstieg und Niedergang der römischen Welt* 11.21.1 (Berlin: de Gruyter,1984).

ANITA MÉASSON is Professor Emerita of Greek at the University of Saint-Étienne. She prepared the volume on *De sacrificiis* for the Lyon edition (volume 4) and is the author of *Du char ailé de Zeus à l'Arche d'Alliance — Images et mythes platoniciens chez Philon d'Alexandrie* (Paris: Edition Etudes Augustiennes, 1986).

JAMES R. ROYSE is an independent scholar in San Francisco. His publications include work on the text of Philo, especially on the Greek fragments, as well as a volume, *The Spurious and the Genuine Fragments of Philo of Alexandria*, forthcoming in the series Arbeiten zur Literatur und Geschichte des hellenistischen Judentums.

DAVID T. RUNIA is a Huygens Research Fellow with the Netherlands Organization for Scientific Research. His publications include *Philo of Alexandria and the Timaeus of Plato* (Leiden: Brill 1986), *Philo of*

Alexandria: An Annotated Bibliography 1937 - 1986 (Brill 1988 — Roberto Radice, co-author), and diverse articles on Philo. He is Editor of the *Studia Philonica Annual* and is currently doing research on Philo's influence on early Christian thought.

GREGORY E. STERLING is Assistant Professor of Theology at the University of Notre Dame and Chair of the Philo of Alexandria Seminar of the Society of Biblical Literature.

ABRAHAM TERIAN is Professor of Intertestamental and Early Christian Literatures at Andrews University (Berrien Springs, Michigan). His twofold contributions to Philonic studies are in the areas of the chronology of Philo's works and the Armenian corpus of Philo. Besides his English edition-translation of Philo's *De Animalibus*, he has contributed two volumes to the French edition: *Quaestiones in Exodum* and *Alexander* (PAPM 34c and 36).

1. INDEX OF PHILONIC PASSAGES

Quaestiones et Solutiones in Genesim

2. INDEX OF BIBLICAL PASSAGES

3. INDEX OF OTHER ANCIENT AUTHORS AND WRITINGS

4. INDEX OF MODERN AUTHORS

www.ingramcontent.com/pod-product-compliance
Lightning Source LLC
LaVergne TN
LVHW091037080826
845145LV00002B/527

9781930675643